I. N Lichtenberg

The widow's son

A story of Jewish life of the past

I. N Lichtenberg

The widow's son
A story of Jewish life of the past

ISBN/EAN: 9783337046224

Printed in Europe, USA, Canada, Australia, Japan

Cover: Foto ©Lupo / pixelio.de

More available books at **www.hansebooks.com**

[COPYRIGHTED.]

THE WIDOW'S SON:

A STORY OF JEWISH LIFE OF THE PAST.

BY I. N. LICHTENBERG.

CHAPTER I.
THE WIDOW'S SON.

The village of Immenfeld is situated in one of the valleys on the Rhine. Two centuries ago the houses, of which not one boasted of more than two stories, already looked as if they were tired of life and inclined to sink down into the abyss of mother earth. The village lay in a deep vale, at whose upper end a high hill rose towering to the clouds, bearing a splendid castle on its peak. This was indeed a contrast, for its gigantic minarets by no means corresponded with the poor huts in the valley. It looked so large and corpulent, so smooth and comfortable, that its aspect involuntarily recalled to mind the old Sclavonian superstition and adage, namely: That the bodies of deceased persons became vampires, and at night sucked the blood from their still living relations, who became weaker and weaker till they, in turn, were consigned to their graves. This castle was a ghost of a time long past; a time in which all these sunken and ruined huts yet looked new and pretty, and did not lean so dejectedly toward the earth. But afterward the castle must have become a vampire and drawn the blood and marrow from the village.

But not alone was the castle in its still, cold majesty a contrast to the village; it also suffered from a like evil, for directly opposite it, with only the length of the village between, was another hill. This also bore a burden on its back—white stones, like those of which the castle was built, but they were tomb-stones, numerous and mostly weather-beaten, half sunken and decayed, as was the whole village. It must have been that many people died, or that the graveyard was very old, for the hill down nearly into the valley was wholly covered with them.

The cemetery was indeed very old. It was the place where even longer than six hundred years ago the Jews of the village laid down their tired heads. Any one who knew of the piety with which the Jews regard their dead, must immediately have recognized this to be a Jewish graveyard, for only these leave their dead to everlasting rest. For other denominations like the soil better than the bones of their relations; they put five or six into one grave, or, perhaps, after thirty years, exhume and consign them to a vault built expressly for this purpose, called the charnel house, and inter new arrivals, under the false representation of everlasting rest, when the old occupants have been violently ejected. For this reason a graveyard so large as that of Immenfeld would have sufficed a populous city for thousands of years. But where two hundred years ago there was a Jewish cemetery in the place to which it belonged there certainly was a "Jews Lane" or a ghetto—that is, an alley or a street in which the Jews were forced to live, suffer and die, before they were laid to everlasting rest.

Such was the case in Immenfeld. Apart from the dilapidated huts in the village lay the Jews' Lane, with its houses, which, with the synagogue at the extreme end toward the graveyard, even less merited the appellation "houses" than the dwellings of their Gentile fellow-creatures.

The Jewish congregation of Immenfeld consisted of sixty *ba'ale batim* (heads of families), unmarried persons who had no household of their own, or widows, not counted.

* * * * * * *

It was a chilly September morning, and the watchman, wrapped in his military cloak, brushed the dew from his beard and knocked at Farmer Hannikel's door, for the farmer wished to be up early, as he wanted to do his threshing that day. The watchman, after he had blown three blasts on his horn, called out the third hour of the morning, which call was responded to by several rash roosters in the neighborhood. Now, having awakened the old farmer, he stationed himself beside the old synagogue in order to send his call down the ghetto, or Jews' Lane, for which favor he received an annual compensation from the Jewish congregation; for, being a Christian watchman, appointed by his congregation, he was not in duty bound to guard the Jewish quarter without any special compensation.

But as he was in the act of applying the horn to his mouth, he became aware of a bowed figure which emerged from the last house in the Jews' Lane, and soon he heard the call for prayer, to him, wholly in an unintelligible cry. The watchman lowered his horn and said, peevishly: "Well, if the sexton already calls to prayer, I need not waste my service on the inhabitants of the ghetto." It is but two weeks to the Day of Atonement, and as they blow the shofar (cornet,) the Jews rise up early at this season for propitiatory prayers and attend service at the synagogue.

Let us peep into one of the most dilapidated huts in the Jews' Lane. In an alcove separated from the room by an old chintz curtain, a boy lay in deep, healthy slumber on an old chest which served for a bedstead; his cherry lips were partly opened, his cheeks glowed with the ruddy hue of health, and a look of pleasant excitement rested on his countenance.

"He dreams so sweetly," said the little woman bending over the sleeper, and holding aloft a little oil lamp, in order better to contemplate his features with eyes which had been sorely tried by tears and cares.

With a deep contented sigh the boy now turned to the wall, thus withdrawing his pretty face from the woman's view.

"I must wake him," muttered she, "I must wake him, so that he can eat something before day, and I don't want to wait for the sexton's second call, for that breaks in rudely upon sleepers!"

She called softly several times, "Joseph! my good boy, get up, it is time; arise, dear, they are calling to prayers already."

But the boy did not stir, and slept on peacefully. The woman pulled his arm gently several times, but without effect; he only turned his face toward her again, and muttered some words in his sleep. Now the woman fairly started with affright—several sharp blows resounded on the rotten shutters. This worked like magic. The boy shot from the bed like an arrow from the bow, and almost overthrew the woman.

"Hurrah! Long live the general!" cried he, but fell back immediately on the bed and stared sleepily on the little oil lamp.

Soon his face lit up intelligently, and he said pleasantly: "Good-morning, mother dear; it is morning, is it not?"

"Yes, yes, although it is still very early, Joseph, but to-day is the first Selichoth day, beginning of the ten penitential days, and as you will be Bar Mitzvah (confirmed) next year, you must fast to-day, and I awoke you in order that you may partake of some nourishment before day-break, and ere you attend service at synagogue."

"Very well, mother," said the boy, begining to dress himself; "but I would rather you had let me sleep a little while longer, so that I could have dreamed out my beautiful dream. Oh, mother, mother, how glorious it was! I dreamed that I had become general of a vast army, and as I rode along proudly on my horse, the soldiers presented arms, and all the drums beat a salute, just like last year in Cologne, and then you marred my prospect by awaking me."

"Your drummer was the sexton who beat on the shutters with his hammer," said the mother, with a smile, while she assisted him in his simple toilet.

"Oh, what a difference," sighed Joseph, "between a drum-major and a sexton; if I was Parnass (President of the Congregation), the sexton would have to call for prayers with a grenadier's cap on his head, and a white leather apron."

"St, st," said the mother; "you must not rail at sacred things, my son."

"But, mother, the sexton is not a reverend; my teacher, Rabbi Mordechai, is so, for he reads the Thorah, while the sexton does nothing of the kind."

"No matter, my child; for you know that one who impels another to do a good deed may expect as great a reward in the next world as the one who has done the deed, and further that any one who tempts another to evil must expect the same punishment as the evil-doer. Now, the sexton is the one who reminds almost all the members of the congregation to go to the synagogue, or that they are to perform some charitable act; he is therefore, properly speaking, the admonisher to good, and for this reason, my child, you must not mock him."

It was not certain whether Joseph was convinced by the argument of his mother. Suffice it to say, that he remained in a contemplative mood, even while he was consuming his warmed oat-meal porridge. (Coffee was then a luxury which only the wealthiest people could indulge in). Still the precept that he who urges another to a good and noble deed lays by the reward for himself, seemed to have made a deep impression on his mind, for he said:

"Mother dear, when in future times I will have become a captain, I will try to urge my subalterns to love God and perform charitable deeds."

His mother, who sat opposite him, raised her eyes and glanced at him almost peevishly.

"Hush!" she said, reprovingly, "hush, with your foolish dreamings; how often have I explained to you that Jews cannot become soldiers, not to say officers."

"Oh, pshaw, they only need *will* it," said Joseph, fretfully; "they only ought to desire it fervently, and take the great kings and judges in Holy Scripture for their prototypes, and they will become as valiant warriors and great commanders as they."

"My son, we are in *galuth* (exile), and it is our duty to be submissive and not enrage our enemies, for *their* power is great, and the wrath of God rests heavily upon us."

Joseph did not answer, for he knew his mother did not approve of plans that seemed so extraordinary and ambitious to a Jew of that time. He got up quickly, put his old cap on his black curly hair, took his prayer book, which he ardently kissed, and was about to depart. But now his mother put a great book, the weight of which almost bore him down, under his arm.

"Here," said she, "take this Machsor (festive volume). It belonged to your father—peace be with him!—and it's the first time since his death that it is carried worthily to the synagogue again."

The good woman dried a few tears and Joseph's lower lip quivered.

"Now go, and God be with you, my Joseph," she then said, patting him lightly on the back. "Next year you will already have taken the *yoke of the Thorah* upon you, and be a man, responsible for your own actions, which you must yourself expiate. When you come home," continued his mother, "you may go to Cobbler Christians' orchard and pick up the fruit which has fallen from the trees during the night. Half of it belongs to you; the other half you must take to the Cobbler; that's what he said to me yesterday. But bring your *Machsor* and prayer-book home first."

Joseph stepped forth from the door of the little hut. It was chilly, and he felt all the more so as he saw no other human being on the street. All the houses in the Jew's Lane were more or less alight, but still Joseph must have started too early, for when he reached the synagogue, which was already open, but there was not a single person within.

The many sayings and legends which circulate in regard to a synagogue are sufficient to infuse a solemn dread and awe, and it seemed very gloomy to Joseph; furthermore, the universal and beautiful belief, that the *Shekinah*, the Divine Majesty, dwells therein; that angels hold their meetings in an empty synagogue, and that therefore, the one who enters first must knock lightly, exercised such a powerful influence on the twelve-year-old boy, that he stepped back, overcome by holy awe, and resolved to walk on a little and wait until a few men had entered the synagogue before him. He therefore strolled quietly on, contemplating the morning sky, which had just spread a light-gray veil over the Jewish graveyard. There stood all the tombstones of many generations, and seemed to look longingly down at the village and at the Jewish Lane. In the doubtful light of early morning, they seemed to nod their heads gravely at the boy; nay, he even thought he distinguished, amid the endless mass of simple, sorrowful monuments, the gravestone which stood over the last resting-place of his father—the man who was so loved and honored, not only by the Jews of the village, but by all the noblemen who possessed estates and castles in the neighborhood; that father who had been known as "Old Bonafit," and whose honesty had become proverbial as his poverty. But his father had been proud of his poverty and adversity, for it proceeded from his exaggerated sense of integrity.

And just a year and four weeks ago, while lying on his dying bed, that father had said to his son, who understood him very well, as he was already able to expound a page of *Gemarah* without the help of Rabbi Mordechai:

"My son, I leave you no earthly goods, but you will inherit a diadem, the most beautiful that can grace a human being, the crown of a good name; for, according to the sayings of our sages of blessed memory, it is a gem more glorious than that of the *Thorah*, of royalty, or of priesthood. This, therefore, I leave you as your inheritance, for I have worn it. At times it is heavy; often it is oppressive, but in the hour of death the rubies and diamonds in this splendid crown shine brightly, make death easy, and inspire a blessed hope of a glorious life in the hereafter. And see, here is your mother; part of the crown is hers, for she has helped in constructing it; she has set many precious stones in the crown of my good name, and whenever its luster threatened to grow dim, she has tried to restore it to its brilliancy. My son, do not rob your mother of her share in this diadem; hold it in particular veneration, for the greater part of the child's good name falls back on the mother!"

How well all this recurred to Joseph as he stood there: he thought to hear again the weak, venerable voice of his sainted father, while his eyes rested fixedly on yonder hill covered with gravestones. But—merciful God! what was that? Joseph's tongue clove to his mouth, his legs trembled beneath him, Machsor and prayer-book slipped from his hands and he sank on his knees, his eyes still directed in fixed terror toward the cemetery!

CHAPTER II.
A FINE SPECIMEN OF NOBILITY.

If Joseph Bonafit had seen by day that which now so sorely terrified him, he would have felt neither fear nor anxiety; but at night, near such a spot, and busied with thoughts of death, after he had barely recovered from the solemn awe with which the empty synagogue had inspired him, it seemed to Joseph as if a gigantic coffin rose from among the tombstones, and that it was drawn by two monsters who moved to and fro uneasily. He could not remove his eyes from the dreadful apparition, and presently he saw it move down the hill straight toward him!

It grew larger and more monstrous the nearer it came, and it came with fearful speed. He wished to flee and could not; he felt as he had often done in dreams, when he wished to escape from some monster, yet could not stir a step, while all the time certain that the awful thing would devour him the next moment. Now the apparition could be barely a hundred paces distant! Joseph drew a long, relieved breath, for what had so terrified him was a coach and pair of horses which rolled down the road leading close by the graveyard with furious speed. But his heart contracted again and fear took possession of him, for he could not hear the least noise. Mutely and noiselessly the vehicle now flew past him; silently the eight horses' hoofs beat the stony ground, and mutely the driver on the box guided his horses.

However, Joseph ventured to glance about him, and look after the ghostly team. But wonder of wonders! The carriage drew up before Cobbler Christian's house; the driver got down from his box, opened the coach door, and then Joseph heard him tap softly on Christian's window-shutters.

What could the poor drunken cobbler have to do with the carriage at early morning? Joseph could not determine; but one thing was certain, that he had to do with actual men and horses, not with phantoms. But now the door was opened, the cobbler—Joseph recognized him by the faint light—came forth, and approached the carriage door, took posession of a somewhat heavy package, and disappeared with it into the house.

The driver immediately remounted his box, turned his

horses, and rolled back the road as noiselessly as he had come, but this time at a very slow pace.

The gray cloud over the graveyard had assumed a rosy coloring; suddenly a golden beam darted forth, illumining carriage and driver, as well as the still kneeling boy.

Not ten paces from him the carriage again drew up, the driver descended from the box and busied himself about the wheels and the horses' hoofs. Now it became clear to Joseph why the coach had rolled so silently. The wheels and the horses' hoofs had been covered with felt, which, as secrecy was no longer necessary, was now being taken off.

Joseph rightly guessed that he had been a witness of a transaction which it would have been better for him to know nothing of. He arose quickly in order to make his way from the spot.

Such a dreadful face looked out at him from the front window of the carriage, that the poor boy's heart almost stood still with fear. It was the face of a man in his prime, but who was so dreadfully thin as to look like a living skeleton. His nose, bent like a hawk's bill, almost touched his upper lip; his gray, pointed whiskers reached down to his breast; but his eyes, of a gray color like that of an owl, were the most awful Joseph had ever seen, and held the poor boy captive by their magic power.

"John," now cried the dreadful figure in the carriage, "catch that fellow there; he has been watching us."

Joseph uttered a cry of terror, and when the man in the carriage opened the door in order to alight, he fled like a frightened fawn, leaving prayer-book and *Machsor* to their fate. He ran instinctively in the direction of the graveyard and nimbly hopped about among the tombstones.

John, the driver, perseveringly pursued him, but impeded by his cloak and heavy boots, he could not gain upon the fleeing boy, who by his agony of fear ran higher and higher up the hill. Suddenly a sharp, piercing whistle sounded from below, and when Joseph looked back, he saw the driver beating a hasty retreat. Joseph sat down to rest on the tombstone, and saw the driver and his master engaged in an apparently very earnest conversation, while the latter held his books in his hands, and at last put them in the carriage.

Joseph knew that the books could not betray him, for there was no name in them; but he was grieved at the loss of the *Machsor* in particular, as it was his heirloom, and he remembered his mother's assertion that it was to come to honor again.

When Joseph saw the carriage set in motion and come up the road, he hastened down the other side of the hill, and thus gained the road which led alongside the village, in an opposite direction from the graveyard, to the hill on which the castle stood.

Joseph was by no means in a happy mood; for, besides the various frights he had undergone, he had to expect at home the most bitter reproaches from his mother for the loss of his books, as well as his absence from the synagogue, which had no doubt already been imparted to her by some kind busy-body. He wished to enter the village from the opposite side, in order at least to carry out the pleasantest part of his morning's work—picking up the fruit in Cobbler Christian's garden—when he suddenly remembered that Christian had played a prominent part in the carriage affair, and he now fairly shuddered at the thought of the cobbler. His curiosity to know what the latter had received did not torment him greatly, for he felt that it could only be dangerous, as carriages did not come at night, nor were wheels covered with felt for trifles. Joseph thoughtfully sat down on the stump of a tree, which stood by the side of the road; he wished to await the time when he could go home without much danger of his receiving a rebuke; he knew that his mother had to go out to nurse a sick person that day; she had, alas! been obliged to take up this employment ever since his father's death.

To the right of Joseph a swamp extended far out to

where a little brook sluggishly flowed through it; this brook was spanned by single trunks of trees laid close to each other, probably the commencement of a once projected bridge. Of course, only the foolhardy boys of the village ventured to balance themselves on those round, slippery trunks; in a better community than that of Immenfeld this poor bridge would have been cleared away long since, in order to prevent an accident; for a fall from the slippery trees was synonymous with a slow, sure death in the swamp below.

Well, at the border of the swamp, which this morning was covered with myriads of frost beads, sat Joseph, from sheer *ennui*, looking up the hill to the castle, a sacred ground which the feet of a Jewish boy durst not tread; for the *rishuth* (hatred of Jews) in the castle since the widowed baroness and her son resided there, had become proverbial. Even the sight of this high-born son, who was of the same age as Joseph, had till now been denied the profane glances of the Jewish boys of the village; but their fathers seldom thought of him without indignation, for the young gentleman indulged in the harmless pleasantry of stuffing pig-bones into the pockets of the Jews, when they were at any work in the castle, and thus rendered the frugal lunch they generally had there unfit for use; or he set his dog on a Jew who was groaning under a load he bore on his back; or he sneaked out behind and thrust burning papers into his shoes while he was engaged in earnest conversation. All this, the poor people were obliged to endure, for they almost all depended on the gracious baroness, who was highly amused by her son's tricks, and called her Egmont (such was the villain's name) a witty little angel. Once only, a Jew, who was not known in this region, had dared to avenge the wrongs of the Jews of Immenfeld, and this constitutes the town talk even to this day. This man carried a large chest, in which were all sorts of fancy wares, on his back. He had come to the castle to try to sell some of his wares to the domestics, and stood conversing with them in the large hall. He rested the chest on his sturdy walking-stick, and then leaned back on it. But the young baron, unobserved by the Jew, tied a rope to the stick and then, stationing himself at a distance, drew away the stick with a strong pull, so that both man and chest lost their balance, and fell back amid the loud laughter of the servants. The Jew was not only a very passionate but an exceedingly strong man. He sprang up, seized the rope, which lay near him, shoved the men-servants, who wished to restrain him, to one side, as if they were feathers, placed the spoiled boy, who yelled death and murder, across his knees, and despite the blows which fell like hail on his own back, gave him such a severe castigation that the young baron had to keep his bed eight days. The peddler's sturdy stick then kept his pursuers at bay, although he had to leave his chest of wares behind him. He escaped, followed by the threats of the servants (who did not really wish to catch him, as the young baron had often ill-treated them) and the loud cries of the gracious lady and her well-whipped son. As the baroness ordered his arrest, he was obliged to remain concealed some time in the Ghetto of Immenfeld; here he received assistance enough from the Jews he had avenged so well to purchase a fresh supply of goods.

But since the young baron had been whipped so unmercifully by a Jew his hate for the Jews knew no bounds, and daily he importuned his mother to allow no Jews to come to the castle, to which, however, his noble mother could not consent, as she was head over ears in debt, and the castle would have long since been sold at auction but for Jewish money.

Joseph thougt of all this while his glances rested on the castle, the gray gate of which he now could plainly see. Thoughts of the brave Jew made his bosom swell with pride; he felt a strong desire to stand opposite this spoilt child, of whose feebleness so many stories were told; he wanted to show him there were more Jews who were not afraid.

Just at this moment a little door in the great castle wall flew open and a boy clad in a blue blouse stepped out.

He looked around warily, then ran down the hill straight to the spot where Joseph was sitting on the stump. There he halted, out of breath, and regarded Joseph with as much malice as curiosity. The latter also looked silently at the boy and perceived that the stories of his feebleness had not been exaggerated; for he knew immediately that this was the young baron. The boy's face had a bluish tint, and its thinness was extraordinary. Scanty hair of a sandy color hung ungracefully about his temples. The watery blue eyes seemed starting from their sockets, and the nose, bent almost to the bloodless lips, gave the boy's face a striking resemblance to that of the man whose mysterious proceedings Joseph had been a witness of.

After the two boys had stared at each other for awhile, the fair one began:

"I am Baron Egmont, what is your name?"

"My name is Joseph Bonafit," answered the other just as haughtily, "and I am *not* a baron."

The fair boy frowned, then said:

"So you are not a baron; consequently, according to mamma's views, I ought not to play with you; but I have run away from my tutor this morning, and I don't care with whom I play; for I mean to be happy for once, to skip and climb as merrily as the children of our servants."

While Egmont spoke he flourished a thin switch, which he held in his hand, and essayed to assume a joyous expression.

"Come," he cried, pulling at the ragged jacket of Joseph, who made no movement to rise, "come, be a horse, I will be a driver!"

"I won't play with you," cried Joseph, roughly.

"Why not?"

"You are not good enough for me, sir baron!"

"Wha-what!" cried Egmont, and his eyes grew even more prominent. "A baron is not good enough for you? Why, you silly fellow?"

"Because I am a Jew; therefore, you are not good enough for me to play with."

Rage and malice distorted Egmont's face even more; he opened and closed his great mouth in order to bring forth some invective, but could not succeed in finding one strong enough for the outrage which had been done him.

He raised his switch for a blow, but Joseph arose quickly and stepped up so close to the boy, that he could not hit him.

"Listen, baron!" said Joseph, his voice trembling with subdued rage; "one blow and I will throw you into this swamp like some loathsome reptile."

Egmont retreated a step, and lowered his whip in a cowardly manner; then he turned and said contemptuously:

"Ah, bah! I will not soil my hands on a filthy boy!"

He glanced over the swamp and discovered the trees laid across the brook. From the windows of the castle he had often watched the boys crossing on these trees, skillfully preserving their balance, and he had often felt a desire to do the same. He therefore approached the swamp and placed his foot on the first tree.

"Do not walk across," cried Joseph, warningly, for he knew the danger, and his good heart thought only of the perilous undertaking of the boy untutored in such pastimes.

But the latter cried back: "filthy Jew; I am not afraid," walked on over the slippery trunks. This abuse failed to sting Joseph, who was completely lost in the breathless interest with which he followed the uncertain motions of the foolish boy.

The young baron walked on for thirty feet on the slippery tree-trunk, and preserved his balance very well; but now he turned around to the Jewish boy, and laughing scornfully, said:

"Do you see, Jew, its quite sa——" The word was smothered by the cry of terror which both boys uttered simultaneously, for Egmont had fallen down into the swamp. Although standing on his feet, he sank rapidly, and the violent movements with which he accompanied his cries of terror, hastened his descent. It cannot be denied that Joseph at first believed to recognize the avenging hand of God stretched out to destroy this enemy of Israel, that he thought how the Jews of Immenfeld would be relieved of this miserable creature, who perhaps in later years would lay an unbearable yoke upon them; for a swamp tells no tales, and does not give up its victims. These thoughts must not be set too hard to poor Joseph's account, for that age implanted vengeful thoughts in the bossoms of the poor, enslaved Jews, and the twelve-year-old orphan boy could not be better than his people, although holy writ enjoins: "If thy enemy falls, rejoice not; be he lowered, thy heart be not glad."

But now milder thoughts coursed through his soul. He heard the dying voice of his father as it conferred on him the glorious crown of a good name, and with one bound he had gained the bridge, was balancing his way easily along, and in a few seconds stood beside the sinking boy who still continued his cries of terror.

Joseph, whom we know to be very strong, succeeded in drawing out the boy so far from the swamp as to enable him to lay his body across a log. Although his legs still stuck firmly in the mud, he could not sink any deeper.

Joseph now heard confused voices, and on turning around, he saw several men storming down the hill, and behind them a lady in a white fluttering garment, who was wildly wringing her hands. Before Joseph drew back to give place to the new arrivals, he called to the boy to hold on tightly till the help which was near had come.

The men—three servants and a gentleman dressed in

black, whom Joseph immediately recognized as the young baron's tutor—threw a ladder to which a board was fastened, across the swamp. The gentleman in black was the first to reach the young baron, and drew him out of the swamp.

"But, my lord," coaxingly asked the tutor of the young baron, "how did you get into this deplorable situation; no doubt you were disobedient again."

"No, no," cried Egmont, in a sobbing voice, looking toward his mother, who, at a distance of about thirty paces from the swamp, had fallen fainting into the arms of one of the servants. "No, no, that Jewish boy there, whom you saw on the tree near me, enticed me to come here, and then drew me into the swamp."

"Accursed liar," cried Joseph, "you shall pay for this some time as surely as there is now war declared between the despised Jewish boy, and the high-born, noble villain!"

The tutor who was carrying the half-drowned boy, and could not make much progress on the shaking ladder, signed to the servants to secure Joseph, but they were so occupied by the fainting baroness, that they did not notice the sign, and when at last the tutor succeeded in attracting their attention Joseph had disappeared.

CHAPTER III.
AN ECCENTRIC PERSONAGE.

ON a decaying bench in front of a hut in the Ghetto sat an old, strange man, an object of horror and superstitious fear to the pious Jews of Immenfeld, and which of these was not pious? The "Old Spaniard" had been excommunicated or anathematized, the Herem pronounced against him because he would not agree to do that which all the Jews of Immenfeld did, not omit what all the other Jews omitted. To be sure he had permission to come to the synagogue, but only into the entrance hall, where the *abelim* (mourners) are obliged to wait, until let into the interior by the rabbi or elders of the congregation. From no one did the "Old Spaniard" receive a kind word, a drink of water or a crust of bread (as no intercouse can be had with an anathematized subject) nor did he ask for any. As the Jews in Immenfeld did not, so to say, consider him one of themselves, been born and reared in the faith, he had often been offered a domicile by the Gentiles of the village, but had always refused, prefering to retain his little house in the Ghetto, and his seat on the bench before the door.

The members of the Immenfeld congregation maintained that he only remained there, after having been excommunicated, in order to vex them; and this must have been partly the truth, for on fine days "Spaniard" sat on the bench before his door, and read aloud from a book filled with strange characters and stranger pictures, in accents so utterly unintelligible to any chance listeners that they were overcome with horror and dread by the awful sounds.

But whence had the old Spaniard come, and what fearful crime had he committed to merit the awful anathema, which had been pronounced against him?

One day—it was a Friday—he had come hobbling into the village, for he had only one leg, reported himself an *orach* (wanderer) to the president of the congregation, and asked for a *plette* (a plette is a kind of ticket for board and lodging, which notifies the master of the house to give board and lodging to a traveler over the Sabbath.

The president had regarded him with surprise, for the traveler's dress was remarkable. He wore puffed black velvet small clothes, whose seams were ornamented with gold thread; a jacket, likewise in Oriental style, trimmed with gold, and on his head a cap with a nodding blood-red plume. On his upper lip he had—contrary to all usage and custom—an immense gray mustache, which extended at least six inches on each side of his mouth, and the long, narrow beard which depended from his chin was twisted so tightly and waxed so stiffly that it resembled the point of a lance.

The stranger—whom, on account of his Oriental apparel, the president's wife dubbed "Spaniard"—a name which, for lack of a better that was never told, he afterward retained—the stranger expressed his thanks to the president, and hobbled off to look for his quarters. Here he established himself as comfortably as possible, washed and combed his hair, after his journey, rubbed his coarse shoes with fat, and oh, heavens! took a little soap-dish from his knapsack, filled it with water from the cistern, and placed it on the oven, close to the dishes. The trembling hostess removed it hastily in order that her dishes might not be made unfit for use from it. When the good-natured old man asked for a little warm water it was given him.

But when the Spaniard took a razor from his knapsack and began preparations to shave himself, the horrified maid-servant ran to the president, and pale with fright, told him that the stranger was either no Jew at all, or certainly an apostate; for instead of piously nipping off his beard with shears, as any devout and pious Jew ought to do, he shaved it with a razor like those did who were not Jews, contrary to scriptural precepts.

This was sufficient to cause the president of the congregation to take prompt action. But he came too late; the mischief had been committed; the Spaniard was shaved. The president then very resolutely requested him to leave his present quarters and travel further on, for the congregation had no desire to harbor him and to call down a heavenly punishment on themselves for the sake of such a renegade and public transgressor of the Mosaic laws.

The Spaniard smilingly looked into the president's face, and then explained to him that, if he were obliged to travel on that day, the Sabbath certainly would have set in before he could reach the next village, which contained also a Jewish community, and that the Immenfeld congregation would be held to account for every transgression he would be forced to commit.

The president was convinced by this argument, and the Spaniard remained. But he received proof how unworthily he was considered to remain in the community or in the synagogue on Saturday morning, for he was not called to the *Thora*—a courtesy which, till now, had not been denied any stranger; and when he strolled through the village that afternoon, all avoided him.

But if they thought to get rid of the troublesome stranger in this manner, they were greatly mistaken.

Sunday morning came, and our stranger, instead of shouldering his knapsack, repaired to the president of the congregation, and showed him a duly drawn-up bill of sale of a house and garden belonging to a person who had once resided in Immenfeld, but now dwelled in Frankford. As the house which now belonged to the stranger had been unclaimed for a long time, it had been considered the common property of the congregation, and the president's rage knew no bounds; all the more because the congregation had preserved the house in very good repair, kept the implements for baking of *Matzoth*, the unleavened cakes, there, and had arranged a dwelling for their sexton in it.

A quiet, sensible man would have agreed to a compromise, for the old stranger spoke in a submissive, courteous tone; but the president, who already mortally hated Spaniard, because he had publicly transgressed the Mosaic law, made bad worse by beginning to abuse him. Now, nothing availed him; the sexton had to quit the house, and Spaniard, after repeatedly and vainly demanding the removal of the utensils for baking the Passover bread, threw them out in the street, thus putting the congregation to an additional expense; for the utensils were rendered unfit for use by their contact with the mud on the street. War was now openly declared. If Spaniard had dwelt one hundred fathoms deep in the earth, he could not have been more lonely than in his little house. Only once more some interest was shown in him; this was when a cart, drawn by two oxen, stopped before his door, and brought his furniture, which, besides some rubbish, consisted of nothing but books.

If, at that time, any one had suspected that a Jew of Immenfeld could think of reading any book but one written in Hebrew characters, all these volumes would probably have been consigned to the flames; but, fortunately, such a thought was too far without the pale of probability. No Jew could be so wicked as to keep a book not written in Hebrew characters within his four walls.

But even worse was to come. One day a boy, who had just become *Bar Mitzvah* (confirmed), appeared before the president, and sank, out of breath, on a chair. When he had recovered a little, he began to tell, amidst tears, and many prayers to God for forgiveness, that curiosity had so tormented and impelled him, that he had peeped through Spaniard's window, and had seen him reading a book on whose pages—oh, horror!—there were pictures of unintelligible characters. Now, the president's endurance was at an end. He summoned a meeting of the board of directors, and Spaniard was notified to appear and justify himself.

He appeared, and when the accusation against him was read, or, rather, screamed into his ears by many indignant voices, he answered pleasantly that the book he had been reading was an edition of "Josephus"; to be sure it was written in Latin, but the pictures and characters represented neither more nor less than the siege of Jerusalem by the Romans. The men with the crosses were Roman soldiers who held the Jewish prisoners of war, of which the honorable board might fully convince themselves, as he would quickly fetch the book and show it to them.

A truly dreadful storm of hisses and protests rose against this proposal, and the next moment Spaniard was out in the street.

On the next morning the unhappy Spaniard's sentence was communicated to him by the sexton; it was excommunication, or the anathema pronounced on him because he not only kept forbidden pictures in his house, but wrote and read a language not in vogue among Israelites.

Spaniard made no response; the narrow-mindedness of that age was so; he seemed satisfied with his sentence, and did not even please the congregation by coming to the entrance hall of the synagogue; he simply remained away altogether; he would not appeal.

He had his meat sent to him from a neighboring village, but when it became known there that he had been "anathematized" the Jewish butcher had to refuse to sell him any meat, as no communication and intercourse can be held by a person excommunicated. He purchased fowls and killed them according to Jewish rites after he had received permission so to do from the rabbis in Frankford.

The relation between Spaniard and the Jews of Immenfeld had now lasted ten years; during this time he had never once failed to salute pleasantly every one he met, be it a man, woman or child, but had never received a recognition.

But no, Spaniard had had one friend, or at least one who kindly returned his nod; this was old Bonafit; yet he had never ventured to speak to him, or invite him to his house, much less to step across Spaniard's threshold.

Joseph Bonafit had once asked his father about Spaniard's books, but received the answer that they were books which generally helped those who were *not* Jews to positions of trust and authority, as they contained important secrets of nature; but just for this cause they must remain forbidden to Jews.

From this day forward Joseph always pleasantly nodded to the old man, and desired nothing so anxiously as just to cast one look into the books of the discarded Spaniard.

Once he partly expressed this wish to his parents; his mother clapped her hands together in horror; but his father gently advised him to learn first what the wise men of their own faith had ever written; then the wisdom of those not Jews would seem mere trumpery to him, and, that it was disadvantageous to Jews, he had an instance of in the Spaniard. His father's death and the preparations for his Bar Mitzvah crowded the boy's wish into the background.

* * * * * * *

Well, on this morning the old Spaniard sat on the bench before his door and read aloud from a great book which he held on his knees. This time the words were German, but such German as was spoken up in the castle, and of which the Jews of Immenfeld did not understand the tenth part.

Joseph, still breathing heavily from his rapid run, came up the street. He had happily escaped from the servants of the baroness, that is for the present; if for the future, remains to be seen.

He had already gone a few steps beyond Spaniard's hut when he halted suddenly, looked about him carefully, and softly glided back to the reader. Looking over his shoulder into the book he saw singular characters, which, like crow's feet, seemed to be creeping back and forth over the paper. His breath moved the Spaniard's gray hair; the latter glanced up, and thus recalled to Joseph the consciousness of his dangerous undertaking, for if any of his people were to see him in his company, it would be all over with him.

For this reason he prepared to move up quickly, but Spaniard took hold of his arm and said in a friendly manner:

"Good-morning, my boy; I suppose you would like to know how to make any sense of this book, which looks so unlike the *Gemarah*" (traditional works).

"Let me go, Mr. Spaniard, let me go for God's sake; you don't know how it would harm me if any one saw me in your company," said Joseph, pleadingly.

"So you also entertain fear of me, although your father did not," said Spaniard good-naturedly, liberating the boy.

The latter looked at him and then said:

"Oh, Mr. Spaniard, how much I would like to know the contents of your books; if I only could or durst learn them!"

"And why do you want to know all that—what good would it do you if you are afraid to speak with me?" asked Spaniard, drawing his forehead into wrinkles.

"Because it must show me the way to become great in the world, enable me in some future time to stand opposite the young baron up there as man to man; because I hope thereby to come out of the *galuth* (exile) in which all the children of Israel languish. Because—because I don't want to travel from village to village with a pack on my back, hawking and mocked at by the peasants, and serving as pastime to the nobles, their ill-bred children and the curs in their stables."

The Spaniard's face had brightened—it fairly beamed.

"Poor boy," said he, "you also would like to rend your bonds; but the time to do this has not yet come. It fares with us as with the crab, which having fallen into a pit fell back at night half the distance which it had painfully ascended by day; yes, yes, often as we essay to climb we always fall back into the night of prejudice and superstition; and not only our antagonists push us back, but even our friends and brothers. But, what is that?" he interrupted himself suddenly; "what is going on at the castle? Policemen are up there, and they are pointing in this direction, the Jew's Lane. Can it be that a *gezerah* (calamity) is drawing near?"

Joseph also looked up. The next moment he had forgotten all considerations not to be seen in the company of Spaniard, and clung tightly to his arm in mortal fear.

"For God's sake, Mr. Spaniard," cried he, "save me, save, hide me! The police are being sent by the baroness to look for me, because she thinks I have thrown her bad son into the swamp."

The Spaniard arose without answering a syllable, and allowing the boy to go before him so that he could not be seen from the street, he hobbled behind him into the house.

"I don't want to know anything, I will not hear a word," he said, as Joseph asseverated his innocence. "Come here, I will do away with you nicely."

Spaniard took the boy into a closet, back of the only room the house boasted of. It was full of books which were piled almost up to the ceiling. He directed Joseph to creep behind the books which he went about building up as a wall.

"Keep quiet, my boy," he said again, "and not a hair of your head will be hurt."

He resumed his crutches, and soon Joseph again heard him read aloud from the great book.

Policemen had in fact been sent to the village to search for the Jewish boy and lead him to the dungeon in the castle; for the baroness lay in convulsions, and the little baron in a high fever. Although the boy was only known by sight to the tutor, who accompanied the policemen, it was quickly found out who had been the attacker on the life of the young baron, all the more easily as Joseph had that morning been conspicuous by his absence in service at the synagogue.

The policemen were not sparing of rudeness and threats against the Jews, for they only too gladly believed that these not only kept the malefactor concealed, but had also instigated him to the attack on the young baron. The noise brought Mrs. Bonafit, who was in attendance upon a sick person, to the street, and here she was immediately denounced as the mother of the delinquent.

It is easier to imagine than to describe the poor mother's feelings when she heard the accusations against her only son—her son whom she had brought up in the love and fear of God. Weeping and lamenting, the poor woman threw herself on the ground, beating her breast and calling on her son. But this was of no avail; Joseph did not come. In the meanwhile all the houses in the Jew's lane had been searched, without the least result.

The police had not been at the Spaniard's; they did not deem it necessary to enter the house. It was generally known on what terms he was with the Jewish congregation; and they were far from suspecting that he would wish to shield the offspring of one of his enemies from righteous punishment.

But now Joseph's mother was dragged to her own hut, and under pretext of looking for the young criminal, not a single piece of the poor furniture was left whole. All, all; even the round window-panes set in lead were broken.

Then, as the son could not be found, they took the mother with them. Her prayers and pleadings, interrupted only by her piteous calls on her misguided son, were not heard by the latter, for the dreary procession did not pass by his place of concealment.

The poor woman was cruelly driven up the hill to the castle, where she was received by the castellan, who locked her up in a small room in the tower, until such time as the bailiff, who was then absent, would grant her a hearing, or the son had been captured.

CHAPTER IV.
DUKE FRANCIS XII

His Excellency, the Duke of Wimmerstein, sovereign of the little country to which Immenfeld belonged, was sitting in his study, reading the papers and letters which the morning mail had brought him. The duke was an industrious, orderly old gentleman; he arose very early in the morning, partook of a simple breakfast, then repaired to his study, and when the clock struck nine—an hour at which many of his lazy subjects still lay abed— he had already answered a number of letters and arranged a great deal for his little, but well-governed realm.

The duke was nearly sixty years old. He had no heir

to his throne, and when he died his duchy would revert to a large empire which lay adjacent to it. Duke Francis XII. was never married; half of his life had been spent in the camp, as general in the Dutch service; the other half in studying, and in intercourse with learned men, of whom he preferred the Jews, on account of their deep penetration and great reasoning faculties. The duke's gray hair, cut short and brushed back from his forehead, his beard arranged in the same style as Spaniard's, combined to give his face a serene, noble, and commanding expression. Despite this, Duke Francis was a good and mild master, who had his peculiarities, but was nevertheless almost idolized by his subjects.

On the morning when we visited him in his study, he sat, as usual, before his papers, reading, writing, and correcting, until the perspiration poured from his forehead. To cool himself a little, he approached the open window and breathed in the fresh morning air, which, at this late season of the year, was already quite chill. The valet, in the antechamber, who could observe all his master's motions, must have thought that his grace had finished working, and would now admit visitors, for he entered the study and coughed softly.

The duke turned around quickly, and asked: "Well, Klas, what is it?"

"Pardon, your highness," answered the old servant; "there's an old Jew, who begs for a hearing, outside."

"Is it a Talmudist?" asked the duke, his face brightening.

"Pardon, your highness, I did not ask, but will hasten to repair my mistake."

"Never mind, just bring him in; for what Jew, unless he be a learned one, would dare to ask for admission here?"

"Is it possible! My good old Moses Benrimo," cried the duke, greatly delighted, as the servant came back, leading a man who had but one leg, and whom we recognize as Spaniard, from Immenfeld. "Is it possible!" again cried his grace, as he hastened forward, holding out both his hands, which Spaniard respectfully kissed.

"Yes, your highness, old Moses has come once again, to prove his allegiance to his sovereign."

"Sit down here, my old companion in arms and teacher, to whom I not only owe my knowledge of Hebrew lore (from which I have culled the purest pearls of wisdom), but who was my faithful friend for thirty years, and lost his leg while fighting at my side.

"Look here, Klas," the duke turned to his servant, "this man here, whom you called a Jew, is my friend, Klas, my teacher, the friend and teacher of your sovereign, Klas!"

"Your highness must excuse me," answered Klas, humbly; "if I had known that I would not have called the illustrious gentleman a Jew."

"You mistake, my good man," said Moses Benrimo, "as does your highness also; the appellation Jew is no insult or stigma to me, for your highness knows how proud it has always made me to belong to a people who have spread and carried the banner and light of civilization into all parts of the world."

"Don't excite yourself, my good Moses," cried the duke, taking a chair and setting down opposite to him, while he motioned to Klas to leave the room. "Do not excite yourself, you cannot think more highly of the Jewish people and their literature than I do, yet when I hear any one I honor called a Jew, it appears to me as if it were an abusive appellation."

"Who made it so," asked Moses, reproachfully; "who first comprehended everything base, vile, everything that has to shun the light of day under the name of Jew; have we done that? Have the Jews themselves dishonored their name that it has become an invective in your mouths; have not you yourselves, to whom we brought the knowledge and light of civilization, rewarded us by base ingratitude; has not the degenerate daughter repudiated her mother? 'The stone which the workmen have cast away will become a corner-stone.' The word Jew will be the pearl of price in the crown of progress and enlightenment when the time will have come your highness, old Moses Benrimo tells you this."

The duke had listened well pleased to the argument of Benrimo, and when he had finished he said:

"My friend, you know we never could agree upon this point; I love the wisdom contained in your books, which you have taught me to read and understand; I admire your history, your glorious literature, your authors, but— but I cannot like the Jews, for although, like the bearer of a dark lantern, they have brought us light, they themselves have remained in the dark. They obstinately shut themselves up from the spirit of the times; they burrow and dig in the wisdom of their fathers, and thus are left behind in that obscure age, which ours no longer is; in short, while we have surpassed them, they have forgotten to understand us, and, as we cannot go back, they do not comprehend us."

"Your highness," said Moses, warningly, "you are accusing your own self. The Jews were always capable of of being educated; they gladly attached themselves to the habits and customs of the country which afforded them a refuge; but your highness forgets that the people to whom they came robbed them of their rights; that the Jews have been shut out from society; that they have been persecuted, slandered, burned at the stake; that they have been crowded into narrow streets; that they have been prohibited to be like other human beings; that they were forced to vanish like a stream in the sand, while they might have enriched the land. But, like such a stream, they will at some future time come to the surface, and then no dam will have the power to obstruct the flow of their free and enlightened thoughts.

"The history of the Jew is the history of civilization; check his progress, he sinks, extend to him equality and privileges, he rises like a thermometer in the rays of the hot sun. Aid him, grant him privileges, and you give the lie to prejudice, silence calumny, by letting him become a yeoman of the land.

"The Jew ever since has been ordained by God himself to carry out his mission under the most adverse circumstances.

"Judaism is destined to plant, first, the seed of true religion and keep it fresh with the moisture of charitable deeds, until it will firmly be rooted in our own hearts. Then it will blossom beautifully, and bear the necessary fruit, and we will recognize God as the Almighty, before whom we all walk, and who will lead us to perfection."

The duke admired Benrimo's eloquence, but began to tire of the subject; it was one which had often been discussed between them, the duke always coming off at a disadvantage, although he never confessed it. It was no rarity that Christians who occupied the highest places, counted Jews among their most intimate friends.

"My Moses," began the duke, "let us drop this unrefreshing subject; tell me rather about yourself: if you have found peace and comfort among your people; if, within sight of a Jewish graveyard, and occupied by your books, you dream away your life as pleasantly as you pictured it to me when, ten years ago, you bade me farewell. At that time you rejected all honors and riches, and left me mourning, in order to pass the remaining days of your life among your people; confess, now, have you found that peace which you sought?"

Moses bowed his head and forced himself to nod an assent, but the duke, who looked at him sympathizingly, noticed two heavy tears drop slowly into the gray mustache of his old comrade.

The duke grasped Moses' hand; he was touched to the heart by his old companion's pain, and said gently: "Moses, you are disappointed, or you deceive yourself; you are not happy; you have not found among your co-religionists what you rejected from me; they are not pleasant to you."

"Oh, yes—yes, your highness," returned Moses, drying his eyes with the back of his hands, "they are good and honest in their intentions, but they do not understand me. They have sighed and groaned so long under the yoke which they are forced to bear, that they have ceased to comprehend who they are."

"You are too good, Moses; you defend your fellow-believers because they are yours, but they have probably found out that all men are alike; that persecution and intolerance strut about everywhere, and that religious fanaticism will appear in the same form over and over again, until in some future time people will have succeeded in liberating themselves from antiquated prejudices. Oh, do not speak of it further, Moses," continued the duke, warding him off, "say no more, I know what oppresses you, although you will not confess it. Stay with me again, you know that you can live according to your inclination and commandments; remain here, and you will have no more disappointments, and should you die before me, I will summon all those of your faith within a circuit of ten miles; they shall carry you to your grave in the Jewish cemetery, there where the mound is highest, and the ten first rabbis in my little country shall say the *kaddish* for you a whole year, and for that whole period shall a lamp be alight for you in the halls of my forefathers; but should it please God to call me first, my testament shall direct the same. Remain here, my friend; my instructor, stay with me."

Moses Benrimo's lips quivered convulsively; he essayed to keep down his emotion, but it was too strong for him; the old man wept. When he had grown a little composed, he said, "I did not come here to complain, yet your highness has divined the state of my feelings. But I came here with a petition; does your highness know the family of the Baroness Weiden?"

"Yes, she lives in Immenfeld, an old, proud family, but very poor. The Baroness Weiden's brother, a Count Witzleb, was banished from court twelve years ago, because he was guilty of an atrocious deed; I think this is the family you mean. There is a branch of it here in the city, an old, very wealthy count, who, but a few years ago, married an accomplished young lady, thus depriving the Weidens of Immenfeld of the prospect of a rich inheritance; however, as the young heir was carried off by gypsies a short while ago, and no trace of him can be found, they have hopes of it again. I think this is the family, is it not?" added the duke.

"Your highness is right," said Moses, nodding his head.

"Well, what of it?"

Moses Benrimo related the story of the young Baron Egmont and Joseph Bonafit, up to the incident of which we already know; it may be imagined that he did not spare the young baron.

"When the poor boy heard," continued Benrimo, in his narration, "that his mother had been imprisoned in the tower, he could not bear to remain concealed any longer. I had to take him to the castle, where he made himself known to the bailiff, who, in the meantime, had returned from a hunting expedition. But if Joseph had thought to purchase his poor mother's liberty, he was sadly mistaken, for the bailiff not only accused the mother of being an accessory in the attack on the young baron, but he even maintained that the whole Jewish congregation had incited Joseph to put the hated young baron out of the way. Your highness ought to have seen the conduct of this base boy when the poor orphan was brought into the court-room to be tried. He poked his fingers into the poor boy's eyes, and overwhelmed him with the vilest invective, and all in the presence of his mother, the baroness, who had recovered from her fright. Dreadful sufferings are in store for these poor creatures, if your highness will not take compassion on them, for the bailiff spoke of tortures to which he would subject both mother and son, in order to find out their accomplices, and the young baron was full of joy at the prospective festivity."

The duke reflected for awhile, then arose, and seating

himself in front of his writing-desk, said: "Moses, I am glad that I can do you a favor, but if I liberate your proteges, I will expect a favor from you."

"Your highness has but to command."

The duke wrote for a few minutes, then handed to Benrimo what he had written; the latter read:

"We, by the grace of God, Duke Francis XII., do hereby request the widowed Baroness Weiden, in whose jurisdiction Immenfeld lies, to liberate, immediately and without delay, the widow of Abraham Bonafit and her son Joseph, and to cease molesting the Jewish congregation in said Immenfeld.

"Furthermore, we request and expect of the widowed Baroness Weiden, to send her son Egmont here to attend the military school, that he may lay aside all vices and wickedness, and learn the military profession, in order to become a good officer to his graciously inclined sovereign. All this do we request to be accomplished as soon as possible, at the risk of our displeasure.

"(Signed)   FRANCIS XII.,
"Reigning Duke of Wimmerstein."

"Hold," said the duke, as Benrimo prepared to put the decree in his pocket; "hold, I have a quicker messenger than you are, and you do not want the poor creatures to languish longer in prison than is necessary. Moreover, I do not intend to let you return to your melancholy village."

The duke rang a bell, and ordered a courier to take the document, to which he had affixed his seal, with all haste to Immenfeld.

But when this had been done, Moses rose, took his crutches and began:

"I humbly implore your highness to let me depart so that I may take the post-coach which returns to my village to-day."

"Stay here, Moses; don't be obstinate. I speak sober earnest; remain and help me in my studies; the sight of you has recalled all the reminiscences of old times, and I cannot spare you any more. I will faithfully keep all I have promised you. Being your sovereign, I might command you, but I don't do it, I only implore you as a friend."

"Your highness, grant me but one year, then will I return and be your most humble servant."

"Wherefore a year, Moses? We are both old, we do not know that we will ever see each other again. And then, I have found a number of questions in the Talmud which I cannot solve, and which you must explain to me; I cannot wait."

"Your highness, I must return for a year to my village, in order to put the boy whom you have restored to liberty into the path which God has indicated to him; there is stuff to make a man of in that boy, but he must be taught the right doctrine, and as much as I know the Jews of Immenfeld, even his own mother will now regard him as an apostate."

"Well, in one year, Moses?"

"In one year, your highness, if God wills, I shall wait on your highness again."

The duke looked on in astonishment as Moses took off the orders and marks of honor which decorated his breast, wrapped them in a paper and put them into his pocket.

"Why do you not wear those orders always, Moses?" asked the duke.

"These marks, which only appertain to the high-born, do not beseem a Jew," answered Moses, bitterly; "nor would my people know how to prize them; because their oppressors wear them, they often take the decorations for the man."

The duke pulled out his purse and handed it to Moses. The latter gently warded him off and said:

"Your highness, I have not a single year been able to use up the pension which your bounty awards me."

"Well then, Moses, take the purse for the poor of your congregation, or for the synagogue of your village."

"They would fear the burning of their fingers by contact with it, and would not take a penny of it from me."

"Poor, poor Moses," uttered the duke, as his old comrade, after a hearty leave-taking, hobbled from the room.

CHAPTER V.
A NOBLE BROTHER AND SISTER.

In the deep embrasure of a window in the antique reception hall of the castle at Immenfeld, sat the Baroness of Weiden, the mother of Baron Egmont. The lady was of a high and stately figure; her features were finely cut and aristocratic, but a careworn expression rested on them. Although she had not yet reached middle age, her high forehead was crossed with wrinkles which could be only attributed to care or grief. The noble lady had, indeed, many cares, for she was poor. A plebeian might not consider this so very dreadful, but to an old, aristocratic family, it is a truly immeasurable misfortune. These people, who had so long persuaded themselves that they were made of different clay and metal to other mortals that they themselves at last believed it, knew no greater crime, next to that of being not noble, than of being poor. To escape this misfortune, and uncomfortable position, they, since time immemorial, had committed misdeeds and crimes which would have brought a man of the people to the scaffold, while they did not cast a blemish on the reputation of a nobleman. We allude to the highly aristocratic freebooters of the middle ages; the special taxes extorted from Jews, and the many similar heroic deeds, which plain people, who have no understanding for the high virtues of those nobly born robbers, now call abominable crimes. But two hundred years ago, all this had already come to a disgraceful end, and in comparison with the preceding century the rights of Jews were now better protected, or, rather, the sovereigns, having perceived how successfully their vassals extracted and extorted money from the Jews, undertook to do this themselves, thus cutting off an income to which the noblemen had till then deemed themselves entitled. If, therefore, a reduced aristocratic family now wished to regain their former wealth, they were obliged to resort to other than the favorite means of the preceding centuries.

Baroness Tekla, of Weiden, had planned and schemed, and to-day she sat in the window planning again, at the same time looking forth expectantly. Her brow grew more and more clouded.

"He does not come," she said; "he does not come; all is lost! This last expedition has turned out a failure, and my poor Egmont will remain a beggar. Oh, I could curse his father in the grave, for not understanding how to keep his son's inheritance!"

The baroness was interrupted in her soliloquy by the beat of hoofs beneath the windows of the castle, and when she impetuously burst open the shutters and looked out, her face cleared, and she cried, joyously:

"Welcome, Brother Kuno, welcome!" The person thus addressed, looked up before he dismounted; he did not, however, think of answering the greeting.

When Kuno entered the reception hall, the baroness hastened forward, holding out both her hands; they were totally disregarded.

"Never mind, Tekla," said Kuno to his sister, very quietly; "never mind; it is not sisterly love which dictates this kind reception and affection, it is curiosity, Tekla—curiosity to know whether your little baron, the good-for-nothing, is to be dependent on his salary as a soldier, or whether he will, as an honored, wealthy vassal, in a splendid castle, be able to defy his emperor. No, my amiable sister, a loving pressure of hands is no bait for me!"

Kuno cast a sarcastic glance from his gray, piercing eyes on the countenance of his sister, which crimsoned with mortification, and awaited her reply, slowly stroking his long beard. The baroness swallowed her rage, and said, gently, although the words came hissingly forth from the thin, blue-tinted lips: "Oh, Kuno, my friend even more than my brother, how can you be so rude and unkind to your only sister. I gave you no cause for such deportment!"

Kuno unbuckled his large sword, and sank down heavily into a chair. "Beloved, only sister," said he, aping the lady's mode of expression, "to what end these phrases? You know very well that I have come on matters of business, although the hated word business falls unpleasantly on the ears of the baroness. You desire to secure a large inheritance for your villian of a son, you have invented a pretty plan how to make this possible; you have looked around yourself for a partner, and found none who could arrange the thing better, nor was more inclined to assist your precious offspring than Kuno, of Witzleb. But as the latter happens to be a brother of the gracious baroness, she naturally has recourse to her sisterly love for him."

"Kuno," reproachfully said the baroness, sitting down opposite him, "Kuno, cease your sarcastic remarks, you know how they grieve me. Your promise to take charge of this matter is as much to your profit as to mine, and if your scheme succeeds, and my Egmont becomes the heir, you will be entitled to full half the fortune."

"Yes, yes," answered Kuno, "but what guarantee have I that your boy will not laugh at my face? His honor, his high descent?—ha, ha, ha!—his honor, ha, ha, ha!—his high descent." Kuno laughed until the tears stood in his eyes.

The baroness trembled with impotent rage, yet she restrained herself. After a pause, during which Kuno had time to recover from his immoderate merriment, the baroness, without recurring to the obnoxious topic, began:

"Well, Kuno, what have you succeeded in accomplishing?"

"Rejoice, sister, for your son is sure of the inheritance,"

answered Kuno as quietly as if the above dispute had not taken place, "the heir of the old Count Weiden has disappeared, and his fond mother is vainly crying out her bright blue eyes for him."

Instead of evincing surprise or joy, Tekla asked coldly: "And the countess?"

"The countess?" asked Kuno, dumfounded, "what of the countess?"

"Is she not dead also?"

"Sister, sister," cried Kuno, "were you brought up in the same school with the evil one's grandmother? What do you want of the countess; is she to disappear likewise?"

"Assuredly; why leave the thing half done?" answered Tekla, as coolly as if she were discussing the sale of a horse in her stable.

Baron Kuno remained lost in thought for a while; then he said:

"Perhaps you are right; the mother ought to disappear as well as the son; but no, perhaps it is better to strike at the root of the evil, and as the count is very old his days may as well be numbered; young people *may* die, old people *must* die."

"No, brother, that would be the most foolish thing to do; as long as the countess lives or remains near the old man, he will bequeath all the property over which he has control to her alone; the estates of course revert to the next male heir. But you know that his wealth and all the property which does not belong to the entail constitute an immense sum, and this would be lost to *me*."

"Ah!" returned Kuno, sarcastically, "how soon you betray your thoughts; you just said that the fortune would belong to you, while all the time you have promised me half."

"Pardon, brother; that was only my mode of expression."

"Never mind, sister, I am acquainted with your noble way of thinking; well, so the old count's death is out of the question, but his young wife must follow her son."

"Exactly, else all thus far accomplished would be to no purpose. But what have you, or rather the gypsies, done with the child?"

Kuno arose, approached his mouth to his sister's ear and whispered:

"*It found its grave within view of its ancestral halls; it lies below in the swamp!*"

The baroness started and grew even paler than she had been before; then she drew a breath of relief and cried:

"Thank God, my Egmont will not need to suffer want."

"Always that serpent of hers, again and again that abominable boy," muttered Kuno to himself, while the baroness remained lost in pleasant reflections, for all her cares were suddenly at an end. It was true that the countess, her sister-in-law, still lived; but Kuno would soon find ways and means to render her harmless, for Kuno was so brave, so crafty and so avaricious.

Kuno arose and buckled on his sword.

"You do not wish to leave me yet I hope," said Tekla.

"I must go away; I have a long ride before me."

"Tell me, Kuno, as we are now friends and allies, would it not, to say the least, be brotherly of you to let me know where you are going to, where you dwell, and what noble employments those are which enable you to keep the most beautiful horses, carriages and a whole army of servants?"

"All these, my dear sister, are in anticipation of the half of the immense inheritance which we hope to receive," answered Kuno, mockingly. "Where I dwell? Oh, now here, now there, as beseems a traveling nobleman. But, sister," said Kuno, suddenly changing his subject, "where is the hopeful heir of the Weidens? I do not see him anywhere, and yet I am accustomed always to see his angelic physiognomy near you."

"He is with his tutor," returned the baroness, disregarding her brother's malicious and sarcastic remarks. "He was disobedient the day before yesterday; he ran away, and I came near losing him forever." The mother who had just listened unmoved by the tidings of the murder of another's only child, covered her face with her hands, and wept at the bare recollection of her own child's danger.

"What happened to him?" asked Kuno, not too sympathizingly.

"Just think, a Jewish boy from the village enticed him to the swamp, and attempted to murder him."

"Bah—nonsense! That is one of Egmont's tricks again," dryly responded Kuno. "Perhaps he fell into the swamp, and, as usual, shoved the blame on some one else. I know his way."

"Kuno," cried the baroness in a rage, "you impute a baseness to my son of which his noble heart is not capable. We witnessed the whole affair from the windows of the castle."

"Who witnessed it—you?" asked Kuno, derisively, as much as to say, "Sister you lie!"

"Yes I, and even if I had not seen it, my Egmont does not lie."

"Hm, hm," growled Kuno, "you can never let alone the Jews, who yet are so necessary to you. Do you know," he continued in a lower tone, "I have never met a Jew who in cold blood caused a child to be murdered so that he might possess himself of his fortune. I have come to know them very well, but the worst among them would not deprive a human being of life; how much less, then, could a boy commit such an atrocious deed!"

"I do not comprehend how you can talk in such a strain," answered the baroness coldly; "have not the Jews often made use of the blood of Christian children on the feast of Passover?"

"Nonsense! Probably this was drawn from charming fellows like your son," responded Kuno. But the baroness had now grown seriously angry; she clinched her hands, and stepping close up to her brother said: "Kuno, you repeatedly wound my most sacred feelings, and only because you revel in my pain. If Egmont has any bad qualities, it is only because, alas! they are an inheritance from his ancestors, for his uncle, the Baron Kuno, was for his misdeeds discarded by his father, banished from court, and his escutcheon was trampled upon by the hangman."

Kuno changed color and put his hand on his sword. He stepped back, but his sister followed him and held her little hand threateningly before his face.

"Dare again to call my child a villian or rascal," cried the baroness, quite beside herself with rage, "and our friendship, scarce begun, will come to a horrible end."

Kuno, who yet was influenced by some few chivalrous emotions, in so far at least as a lady was concerned, attempted to pacify his sister, but did not succeed until he assured her that he did not have so very bad an opinion of the last descendant of his family, for, as proof, did he not wish to procure the half of an immense fortune for him?

"Go to the prison," said the baroness somewhat mollified; "take a look at the old Jewish hag and her degenerate son, and then tell me whether this boy with his curly, black hair, his piercing eyes and his robust frame looks like a good-natured child or a criminal."

His sister's description of the boy had attracted Kuno's attention; he asked her to repeat it, and then left the apartment to go and look at the Jews in the dungeon. When the door closed behind him, the baroness raised her hand threateningly.

"Wretch!" cried she, "just work for me, murder for me, but you shall not have a cent from my son's inheritance. You deem yourself clever, but a woman, a mother who works for the welfare of her son cannot be outwitted. Just dare, when we have gained our end, to lay claim to the fortune and I will show you the swamp beneath the windows of my castle, and dread of the executioner will seal your lips!"

Kuno of Witzleb, as he walked though the corridors toward the prison, also had his private thoughts.

"Just wait, serpent," he thought; "you err greatly if you believe that your good-for-nothing son will ever see a cent of the whole inheritance. But I thank you for having brought me to the right track. Do you think that Kuno of Witzleb is so foolish as to kill the goose which lays golden eggs? Do you think that he would throw the heir to such a fortune into a swamp and then go and tell it to his amiable sister? No, no, then my name would not be Kuno of Witzleb; the money and private property shall all be mine; your boy shall not even have the entailed estates; sooner would I give them to the Jewish boy who is imprisoned here. Oh, my dear sister, if you would have bridled your tongue, and not called up old reminiscences for my edification, I might, perhaps, for the sake of the name to which I once had a right, have become lenient; but now, you and your sweet son may go a-begging for all I care."

Soliloquizing thus agreeably, Kuno had reached the entrance to the prison, a large, strong, iron-bound door, which was guarded quite unnecessarily by the old jailer, who, searching among a bunch of rusty keys, asked·

"Does your lordship wish to see the woman or the boy?"

"Are not both locked into the same cell?"

"O, dear, no; both are in subterranean cells, there where neither light of day or night penetrates; but do you think that these two murderers would be put into one cell, so that they could take counsel with each other?"

"Well, then, lead me to the boy."

The jailer opened the iron door and stepped into the interior, followed by Kuno. It was a small, circular room, from which a flight of stone steps led to the dungeon beneath. The jailer seized a lamp, drew flint and steel from his pockets, laid a piece of a sponge on the latter, struck the steel on the flint until a spark, darting forth, ignited the sponge; then took a thread which had been immersed in sulphur, and, holding it over the sponge, blew on it until it caught fire, finally lighting the wick of the lamp with it—altogether a tedious operation, of which our century, with its parlor matches and gas-jets, is happily rid. The jailer led the way, and Kuno followed, down a flight of at least thirty steps.

Arrived below, Kuno saw, as far as the lamplight fell, nothing but heavy iron doors, let into massive walls, from which small streams of water trickled slowly. The jailer again searched among his bunch of keys, and when he had found the right one he opened the first door, which turned back, creaking on its hinges; the jailer held aloft his lamp, thus illuminating the dark cell.

Kuno had hardly glanced in when he uttered a low cry, which was answered by a shriek of dread. Kuno had recognized the Jewish boy who had watched him a few days ago, and the latter remembered him as the man whom he had seen in the mysterious carriage!

CHAPTER VI.

KUNO'S TRIUMPH.

Kuno remained standing in the doorway for a moment, and contemplated the poor boy, who, shivering with fear, crouched on a stone bench, the only piece of furniture the vault contained; then, taking the lamp from the jailer, Kuno signified to him to ascend the stairs again, and await him in the circular room above.

The baron then approached the boy, placed the light on the lower end of the bench, and sat down next to poor Joseph, who fairly clung to the wall.

"Why are you afraid of me, my boy?" asked Kuno, in a gentle voice, quite contrary to the tone the poor boy had expected. "Why are you afraid?" repeated Kuno, as Joseph still remained silent.

"Because — because you — because I——" stammered Joseph.

"Because—I will tell you why—because you have a bad conscience; because you have concerned yourself about things which are of no consequence to you; because, with unpardonable curiosity, you watched, and tried to fathom the secret of another—a crime next to that of theft, and which already has cost many a one his head. Listen, my boy: although I myself am no angel, I may tell you that curiosity is a most reprehensible thing, and that eavesdropping and watching, turn a person into the most miserable creature in existence, not only in my eyes, but in the eyes of all who still have a spark of honor in their hearts. Remember this, and should you ever be released from this dreadful dungeon, think of this hour, and of my warning. But tell me," continued Kuno, in a lighter tone, "how was it that you came to watch me?"

In a trembling voice, which gradually grew firmer, Joseph proceeded to relate his adventure, even mentioning the fact, that he had thought the carriage a phantom, and had been greatly afraid of it; amid sobs and tears, he added: "I know it was wrong to remain away from synagogue, and I even had in mind not to tell my mother of my remissness; these two crimes led to my misfortune, into which my poor, dear mother was dragged as my companion. Oh, if ever I should be released from this horrible prison, I would never again sin against my dear, precious mother."

"Compose yourself, my boy," said Kuno, with a heartiness no one would have credited him with, "compose yourself, and tell me if you can keep my secret."

"Yes, my lord," answered Joseph, proudly, "I can be silent."

"But prying people cannot be silent."

"I am not prying; I have told your lordship how it all came about, and I never told a falsehood."

"Well, then, will you swear that you never will betray a word of what you saw that night?"

"I promise it, but I cannot swear, your lordship, for God will not leave unpunished the one who takes his holy name in vain."

"But," returned Kuno, and a sort of respect for the devout boy expressed itself on his countenance, "you will not swear in vain; your liberty, nay, your life, may depend upon this oath."

Joseph ruminated for a while, then said: "I really think that this matter is important enough to give me liberty to take an oath. I will swear."

The baron drew forth a heavy golden cross, which he held to the boy, who shrank back in horror. "I do not swear on the emblem of a cross," said he.

Joseph heaved a deep sigh; then the words came from his trembling lips, "May God in His mercy protect me, but I would rather languish in this dungeon all the days of my life, ere I would swear."

A smile flitted across Kuno's emaciated face; he quickly put the cross away and said:

"Were I to weigh the manly character of this despised Jewish boy in the balance with that of my good-for-nothing nephew, I do not doubt which way it would incline." Then he said aloud: "Ah, I forgot that you are a Jew, else I would not have placed such an emblem before you. Well, take my hand and swear that you will keep secret all that you saw that night, and anything that in the future you may discover in regard to it, until I give you leave to speak."

Joseph hesitatingly placed his hand into that of the baron, but he drew it back quickly, and said: "No, no, I will not swear."

The baron's eyes flashed angrily. He sprang up and stood with drawn sword before the boy.

"Miserable fellow," cried he, grinding his teeth, "why will you not swear, do you want me to run my sword through your body?"

"I cannot," returned Joseph, with bated breath; "how do I know but what some wrong has been committed, to keep which secret would make me an accomplice and accessory, for on that morning my poor mother said to me, 'One who instigates or conceals a crime commits it as much as the criminal himself.'"

Joseph's mention of his mother gave the baron a good idea.

"Look here, my boy," said he, "I should like to procure you your liberty, for you are a brave little fellow, and might become a good, great man; therefore I require your oath, otherwise my secret could remain forever buried with you and your mother in these walls. I gave you the opportunity, not only to save yourself, but your innocent mother; you refused to take it; remain here and add to your other crimes that of being the cause of your mother's death.'

Kuno turned away hastily, and acted as about to leave the cell.

Joseph uttered a heart-rending cry and convulsively clung to the baron's cloak. The latter turned around again, and the boy fell on his knees.

"Oh, have mercy, your lordship!" cried he; "spare my dear, good mother, she is innocent; do with me what you will, but have mercy on my dear, good mother."

"No, no, there will be no mercy for your mother unless you swear!" cried Kuno, hastily tearing his cloak from the boy's hands, and seizing the door knob.

"Pardon, sir! pardon!" wailed Joseph, "I will swear!"

Kuno turned to the boy, who was sobbing violently, and again held out his hand.

Joseph placed his within it and repeated word for word the dreadful oath which Kuno dictated; then he fell back sobbing on the stone bench and cried again and again:

"Oh, what a sin! what a terrible sin!"

Kuno stepped nearer to Joseph and asked him:

"Tell me, my boy, what impelled you to throw the young Baron of Weiden into the swamp?"

"I did not do it, your lordship; on the contrary, I warned him not to undertake the breakneck venture, I drew him forth when he fell in, I saved him, for it would have been too late when help from the castle arrived. Believe me, your lordship, believe me!"

To Joseph's intense astonishment, Kuno said indifferently:

"Of course, I believe you; I would believe a worse boy than you more than my *noble* nephew, and depend upon it I will do all in my power to liberate you as well as your mother from this dungeon, for you are a boy such as I have need of."

"Oh! my lord, you promised to release me if I would swear, and now you already break your word," said Joseph, crying bitterly; "but I might have known it; even a nobleman does not feel bound to keep his promise toward a Jew."

Kuno frowned darkly and said:

"Guard your tongue, my boy, guard your tongue, you do not know what you speak; but be assured of this, that were you of my belief you would languish here as long as it pleased Heaven and the baroness; yet just because you are a Jew you have found a protector in me." In a tone inaudible to Joseph the baron continued: "All that I would refuse to people of my religion I grant to Jews, for there is a great resemblance between their condition and mine. They are the Pariahs of the community; I am thrust without the pale of aristocratic society."

"So you will release us, noble sir, you will really release us, and not detain my poor mother and me in this dungeon?"

"Yes, yes, my boy, whatever Kuno of Witzleb may be, his word is sacred to him; and if it were only to plague young Egmont, I will snatch you from his power."

Here the sudden appearance of the jailer interrupted the baron.

"Your lordship," cried he, "the baroness desires to see you immediately; something dreadful must have happened, for the servant told me that the baroness is quite beside herself with grief."

"You will hear from me soon," cried the baron, hastily leaving the cell, which the jailer again securely locked, thus leaving the poor boy to the gloomy despair on which a momentary ray of hope had fallen.

When the baron re-entered the reception hall, he could hardly recognize his sister. The noble lady ran like a crazed hyena up and down the apartment, followed by her hopeful son, who wailed incessantly: "Boo-hoo, boo-hoo-hoo."

Torn bits of paper were scattered on the floor, and a great red seal, broken in the center, lay on the table.

"Why, what is the matter, dear Tekla," asked Kuno, in surprise.

"Here, read!" cried Tekla, shrilly.

"Well, what shall I read?" asked Kuno.

Tekla suddenly remembered that there was nothing to read any more, as the torn bits of paper on the floor plainly testified.

"Boo-hoo-hoo!" wailed the young Baron of Weiden.

"It is shameful, it is atrocious, it will kill me and my poor defenseless, fatherless child," cried Tekla, wringing her hands, while heavy tears coursed down her cheeks.

"Boo-hoo-hoo!"

"Do come to your senses, for Heaven's sake, Tekla; and you, you puppy, cease your whimpering," cried Kuno, now seriously vexed. "What has happened?"

"A courier from the duke, boo-hoo-hoo," howled Egmont."

Kuno grew pale, for no good to the house of Weiden could come from the duke, with whom he had long lived in open enmity. For one moment he was really foolish enough to believe that his sister and her son were overcome with grief on his account, and that the duke's message concerned him; but he quickly cast away this thought.

"Well, what did the courier bring?"

"A command from the duke to release those miserable Jewish murderers, and not to molest them any more," cried the enraged baroness.

"Boo-hoo-hoo, and I anticipated their torture so much," whimpered her grievously disappointed son.

"Yes, I believe you, kind heart," said Kuno, mockingly. "But how did this come about?"

"How do I know?" cried Tekla. "The devil must be their ally; but I will not release them; I will let them starve, and then say they died before the courier's arrival."

The young baron's face grew brighter and he said:

"Yes, yes, mamma, let them starve; that is right, mamma!"

"Reptile! muttered Kuno; then turning to his sister he said: "Dear Tekla, I hope you will deliberate a while before you execute your humane plan. Consider what influence must have been at work to cause the duke not only to order the release of your prisoners, but to send a special courier with the decree."

"Oh, brother, you do not know all! Oh, these accursed Jews! My poor little Egmont——."

"Boo-hoo-hoo!"

"My poor little Egmont is to go to the military school, in order, as the old tyrant says, to be cured of his naughtiness. How low, how absurd—my poor Egmont naughty!"

Kuno gave vent to a long whistle. The tidings surprised him, but his face fairly beamed with malicious joy.

"H-m—h-m!" said he, consideringly; "whose hands must have been at work here; how has the duke been informed of the whole affair? Kuno, Kuno," he muttered, "if you understand aright which way the wind blows, remain good friends with the Jewish boy, for a new star is arising in Israel!"

The baron comfortably seated himself on a chair; his

sister and her hopeful son were still running frantically up and down the apartment.

"Well, dear sister," he said, in high good humor, "what have you resolved upon?"

"I suppose I will have to release the dirty pack; don't you think so?"

"Certainly, certainly; there is no question about that; but hasten to do it, for the duke is an old soldier, and requires strict obedience to his commands."

"Well, then, I must send to the dungeon," said the baroness, biting her lips with rage.

But this did not suit Kuno's plan: the Jewish boy must owe his liberty to *him*, and remain *his* friend; for who could know what might happen; and, besides, his sister must not profit by that which could be of use to him. For this reason, Kuno said: "Let them grumble a while longer. I do not want you to excite yourself any more by giving the command for the release of the prisoners; I will go down myself, by and by, and see to it. But I did not allude to this. I mean, what have you resolved upon doing in regard to your vil——Egmont?"

"Boo-hoo-hoo!" howled Egmont again.

"I have decided. I will not deliver the poor, delicate child to the rough hands of soldiers."

Kuno shook his head, doubtfully; then, as if trying to persuade her, he said: "Dear Tekla, if I were in your place, I would rather not do such a thing; it is somewhat dangerous to oppose the old gentleman's will. I have had occasion to find that out."

"What can he do to a woman? He cannot banish me from court, because I do not go there; nor exile me to my estates, for I have none!"

"But your ras——your Egmont's future lies in the hands of this tyrant!"

"Alas! yes," sobbed the baroness.

"And the duke is a genuine tyrant—a second Caligula, when his will is crossed," related Kuno. "I remember how, about thirty years ago, he ordered one of his cadets to be whipped unmercifully."

"Almighty God, support me!" shrieked the horrified baroness, covering her face with her hands, while Egmont again took up the refrain:

"Boo-hoo-hoo! whipped unmercifully—boo-hoo-hoo!"

Kuno forcibly kept down his merriment, and went on to comfort his weeping sister, now and then interposing some anecdotes of the old duke's cruelty, so that altogether his soothing words did not take much effect.

Finally the baroness asked Kuno if he knew how the cadets in the military schools were treated.

"The duke," recounted Kuno, "causes his cadets to be trained strictly in accordance with the Spartan model; I need not tell you, Egmont, what this means, for your tutor has without doubt made you very well acquainted with the history of the ancients; but you, dear sister, may not know much about it."

"Oh, my God, no!" wailed the baroness; "I do not, but yet I shudder."

"You need not shudder, it is nothing so terrible," returned Kuno, assuming a soothing tone; "it is a mode of training that hardens boys. Their food consists of the so-called black soup, a mixture of stale bread and goodness knows what other ingredients. In order to sharpen their appetites the cadets must saw wood, mold bricks, cut hay, in short exercise their bodies in many similar ways, which no doubt your Egmont will be greatly pleased with. After every meal each pupil is treated with a whipping——."

"Boo-hoo-hoo!"

"And if he cries he is beaten until he is quiet."

"Oh, brother, this is inhuman; but you are joking."

"Just ask Egmont whether the Spartan boys were not subjected to like treatment."

"Yes, yes, mamma; just about the same," howled Egmont, who knew as little about the Spartans as his mother, but did not like to confess his ignorance.

"No, no," cried his mother, "I will never let my only child go there."

"Just think of the whipping, mamma," cried Egmont in despair.

"You may dispose of your child as you like," said Kuno, "but I would advise you to swallow this pill, bitter as it is, and send your boy to the duke. It may be best for all concerned."

"Oh, who has done this," cried the baroness; "who has so shamefully maligned, traduced me to the duke?"

"Your own son is to blame, and now he may bear the consequences, whippings, black soup, etc."

"But how? what has the poor child done?"

"Probably an disinterested person witnessed the whole occurrence," said Kuno, "and reported to the duke how abominably Egmont lied when he said that the Jewish boy attempted to murder him."

"Oh, if I had known that," howled Egmont, "I would not have said it."

"Are you convinced now that I guessed aright?" cried Kuno; "the rascal has lied from beginning to end, and a mitigation of his fate can only be brought about by a full confession, for it is my opinion that the duke only desires his presence at court in order to force a confession of his lie from him by means of torture."

"Oh, pardon, pardon!" cried Egmont, "I am ready to confess everything. I fell into the swamp by accident; the Jew had warned me not to step on the slippery logs; I did so, nevertheless, and when he saw my peril, he, at the risk of his own life, came to my rescue, although I had derided him."

"I knew it," cried Kuno. "What do you say now, sister? The sooner you deliver the boy to the duke's keeping, the better for you. I only frightened him a little, and now his black heart is plainly revealed. Fare you well; I go to release the Jews from their confinement."

CHAPTER VII.

THE PREPARATION DAY OF THE HEBREW NEW YEAR.

When Joseph and his mother reappeared in the Jew's lane, they were welcomed by demonstrations of triumphant joy. The whole Jewish population, young and old, men and women, hastened forth to greet them. It was the eve of New Year, and every one had remained in the village in order to make due preparations for the holy festival.

It seemed as if the hand-shaking and congratulations would never end. But it cannot be said that the joy of the Jews of Immenfeld was not egotistical, and that they rejoiced so immoderately at the widow's and her son's release; no, each one was glad on his own account. Any one who knows the danger which in those days threatened a whole Jewish community when one, be it even the least among them, was seized by the hands of justice, will easily comprehend why the Jews of Immenfeld were so joyful. In most cases the crime of one single person was with the most refined cunning thrown to the blame of the whole community, thus affording a pretext to wreak vengeance on the hated Jews. Although considerably weakened, this practice is not unusual even at the present day. When some one who happens to belong to the Jewish race commits a dishonest act, how often is not the judgment heard: "Yes, yes, the Jews are swindlers!" while no one will think of holding a whole people of another faith responsible for what one of them has committed.

Soon old Rabbi Moses Benrimo also came up to the released prisoners. He stretched out his hand to the boy, who seized it eagerly and kissed it in the face of the whole congregation. Mother Bonafit uttered a cry of horror, and violently tore her son away, while murmurs of displeasure arose among the bystanders.

"Almighty God, what are you doing?" cried Mrs. Bonafit, "to kiss the hand of an unbeliever. Have you forgotten that you are a Jew, and do you want to draw the wrath of God on Israel again?"

"Let me alone, mother," cried Joseph, blushing with shame, "let me alone; this man is no renegade, he is a good, noble man."

"How can you sin so against God, against your mother and against Israel, as to call a person who has been excommunicated by the congregation a good man."

Benrimo smiled painfully; he signed to Joseph to put an end to the scene, but the boy, suddenly overcome by a singular stubborness, clung to the hand of his benefactor. An undefined suspicion arose in him that this man had done more for him than his abusers.

His mother again attempted to draw the boy away, but the latter was ashamed to turn his back in such a cowardly manner on the Spaniard, whom he had but now greeted so gladly.

Mrs. Bonafit burst into tears and sobs.

"God be merciful to me," she wailed, "my boy is done for; first, he brings his poor mother into imprisonment, and then he remains standing with that renegade in the open street."

The women on beholding Mrs. Bonafit's tears fell on her with many soothing and pitying words, and led her back to her little hut, in which, as we know, everything had been ruthlessly destroyed.

The boy's heart was for the first time filled with anger against the people among whom he had been born, raised, and with whom he had spent his childhood; he dropped the Spaniard's hand and with head bent was about to follow his mother, when he was again detained:

"Joseph," said Spaniard, "you and your mother cannot keep yom-tob (holiday) in that house; I have furnished two rooms nicely for you; come and take possession of them."

Joseph shook his head sorrowfully, and while the tears filled his eyes he turned to follow his still lamenting mother.

"Bitter is the fruit from the tree of knowledge," muttered the Spaniard, as he likewise turned his steps homeward; "you will find this out soon enough, my boy; *but if you are ever destined to enter into the path of glory, you have to-day cleared away the first obstacle in your way!*"

To the credit of the Jews of Immenfeld, be it said, they went to work with a will at rendering the widow's little hut as habitable as possible before the holiday set in. One brought a piece of furniture, another bread, a third cake, a fourth and fifth meat; several families sent their maid-servants to scrub and clean the interior of the little hut; some young men temporarily stopped up the gaps in the window frames with oiled paper; in short, every one lent a helping hand, and before the sexton went the rounds to summon the people to the synagogue, the little house was as comfortably furnished and provided with all necessaries as it had ever been.

But something which had never failed to be there was wanting in the little house—a link which had never been lacking as long as the widow could remember—something that gave brilliancy to the Sabbath lamp, brightness to the table-cloth, warmth to the heart; that was—peace.

Joseph had essayed several times to approach his mother, but she waved him back each time, while breaking anew into sobs and lamentations.

Joseph sat down in the doorway of the hut and hid his face in his hands. Now and then some curious person, or some of his comrades, stopped to question him about his imprisonment; but he did not answer. This tended considerably to heighten the displeasure which his familiarity with Spaniard had called forth. Evening set in, and when Joseph at last lifted up his head, he saw men and women, in holiday attire, hurrying past to the synagogue; he arose and went into the house to wash and dress himself. His best clothes were already laid out; he quickly donned them, and when he again stepped from the house, he became aware that his mother had not awaited him as usual, but had gone on alone to the synagogue. Sorrowfully, and with a heavy step, he walked along to the festive service, where the greater part of the congregation were already collected, and, in subdued silence, were awaiting the commencement of the solemn devotions.

Joseph walked to the seat which had once been his father's, and looked longingly over to where his mother sat in the women's gallery, which was screened by a high railing.

Joseph's thoughts were more with his mother than with his prayers. Finally, the closing prayer, the *Yigdel*, was sung, with a mournful cadence, as it is sung only twice in the year—on New Year and Day of Atonement. The members of the congregation wished each other a "Happy New Year"; mothers kissed their sons, laid their hands in blessing on their heads, saying: "May God let you become like Ephraim and Manasse!" Joseph wept aloud; thus had his father blessed *him*, that father who had been so enlightened, and had never called the Spaniard a renegade.

All, all were joyous; all were happy; only the poor orphan, who had no father to bless him, was neglected. The glory which had surrounded him that morning was gone; nay, it seemed to him that disagreeable and even contemptuous looks were directed at him.

Sorrowfully as he had come, Joseph walked home again. He was the last one to leave the house of prayer.

When he passed the Spaniard's house, he saw the windows all alight. He peeped in guardedly and saw the great Sabbath lamp hanging from the ceiling. The Spaniard himself, attired in festal garb, stood beneath it, completely absorbed in his prayer-book.

"And this man was excommunicated, and is called a renegade," murmured Joseph, as he sorrowfully proceeded on his way home. When he reached his mother's house, he saw there also the bright rays of the Sabbath lamp streaming out into the street. Softly, softly like a thief he stole up the stairs, gently he laid his hand on the knob, the door flew open, and he saw his mother, all dressed in white, with the full glow of the Sabbath lamp falling on her. She had just laid down her prayer-book. Joseph uttered a cry. Never had New Year seemed so painful to him before. He threw away his book, and with a cry: "Mother, dear good mother!" he rushed forward to embrace her; and she opened her arms and held him close. The tears choked her voice as she whispered: "A happy, happy New Year, my life, my son, my all!" And then she placed her hand on his head and said: "May God let you become like Ephraim and Manasse!"

And when later on they, according to usage in vogue, were eating the sweet apple dipped in honey, Joseph said: "Oh, mother, may God sweeten this year and all the years of our life, amen!" After supper mother and son discussed their recent dreadful adventure, and again the mother warned her son to remain pious and godly, not to walk in the ways of the wicked, and to keep afar from such men as the Spaniard.

The evening advanced, and Joseph's mother bade him to retire to rest. He took his prayer-book and devoutly repeated the night prayer, that most beautiful of all devotions, which, besides the psalms, contains so many pure, angelic sayings.

When Joseph came to the part in the psalm: "He will surely deliver thee from the snare of the fowler and the plague of wickedness," he fervently raised his eyes and thanked God that He had released him from the dark dungeon and restored him to light and liberty. Joseph ardently prayed for God's protection, and that his couch might be surrounded by angels—at his right hand the angel Michael, at his left hand the angel Gabriel, Uriel before him, the guardian angel Raphael back of him, and God himself, in His glorious majesty above him.

Joseph's mother had gone to bed before he finished his prayer; tired and exhausted from all the horrors she had lately undergone, and the work of preparing for the holiday; she soon fell into a deep slumber. Joseph closed his book and looked thoughtfully into the few remaining lights of the Sabbath lamp still struggling for life, which yet was no life, but rather a slow and painful death. Now one of these went out, the room was wrapt in partial darkness, and wonderful shadows caused by the uneasy flickering of the two remaining lights flitted along the wall.

Despite his mother's warning, Joseph could not forget the old Spaniard to whom he felt himself powerfully attracted. His childish imagination repeatedly called up the old man's kindly face. At times it seemed to him as if he had found a second father, one who combined with his own father's kindness of heart a higher intelligence of mind and more of wordly wisdom.

Joseph could not sleep. He looked unceasingly into the last lights of the Sabbath lamp, which, almost exhausted, hastly consumed the remaining oil and flashed up repeatedly like the last sighs of a dying man. In the partial darkness of the room the lamp appeared to him like a great head and the two lights like the eyes of the Spaniard which winked at him continually and beckoned a magic "Come, come."

"Yes, I come!" cried Joseph, and with one bound he had reached the door.

The lights had gone out.

Joseph slipped off his shoes and glided down the stairs. Arrived in the street he put them on again and looked around carefully in all directions. There was not a human being in sight; the few remaing lights from the various Sabbath lamps looked out like sleepy little eyes into the deserted street. Joseph hastened down the street and halted before the Spaniard's house. Here also but two lights were still burning. The Spaniard himself was fast asleep in a chair by the window. Joseph considered for a while; then he knocked softly with bent finger on the window pane, which, as on the ground-floor of most houses of that period, lay within his reach.

Although Joseph's knock was almost inaudible, the Spaniard started up and growled such a "Who's there" that the boy almost fainted with fear. But now the window was thrown open, the Spaniard put out his head and recognized Joseph. A cry of joy escaped him and he called out softly:

"Ah, it is you, my dear boy; and you are come to wish me a happy New Year."

"Yes, yes," whispered Joseph, hurriedly, "but please open the door for me, I must speak to you; oh, hurry, sir, before the night-watchman comes to this corner and perhaps catches sight of me."

"Here, take the key, and spare me the journey to the door," said the Spaniard, handing a large iron key to Joseph. "You know that I am not fleet of foot."

Joseph did as he was bid, and at the next moment was in the room and holding both of the Spaniard's hands.

"Pardon me, Mr. Spaniard," said Joseph, timidly, "for coming at such a late hour."

"No excuses; come, take a candle from the bureau and light it."

When the candle was lit and replaced on the bureau, the Spaniard asked:

"Well, my good boy, what do you wish to say to me?"

"Mr. Spaniard——"

"One moment, Joseph," broke in the old man, "I will intrust you with a secret; my name is not Spaniard, and I think it is ridiculous for people who have a liking for me to address me by a name which my enemies have given me. Call me Moses, for my name is Moses Benrimo."

"Then allow me to call you Rabbi Moses, and excuse me that I have hitherto called you Spaniard, but I thought that was your name."

"I excuse you, my boy, and also give you permission to call me Rabbi Moses, for it is a title I am proud of, as it was conferred on me in the *Yeshibah* (Jewish high school) of Amsterdam. But here I am chatting away, and do not yet know what I can do for you."

"Rabbi Moses, I want to learn," cried the boy, enthusiastically. "I want to learn everything—all the sciences which the people of the land learn."

The face of old Moses beamed with joy; he agitatedly stroked his majestic mustache; then, in deep emotion, placed his hand on the boy's head, and blessed him with the blessing Joseph had that evening so sorely missed in the synagogue; and the boy devoutly bent his head before the man who was outlawed by his people.

A holy awe overcame the boy; a father's hands had blessed him; he kissed them ardently.

"When, my son, will you begin your lessons?" asked Moses, kindly.

"I can only come at nights, and will gladly sacrifice a few hours' sleep, if it would not be too troublesome for you, Rabbi; for I would not like to grieve my mother again," returned Joseph.

"That is right, my son. I do not require much sleep, and your self-sacrifice will be repaid doubly and trebly. Our great teacher Hillel studied only by night, for he had to work for his sustenance by day."

* * * * * *

The sky was gray in the east, and the sexton's shrill voice was summoning worshippers to assemble for prayers, when Joseph entered his little room and threw himself on his bed; and his mother had the greatest trouble to rouse him from his apparently deep sleep.

CHAPTER VIII.
THE APPROACHING FEAST OF CONFIRMATION.

On the first day of New Year the news that Cobbler Christian had disappeared, spread like wildfire. All the Jews of Immenfeld knew the old drunkard, many were unpleasantly surprised by the news, for ignorance of the fate of the torn boots and shoes intrusted to the cobbler's skill spoiled many a one's enjoyment of the holiday, and this they would not desecrate by instituting inquiries.

But soon they received the comforting news from the Gentiles of the village that the cobbler had left everything behind him, even his furniture, and that nothing would have led to the supposition of Christian's departure, had not a note, fastened to the door, given notice thereof. This note, which, however, could not proceed from Christian himself, as he did not know how to write, contained news that he was gone never to return.

Joseph Bonafit was powerfully affected by this startling intelligence. Vividly it occurred to his mind that this had a close connection with the mystery he had been a witness of. He tormented himself unmercifully to find the right clew, but in vain. What would he not have given to be at liberty to confide his secret to Benrimo, but he was bound by his oath.

When Joseph's mother had retired to rest that evening, he, as on the night before, rose from his bed, which he had sought at an early hour, and repaired to Benrimo's house. And thus Joseph continued to pay his nightly visits to his learned patron and friend, never failing to appear at the appointed hour. After surmounting the difficulties of the German language, both in reading and writing, he studied history, geography, arithmetic, and listened with strained attention to his master's discourse. And when the old rabbi explained in a natural manner the many miracles of the Bible, when he spoke of the science of chemistry, which, although then in its infancy, could already work greater miracles than those of which the ancients told, Joseph was completely carried away by admiration.

"You are like a prophet, Rabbi Moses," murmured the boy, a sacred awe upon him, "like a prophet who has the power of seeing into the future."

"It is no wonderful thing nowadays to be a prophet," returned Benrimo, "just as it never was difficult to wise and thinking men of all times and countries to foretell the future, for he who compares past and present aright, and understands how to infer the effect from the cause, can easily foresee what is to come. Nature forever moves in accordance with fixed laws, and we have but to subordinate ourselves to these; therefore, any one who thinks must be able to calculate how long, for instance, it would take the inferior of two neighboring tribes to raise itself to the other's might and power, and to successfully attack and conquer it.

"He who observes and thinks will always find some place in history on which to base his prophecies; he sees, for instance, how one nation, in the continuous struggle for pre-eminence, reached a zenith of glory, then quickly deteriorated from it, thus giving room to some other.

"In olden times, the reverence with which the people regarded their prophets was fully justified, for they far exceeded the common masses in wisdom and knowledge, and the one who acquires knowledge because he thinks it something infinitely desirable, is at all times a prophet, for the masses regard him with veneration, his equals with respect, and those high in office with favor. As in former times the world belonged to the mighty, as it now belongs to the wealthy, a time will come when those who are rich in knowledge will rule it absolutely."

If the Jewish citizens of Immenfeld had listened to this discourse, they would have excommunicated Benrimo at least half a dozen times more; but they did not hear it, for the night-watchman was just calling out the second hour after midnight, and Joseph arose to depart.

*　　*　　*　　*　　*　　*

While with Benrimo, Joseph had completely forgotten Cobbler Christian and his secret; but in his little bed it oppressed his heart again like a heavy weight. If he could only have spoken about it, but he durst not!

As his thoughts continually revolved about the same axis, it was but natural that, as he and his mother were sitting at their breakfast, he suddenly asked:

"Mother, dear, do you know the gentleman to whom we owe our liberty?"

"Lead me not into the way of the wicked," murmured his mother, instead of an answer.

"But you seem to know him?" urgently asked Joseph again.

"He is the brother of that wicked woman who persecuted us," his mother now answered.

Joseph clapped his hand on his forehead. Why did he not think of this before? Had not the baron's resemblance to the gentleman already surprised him?

"Can you tell me some particulars about Cobbler Christian?"

"My son, what nonsense you talk; these two persons must not be spoken nor even thought of!"

"It's remarkable," muttered Joseph; "even mother puts the nobleman and the cobbler into one category."

"Do you not know," began Joseph aloud, casting down his eyes in order to avoid meeting his mother's reproving look, "as you know the gentleman, whether he is on good terms with young Baron Egmont?"

"I forbid your mentioning the name of this young enemy of Israel within my four walls. I have grown old enough to know that you have in him a persecutor who will render your life a constant fear."

"I fear no one. I need not shun the light of day. I leave those whose deeds are dark to fear," returned Joseph, sullenly.

He arose and, taking his prayer-book, prepared to go to synagogue, whither he was accompanied by his mother, for it was a Sabbath eve. It was still very early, and when the two passed Benrimo's house it was quite dark, while lights twinkled from all the other houses in Jew's Lane. Mrs. Bonafit remarked to her son:

"This is also one of whom you must beware, as he has been excommunicated by our congregation."

* * * * * * *

Hard times had come to Joseph. During the day he

studied for his bar-mitzvah and attended the *heder* (school), and at night he stole away to his new instructor. But above all he was tormented by the criminal to him.

Gradually he came to the resolve to fathom it, even were it to be his ruin.

He was very well aware that a never-ending enmity existed between the young baron and himself, but the former could not have a more bitter feeling against him than he to Egmont. He thought and calculated, and as Benrimo's instruction had sensibly sharpened his intellect. he came to the conclusion that sure preventive against the malevoence of the nephew.

Joseph's nightly visits to Benrimo's house were regularly continued; the lessons which he there received could not fail to give him a polish and style of speech very unusual in the Ghetto. Mrs. Bonafit was the first to notice this change in her son; she vainly tormented herself as to what could have caused it, and resolved to observe him closely, but as her duties—nursing the sick— left her very little leisure, Joseph was enabled to continue his nightly journeys unmolested.

Six months had passed in this wise, spring had come, preparations were already being made for the feast of the Passover, and Mrs. Bonafit was soon to have that happiness, which most parents so longingly wish for, the pleasure of seeing her son take the "sweet yoke of the Thorah" upon himself for the first time; he was to become *bar-mitzvah*. Evening after evening mother and son sat together, and the former warned her son to deliver his *Sidrah* (section of the Thorah) in a creditable manner, and to show no timidity, for it would bring her to her grave if the people would say of her son, her all, that he had not learned his assigned portion well; all the more as the whole congregation did not look upon him very favorably since the day before New Year when he had shown such familiarity to the Spaniard. If ever a poor woman, whose only possession in the world was her child, felt happy, it was the mother of Joseph. She had erected the most beautiful air castles: on the day after Joseph's confirmation, she would, with the few florins she had saved, buy some little fancy wares; with these he could begin a little trade, which in time would make him a rich man and enable him to brighten the days of her old age. But three days were wanting to the eventful Sabbath; then only two—now it was Friday evening and to-morrow —to-morrow Mrs. Bonafit would have a son looked upon, in a religious point of view, as being of full age; a man, yoked with the fulfillment of the laws contained in the Thorah.

That evening Mrs. Bonafit sat up later than usual, speaking to her son of the eventful morrow. But at last, much to Joseph's relief, she retired to rest. He was quite happy when he heard her regular breathing, for this was to him the signal that he might safely leave the house. He arose from his couch, slipped out of the door and hastened to his kind teacher, who had promised him to make use of his right, for the first time in ten years, on to-morrow, in order to listen to Joseph's delivery, from the entrance-hall of the synagogue.

The morning sun shone brightly into Mrs. Bonafit's room; its rays fell on her peaceful countenance, as if wishful to arouse her on her only son's day of honor. And they succeeded in doing so. The good woman opened her eyes, ruminated a moment, then with the glad words: "Praised be God" she jumped up briskly. While she was dressing she repeatedly called out her son's name with the loving intonation only a mother's voice can express. Pure, unalloyed happiness rested on her countenance.

"I don't know," said Mrs. Bonafit to herself, "why that boy needs so much waking, and just to-day, on his gala day; but the young sleep soundly."

Mrs. Bonafit stepped into the alcove which we described once before, and mechanically lifted her hand to awaken her son. But suddenly her eyes grew fixed, her face paled to the hue of death; trembling, she clung for support to the bed. It was empty!

"Oh, God, punish me not so severely!" she murmured weakly. "Perhaps the sun did not let him sleep and he is gone out; he may be in the street; why do I fear? I *will* not be anxious, he is no baby any more; no doubt I will often miss him morning and evening after he is confirmed, why should I be anxious?"

But the poor woman's face and tottering walk contradicted her words. She dragged herself to the door, looked up and down the street; her voice grew more and more anxious; her trembling knees threatened to give way beneath her. "Joseph! Joseph!" she cried, at first with smothered voice, then louder and shriller, at last frantically, as no Joseph appeared. The neighbors, startled by the unwonted sounds, came forth from their houses; they helped to search and call, but no sign of Joseph could they discover. The morning advanced, the men assembled in the synagogue, the service began, but still no Joseph made his appearance. The *Hasan* (reader) took forth the Thorah, and was himself obliged to read the section the truant boy ought that day to have delivered; and as he had depended on Joseph, and thus failed to prepare himself, for this Sabbath the congregation had to listen to a rather bungling recitation instead of the smooth one they had confidently expected.

In the meanwhile all this anxiety and grief had completely prostrated poor Mrs. Bonafit. She lay tossing about on her bed in a high fever, unconscious of what was transpiring around her, recognizing no one, yet constantly repeating in her delirium the *sidrah* which she had heard Joseph study every night during the past preceding months, and had it been Joseph's fate to read it that day in the synagogue, it would have redounded immensely to his credit, if he had intoned it as correctly as his poor mother now did in her delirium.

CHAPTER IX.

THE IRON DOOR.

In the city where Duke Francis XII. of Wimmerstein dwelt, there was a street called Rubbish lane. It formed part of the Ghetto, which consisted of several gloomy and dirty streets. The ground floor of each house was filled with all sorts of rubbish and lumber. Here they could buy some tarnished ornaments that had once adorned a nobleman's castle, or a broken table that had disfigured a peasant's cot. Here the beggar exchanged his rags for others, the reduced nobleman purchased a worn velvet cloak or a moth-eaten cap, and pawned his rapier in a shop close by. Here the school-boy bought copy-books, the soldier brandy, the juggler cards, the gambler loaded dice, the burglar tools, the pickpocket scissors. Everything you saw was old, faded, bent or torn. Hence a splendid show-window, in which brightly-polished weapons were exhibited to attract purchasers, excited all the more attention. And even more remarkable than the splendid show-window was the handsome sign, painted in blue and gold, which hung over the door, and bore, in striking contrast to all the Isaacs, Samuels, Davids, etc., on the other dirty signs, a genuine Gentile appellation. "Augustus Heberline, Furbisher," was the inscription on the handsome signboard.

Did you enter the store of this armorer, you encountered an aged man, with a long, waving, white beard, who courteously inquired your wishes, showed you weapons, but always demanded a price so exorbitant that you could purchase nothing.

None of the Jewish traders in the neighborhood had ever seen a customer depart from Heberline's store with a weapon he had bought there; all came forth vexed and disappointed, and generally directed their steps to one of the numerous second-hand shops where they could purchase at more reasonable rates.

At first, which was now some time ago, there was much

laughing at the expense of the Gentile armorer, who thought to compete with all the surrounding Jewish tradesmen, and a speedy ruin was predicted for him; however, since then, many of the other shops had time and again changed owners, while the armorer maintained his post, kept his windows bright and his weapons polished, although he never took in a cent of money.

It is conceivable that such sagacious people as Jews are —people who can so accurately calculate receipts and expenses—should soon feel astonishment at such a business and its owner, and in Rubbish lane it was quite openly rumored that the brightly polished weapons in the show-window only served as a blind for something not quite so bright as they.

As the Jews of that time went very early to the synagogues at a certain season of the year, they could not fail to see men, who, to judge from their dress, were armorers, enter and leave the house of Augustus Heberline. But, where so many armorers were employed, and especially at a time when other people still sleep, there must either be a considerable sale or an ample stock. All the Jews in Rubbish lane very well knew that the former was not the case; and that the latter was likewise improbable was proven by the fact that the weapons in the show-windows were never increased by any addition, nor the shelves in the store enriched by as much as two pistols or swords.

That a Gentile at that time settled among Jews was in itself a rare occurrence enough, but that he should keep a secret to himself, the inhabitants of Rubbish lane could not endure. The most inquisitive of all was Levi Pinkus, a man, who, by virtue of his position, ought to have been least troubled by this vice; he was the president of the congregation. At first, Pinkus had made friendly advances to Mr. Heberline, who was his next-door neighbor; but " Good morning, gracious sir!" was never answered, save by a scornful, contemptuous glance; and once, when Pinkus had even had the assurance to waylay the old gentleman and offer him a pinch of snuff, Mr. Heberline had said, shortly: "Neighbor, if you ever stop my way again, or dare to address me, I will wring your neck for half an hour; now act accordingly."

But Pinkus could not rest; to what purpose was he president if he could not keep his congregation informed of current news, or bring the only Gentile who dwelt among them to listen to reason.

Therefore, Pinkus, while he sedulously avoided to openly encounter the proprietor of the mysterious store, secretly watched and spied on him night and day, but without result. He saw what the others saw—no more.

Now there was a cellar beneath Pinkus' shop, and, according to his calculation, there must likewise be one in the adjoining house. All of a sudden the way he ought to take became very clear to the good, inquisitive man. Without delay, Pinkus procured a candle, and repaired to the cellar, which, however, was so full of old rubbish that it took him half a day to clear the way to the partition wall between his and his neighbor's cellar. He knocked along the wall with a small hammer, in order to discover if any of the huge stones were loose and might be displaced. Thus he had arrived at the extreme end of the vault, and, vexed at his ill success, he raised his hammer and brought it down with all his might on what he took to be a huge square stone, but—oh horror!—there was a sound far louder than the beat of a hammer on an anvil; a sound as of iron on iron. Simultaneously the wall turned inward, a bright ray of light darted forth from the adjacent cellar, Pinkus fell on his knees, but in the next moment felt himself hurled far back into the cellar, where he fell over barrels and chests; and remained lying motionless, paralyzed with fear. When he ventured to look up, his dreaded neighbor stood over him and uttering the words: "Just wait, you rascal, I'll give you a lesson for stealing Christian children." He began to beat him so unmercifully, that poor Pinkus thought he would never survive. His dreadful cries of anguish were not heard in the upper world, and his neighbor continued to inflict a hearty chastisement, until he observed that Pinkus was about to swoon, when he vanished through the door where he had so suddenly made his appearance.

Now, Mr. Pinkus had neither wife nor child, but kept bachelor's hall in the small apartment back of his shop. Thither he now painfully made his way, and threw himself on his bed, where he writhed about in indescribable agony.

But poor Pinkus' sufferings were not at an end, they had but just begun.

When it had grown dusk, Pinkus heard a terrible knocking at his door, and the cry: "Open, open, in the name of the law!"

Trembling in every limb, the suffering man arose from his couch, dragged himself to the door, and pushed back the bolt. He fairly bounded back, for before him stood a finely dressed gentleman, followed by a servant bearing a torch, and four men who looked startlingly like police-officers.

The gentleman drew Pinkus into the shop, the others followed one by one, the last closing and bolting the door.

"For God's sake, my gracious sirs," groaned Pinkus, "what do you want of me—what have I done to bring the police to my house?"

"To begin with, my good friend, I do not want to be taken for a policeman. I am a nobleman; look at me and say whether I resemble a myrmidon of the police?"

Pinkus ventured to look up, and the face of the nobleman did not by any means inspire him with confidence. It was the face of a man in his prime, but who was so dreadfully thin as to look like a living skeleton. His nose, bent like a hawk's bill, almost touched his upper lip. His gray, pointed whiskers reached down to his breast; but his eyes, of gray color, were the most awful Pinkus had ever beheld, and their glances made him shudder all over.

"But if the gracious gentleman is no policeman, why does he come in the name of the law, and what does he want of me?"

"I was notified that you generally slay Christian children and make use of their blood at your sacrifices."

Pinkus was obliged to lean against a chest in order not to fall. This was always the pretext for instituting anew persecutions of the Jews, the excuse for robbing and cruelly murdering them during all the middle ages.

"God have mercy on us," muttered Pinkus; "happy the man who is not president of a congregation now."

But the measure of his terror was not yet full.

"You are president of the congregation?" continued the nobleman, in an inquiring tone.

"Alas, yes," returned Pinkus.

"Know then, that I have been informed that you have a little Christian boy concealed in your cellar."

"Oh, what a lie, what an infamous falsehood," cried Pinkus, raising his eyes to the ceiling.

"I myself did not believe it; but to convince the people how groundless their accusations are, I must institute a strict search here."

"Be it so, in the name of God," replied Pinkus, greatly relieved. "I know that the noble gentleman does not for a moment believe what the silly people say, for the gentleman is a nobleman, and a nobleman has had some education. I know, gracious sir," continued Pinkus in a pleading tone, "that when you have convinced yourself of my innocence, you will let me and my congregation go forth pure and unsullied from this trial."

"As unsullied and white as a swan, Pinkus," returned the nobleman, with a scornful smile which boded no good for the poor man. "But now, Pinkus, light us down to your cellar so that I may convince the people of the groundlessness of their talk," said the nobleman moving toward the back room.

Pinkus hastened to raise the trap-door, and descended the steep stairs in advance of the others.

"Christian," said the nobleman to a man standing near him, "search the cellar well, you have been brought up among the lower classes, and you shall convince your own self that your talk is nothing but malice."

At this moment a cry was heard which froze every drop of blood in the veins of poor Pinkus, and caused all present, the nobleman at their head, to hasten to the extreme corner of the cellar. The cry was that of a little child. Pinkus lost all control over himself, and shaking in every limb, he sank on his knees and tore his hair in bunches from his head.

Soon the nobleman and his followers returned, the former bearing a little child in his arms.

It was a wondrously beautiful, golden-haired little boy of about a year old. When he caught sight of all the strange faces he broke into lamentable crying. The poor child was clothed with but one little garment.

"You rogue of a Jew," roared the nobleman, "do you see now that the voice of the people is the voice of God?"

"Hear, O Israel!" cried Pinkus, his teeth chattering! "I am lost, all Israel is lost! God Almighty take pity on us in this hour of peril!"

"Yes, the mercy of God will be very needful, very needful indeed, if one Jew of all in the city is to remain alive this time. Your fate is sealed."

"Mercy, gracious sir; mercy for God's sake! I am innocent, the whole congregation is innocent; the child has been placed here to effect my ruin," cried Pinkus, essaying to embrace the nobleman's knees.

"Has your cellar any entrance besides the one through which we descended?" asked the nobleman, in a somewhat softer tone, while he handed the shrieking child to Christian, and signed to him to carry it up-stairs.

"Yes, gracious sir, yes," cried Pinkus, to whom these words had given new life, as he now saw a prospect of escape, "there, my dear sirs, there in the corner is an iron door, which leads into the cellar, and through that door the child was brought here."

"Show it to us, Pinkus, show us but a grain of sand which may lighten the load of suspicion resting on you, and it would be welcome to us."

Pinkus arose quickly; although his face still bore an expression of deep despair, the prospect of possible escape rendered his gait firm. The nobleman and his followers, exchanging smiling looks, followed him closely. Pinkus held his light aloft and pointed to the spot where Mr. Heberline had entered that morning. "Here, gracious sirs, here," he cried, triumphantly.

"Where, where?" cried all.

"Here, don't you see?" and Pinkus knocked once on what he had taken to be an iron door; then the hair on his head bristled with horror, his uplifted arm grew rigid! What he had seen was supernatural—a miracle that God had worked to destroy him and all the Jews.

CHAPTER X.

A CAPITAL JOKE.

THE iron door, of whose existence he had that morning been so profoundly and *feelingly* convinced, was not to be discovered, only the cold, gray wall stared blankly at him. Pinkus sat down, rolled his face in the dust, and cried: "Oh, God, dost Thou still work miracles for the destruction of Thy people?"

"Where is your iron door, you Jewish rascal?" roared the nobleman, smiting the solid wall with his sword. "Is it not enough that you slay Christian children? must you deceive us so basely? Away with him!" cried the nobleman to his band, "away with him, hang him to his own door-post, and then report to your friends; by to-morrow the whole Ghetto must be razed to the ground, and ere the duke awakes the Jews must be exterminated and annihilated."

Who can imagine the mortal fear of poor Pinkus when the myrmidons seized him? Who can describe his prayers, his lamentations, his promises, his asseverations of his innocence, and that of all the Jews? It was truly heart-breaking. The unfortunate man clung to every barrel, every chest, even to the jagged stones which formed the wall, until his fingers were bruised and bleeding, while he was dragged to the cellar stairs, nearer and nearer to his dreadful doom.

When Pinkus had been brought to the foot of the stairs, he was suddenly released, and his captors vanished one by one through the trap-door into the shop above, the nobleman alone remaining below with the half-dead prisoner.

It was an awful scene.

The torch which Christian had left behind him diffused a ghastly light in the low vault, and the long, attenuated figure, bending over the writhing sufferer, bore a striking resemblance to the devil our fancy paints. It was a meet subject for a picture.

"Jew," cried the nobleman, "arise! perhaps it is not yet too late to save your accursed life!"

These words sounded like joyful pæans to the ears of the sufferer. He partly raised himself, and his fixed eyes regained some of their wonted expression.

"I will grant you your life," said the nobleman, "and the lives of those of your faith, but only on conditions."

"I agree to any conditions in advance, gracious sir," sobbed Pinkus.

"Very well; the Jews of this city must pay an indemnification of ten thousand florins by to-morrow, and you are to deliver the money to your neighbor, Heberline, the furbisher."

"Oh, oh! your lordship, do it a little cheaper," sobbed Pinkus, "a little cheaper." Instead of an answer, the nobleman whistled, and immediately a great tramping of feet was heard from above. "Granted, gracious sir, granted!" howled Pinkus, excitedly.

"Very well; the next condition is that neither you nor the other Jews of the Ghetto are to concern yourselves about the armorer's business, nor try to discover it;

quite on the contrary, you must assist him as much as lies in your power, for his misfortune will bring about that of the whole congregation. On the day when the armorer disappears from your street, or falls into the hands of justice, on that day your crime in regard to the Christian child will be made known, and I need not tell you what the consequences may be."

"Agreed, gracious sir. Mr. Heberline may do what he pleases; we will not concern ourselves about him, and we will protect him as we would one of ourselves."

"Very well; but now I demand a security, so that at some future time you will not be able to deny what we have seen to-day."

"More money," groaned Pinkus, "more money! we can procure no more."

"No, no; be at ease; no more money. I shall leave the little boy to your care; you must adopt him, and rear him in your faith."

When poor Pinkus had reluctantly assented to this also, he was dragged up-stairs and thrown on his bed; his persecutors helped themselves to what pleased their fancy, then left the house, and Pinkus heard them enter that of his neighbor, and indulge in hearty fits of laughter.

The first rays of the morning sun were just faintly lighting up the room of Pinkus, when he heard a small voice beside him cry, first "papa," then, "mamma!"

It proceeded from the child that had been left to his care. Pinkus jumped from his couch as if bitten by a tarantula. An indescribable rage took possession of him. He raised his clinched hand, but the little unsuspecting creature smiled sweetly, lovingly stretched out its arms, and repeatedly cried: "Papa, papa!"

Pikus allowed his uplifted arm to droop, and murmured: "*Gam zu l'tobah*" (this is also for the best). The compassion which dwells in every Jewish heart filled that of the sorely-tried man. He raised the crowing, merry little fellow, went to the cupboard, poured some milk into a saucer, and gave it to the child. Then he put a piece of cake into its little hand, replaced it on the bed, and—honor to the compassionate heart of the Jew—kissed its cherry lips, and muttered: "Poor little thing; you are innocent, you are not to blame for this great *gezerah*" (misfortune).

Suddenly Pinkus remembered the engagement he had entered into with the nobleman, and that he was in need of the speedy help of the whole congregation to enable him to fulfill it. He accordingly hastened to the synagogue, where his late appearance created no little sensation, which was augmented by the expression of his countenance; for the sufferings he had undergone since the day before had not failed to leave their mark.

It was still quite early, and when the services were ended, Pinkus arose and related to the terrified assembly his adventure—how nearly destruction had overtaken them.

But he wisely kept to himself that the principal cause of this calamity was his own pernicious curiosity.

The sum which Pinkus demanded was an immense one to the inhabitants of the Ghetto, none of whom were greatly encumbered with worldly goods. The men wrung their hands in mute despair; but it concerned the lives of their wives and children, the most valuable treasure they possessed, and they were obliged to determine upon some mode of action. Various proposals were made, among others that a deputation should be sent to the duke to lay the whole matter before him. But this was overruled by Pinkus, who very justly remarked that, as a nobleman had been mixed up in the affair, the duke had probably already been informed of it, and in a manner unfavorable to the Jews; the money was no doubt destined for his own private purse.

The Jews only too well knew, that when any of their reigning sovereigns was in need of money, he procured it in a justifiable or unjustifiable manner from the defenseless sons of Israel. Of course, if the Jews of the Ghetto had known that the nobleman, who plunged them into this dilemma, was no other than Kuno of Witzleb, and if they had suspected in what relation he stood to the duke, their sufferings would have been at an end; but they did not know anything of this, and were accustomed to similar treatment in extortions in those days from the nobility.

The members of the congregation contributed all the money they could spare; they counted and calculated, but could not succeed in collecting more than half the required sum.

Now the rabbi of the congregation, a venerable man with a long waving white beard, arose and thus addressed the members:

"All Israel are brethren, my friends; never forget this, be it in suffering or joy. Never has it happened in Israel that a helping hand was not extended to a brother in distress or misfortune. My proposal is the following: Send me and one other member of the congregation to our brethren in the country. We will report our grievous situation, and will surely succeed in procuring succor and aid. We will bring back enough to satisfy our enemy, and he will not further persecute us. It is true that I am old and weary of foot, but God will strengthen me, for I go forth in His name and for the weal of my people. This evening our president, Mr. Pinkus, shall take the money, which will have been collected by that time, to the foe of Israel, and as security for the rest of the amount our wives and daughters will carry their jewels and dishes of silver and gold to Pinkus, who will deliver them to our enemy, that he may be satisfied; and this he will be all the more when Pinkus gives him our assurance that we will try to please the armorer in every way, and bring up the little child among us, as a pledge of our faith and constant reminder of our compact, a compact which Haman could have devised none better."

All had attentively hearkened to the venerable rabbi's words, and they found an echo in every heart.

One of the rabbi's pupils, a sturdy young man, volunteered to accompany him, and they departed amidst the blessings and good wishes of the congregation. Without anticipating our story, we may here remark that the two delegates returned in three weeks, bringing with them the immense sum of five thousand florins, a proof of how open they had found the hearts and hands of their brethren in faith in the country.

At that time the press, that winged messenger of civilization, had very little influence; no Jewish newspaper published the events that occurred in Jewish communities, and the latter kept strictly secret any wrongs inflicted on them by the Gentiles, for well they knew that rapacity was easily excited, and only awaited a pretext to seize its prey. Hence it was that the baron's disgraceful act did not become known in any of the other Jewish communities.

But to take up the thread of our story. On the evening of that eventful day Pinkus entered the armorer's store. Old Mr. Heberline came out of his little back room and inquired what his neighbor wanted. Pinkus stated why he had come, and the armorer returned quite indifferently that the baron had commissioned him to receive the money; he also agreed to take the jewels as security until the return of the two delegates. This was an immense relief to poor Pinkus, who had feared that the armorer would not accept the jewels, although their value far exceeded that of the remaining sum, as not one woman or maiden had hesitated to bring every ornament she possessed.

Despite the severe lesson he had received, Pinkus had not unlearned his curiosity; he attempted to question Mr. Heberline about the nobleman, but the latter grew insolent, and bade him depart.

Pinkus was about to retreat in affright, when Heberline called him back, and asked him:

"Well, Mr. Pinkus, what about the little boy—what are you resolved upon doing with him?"

"I am going to keep him; the congregation has already

hired a woman to take care of him, and I should like to thank the nobleman for leaving him with me, for he is a dear little creature. If I only knew to whom he belonged, I should feel satisfied."

Heberline seized a pistol and aimed it at Pinkus. The latter sank on his knees in terror, and begged for mercy.

" Remember, you rascal," cried Heberline, " that your inquisitiveness and curiosity nearly brought down ruin on all the Jews of this city; remember this, and bridle your tongue. Now go, else I will give information that you wish to bring up a Christian child in your faith."

Pinkus departed hastily. Arrived without, he muttered inaudibly:

" By my soul, that was the voice of the nobleman! I should dearly like to know what connection there is between the two."

You see, Pinkus was incorrigible.

Hardly had Pinkus left the store, when Heberline ran with his treasure to the back-room, pulled off his long white beard, and, sinking into a chair, laughed loudly and heartily.

This awakened a sleeping man, the same whom the nobleman had last night addressed as Christian. The latter yawned, stretched himself on the sofa, and looked at the laugher with eyes heavy with sleep.

" Well, drunken cobbler, what are you staring at?"

" Pardon, your lordship, but I cannot imagine what cause there is for amusement."

" I should like to know any one who would not laugh," returned Kuno, the ex-armorer. " Never has masterstroke of mine been more successful."

" Very true, baron, but I cannot comprehend how you can act so, as I often heard you express a decided preference for the Jews."

" It is true that I like the Jews," returned Kuno, " but I also like their money, and no one can prevent a joke well-meant. I would have played the same little game with Gentiles, but it is difficult to impose on them.

However, Christian," continued the baron, "it is high time for you to depart on your journey, and enter into the situation I have promised you as a reward for your services. Truly, I should like to be as well off as you— nothing to do but to eat, drink, and laze. You are a lucky fellow!"

Christian did not answer. He arose, grasped a sturdy stick which stood in a corner, slung his knapsack on his back and approached the baron, who put a heavy purse in his hand.

"Of ours?" asked Christian, morosely.

"No, sheepshead, it is solid Jewish coin."

"All right, baron," said Christian, putting his purse in his pocket; "but what is to become of my house in Immenfeld?"

"I suppose we can sell it to some one in the course of time; for the present we will leave it closed up."

"Have you no commands for me?"

"No; tell the holy fathers that I will visit them in the spring, and will probably bring with me a guest and some Jewish money of full weight. Now, farewell, Christian."

On finding himself alone Kuno again gave way to hearty laughter.

"Delicious, delicious!" cried Kuno, again and again; "there is no fear that the holy fathers will let the drunken cobbler go; he is safe not to blab anything where it might become dangerous. From the Jews I have taken money and given them in return a child, who will be brought up in their faith as equivalent for the soul I intend to wrest from them. Oh, it is too good, by my sword! I grudge the enjoyment of it to myself alone!"

The store-bell rang, and Kuno, resuming his false beard, entered the store as armorer Heberline.

CHAPTER XI.
A FRIEND IN NEED.

It is time that we return to Immenfeld.

During the delivery of the *Sidrah,* the portion of the

Sabbath lesson, many whispered remarks were interchanged concerning the mysterious disappearance of the widow's son. It may be imagined that these were not always favorable to the poor boy. When the services were ended, members congregated in little groups, some standing before the synagogue, and others slowly strolling on their homeward way. The majority maintained that as Joseph was already so much of an apostate, he had shrunk from facing the Thorah, looking into God's countenance, as it were, and had secretly run away; a very small minority ventured to express the opinion that something might have happened to the boy.

The first group, talking energetically and walking slowly along, stopped short before the Spaniard's house; the other groups coming up, gradually increased the circle of excited talkers, and so it came about that the whole congregation was soon, almost unintentionally, assembled before Benrimo's house.

Suddenly a prying boy stooped and picked up an old cap which lay on the step at Benrimo's door.

"Look here," cried the boy, "as sure as I live and breathe, this is Joseph Bonafit's old cap."

All looked at the cap in breathless suspense, and many identified it as Joseph's property; and now the crowd seemed to comprehend where they were; instinctively they retreated into the middle of the street; all glances were directed to Benrimo's windows, which, strange to say, and in direct contrast to their wonted manner, were closely curtained.

Benrimo himself, however, was wholly ignorant of what was happening before his door. His pupil had left him at a very late hour, and he slept so far into the morning that he missed the *Shacharith* (morning) prayer.

The curtained windows had contributed no small share to Benrimo's long sleep. These very curtains, however, which now excited so much astonishment, were by no means an innovation; they had never been remarked because the members of the Immenfeld congregation did not dare to look up at the excommunicated Spaniard's windows. Their origin may be explained easily enough. Joseph Bonafit had observed, or thought he had observed, that some one passed the windows every night while he was at his lessons, and once he even believed to have seen Cobbler Christian's face pressed for a second's time against the window-pane. Partly to quiet the boy's fears, and partly to keep his attention from wandering from his studies, Benrimo had put up curtains which he drew close every time Joseph came.

It was about noon when Benrimo arose from his couch, greatly wondering that he had so overslept himself. As he did not cook on the Sabbath, he partook of a cold breakfast, and then sat down over his books, in whose contents he soon became so absorbed that he did not notice the unusual number of shadows which crossed his window on that day.

In the meanwhile the crowd before the door had been admonished by the rabbi not to break the peace of the Sabbath by any unusual demonstrations, but to disperse quietly to their homes, and reassemble at his house in the evening, in order to consult about what steps they ought to take in the matter.

When evening arrived all the *ba'ale battim* (members of the congregation) hastened to the place of meeting, and as every one had something to say, and all said it at the same time, a regular hubbub and babel ensued.

Finally all the screaming and gesticulating resulted in the following resolution: A deputation, consisting of the president and two of the most influential members of the congregation, was to go to the Spaniard's dwelling to investigate Joseph's absence and whereabouts; also to make the necessary inquiries.

They received accurate instructions how to act, and the meeting resolved to remain in session until the return of the deputation, in order to await the latter's report.

But hardly had the committee of three departed when the members on some pretext or other successively left the room. At first single members slipped out, then they went by twos and threes; finally none wished to be left behind, and when the deputation arrived at Benrimo's house (it must be confessed that their hearts beat quite violently) they saw the whole congregation trail like the tail of a comet after them.

This was far from being disagreeable to the deputation. A singular feeling of awe overcame them on crossing the threshold of a man whom they had persecuted for ten long years, and to whom they were even now coming with a purpose far from friendly.

The president had foreseen this feeling, and had therefore spoken at length in the meeting, that the Spaniard should be summoned to appear before them. However, it was very justly maintained that the Spaniard would not come, and then the matter was very urgent, for the Widow Bonafit lay on the point of death. Well, when the president stopped at Benrimo's door, he hemmed, hawed and scraped his feet on the sill, in all which actions he was faithfully supported by his companions, and then knocked pretty firmly on the door. Immediately a stamping and pounding was heard, and the hearts of the valiant three fell some inches, for they recognized the beats of Spaniard's crutches which were approaching the door from within.

The deputation expected that they would be questioned from within, and this would have just pleased the president, as it would have given him an opportunity to unfold his diplomatic talents; but nothing of the kind occurred; a bolt was drawn back and the next moment the three were face to face with the outlaw, the anathematized.

The latter did not immediately recognize his visitors, for the hall was in partial darkness; despite this he gave them a somewhat surprised "Good-evening," and invited them to enter the room. In his desire to know who these late disturbers of his solitude might be, he forgot to close the the house door. When Benrimo hobbled into the room he almost dropped his crutches, so utterly astonished was he at the sight of the president and two of the most esteemed members of the congregation. The latter did not fail to note the Spaniard's surprise and nodded significantly to each other.

Benrimo quickly regained self-possession, and offered chairs to his visitors, which were, however, not accepted.

"Then permit me to sit down, gentlemen; you have each of you two feet, while I must always stand on one."

Thus saying, Benrimo seated himself and looked expectantly at the three men, who were completely at a loss how or when to begin.

"Well, what have you to say to me?" at last asked Benrimo.

"Nothing good," stammered the president.

"That I believe, gentlemen; what good can come from antagonists?"

Had not Benrimo already been excommunicated, this one expression would certainly have sealed his fate; the three men reddened with anger, their eyes glared fiercely on Moses, for he had spoken words foreign to them, words which were only used by the tormentors when speaking of Jews.

The president advanced close to Benrimo, and in a voice quivering with rage, he asked: "Say, what have you done with Joseph Bonafit?"

"Ah! so," said Benrimo, lightly; then he continued, scornfully, "so the wise congregation has at last discovered this!"

"Of course," shrieked the president, "and for that reason we have come here!"

"Well, as you know all, you might have dispensed with the journey here. Why do you come to me? Do you, perhaps, wish to wrest from me the soul I have stolen from you?"

"Exactly," one of the deputation ventured to remark, gathering courage from the fact that the hall and room were fast filling with men, unobserved by Benrimo, who sat with his back to the door, "exactly; you have stolen his soul, and we demand it back."

"You must ask the boy himself if he wishes to give it back."

"Hear the renegade! hear the kidnapper!" cried the president, who was well aware that help was at hand; "he derides us!"

Hardly had these words escaped the president, when Benrimo stood on his one foot, and threateningly brandished aloft his crutch. "You are in my house, miserable slanderers," he cried, in a voice like thunder; "even though I am a cripple, I can defend my honor against the whole good-for-nothing crew."

The three men retreated with very pale faces; but now another man, a cattle dealer, who was noted and dreaded in the village for his roughness, and who had slipped into the room among the rest, stepped up to the aged man and said:

"Just put down your crutch; you are a renegade. Joseph is nowhere to be discovered; he disappeared last night, and his cap was found on your doorstep; now, who has done away with him? You, and no one else!"

Benrimo dropped his crutch, and sank down in a chair. Great drops of perspiration oozed out on his forehead.

"Wha—what do you say? Joseph Bonafit has disappeared? That is impossible; it cannot be; he asked me to come to his *bar-mitzvah*. I promised to do so, and forgot."

"Do you hear it? Do you hear it?" cried numerous voices, and Benrimo was surrounded by red and angry faces. "Do you hear it? He was here last night! The Spaniard's fear and surprise, when he heard that we knew of his crime, have betrayed him!" howled the cattle-driver.

"Gentlemen!" began Benrimo, and his voice trembled, while he painfully supported himself on his crutches, "believe me, this dreadful news has moved me more——" A burst of contemptuous laughter overpowered his voice. Benrimo wiped the perspiration from his forehead with the back of his hand. His words were not credited; he became anxious for his safety. Carefully giving way before the crowd pressing in on him, he maneuvered so well as to reach the wall, thus gaining a shield for his back. Beside him hung an unsheathed cavalry sword.

"Rabbothai!" (gentlemen) now began the president. "here, before you stands a blasphemer, an apostate in Israel; he has purloined a boy, the only son of his mother, and she a widow; what shall we do with him?"

"Flog him," howled the cattle-dealer, and some of the younger men joined in the cry.

"God shall not punish us so severely," said the president, "we will not lay violent hands on one of our people!"

"But he is no Jew, he is an apostate and is anathematized," cried the cattle-dealer; the foam standing on his lips. "He is excommunicated, he does not belong to us." And ere the others could prevent him he rushed forward with uplifted arm; Benrimo tore the sword from the wall with the rapidity of lightning, and, anticipating his opponent, inflicted such a blow on the latter's arm, that he sank to the ground howling with agony. This was a signal for a general attack; Benrimo whirled his sword like a wheel about his head, and thus kept his assailants at bay; the latter finally took up the large folios which lay about the room and began to throw them at Moses; one hit him so violently on the breast that he tottered, and the next moment would have decided his fate, had not all remained standing as if magically rooted to the ground. A fanfare—the shrill blast of a horn resounded from the upper end of the street; there was a trampling of horses, which ceased before Benrimo's house; the crowd in the hall was pushed to one side, and in the doorway appeared the tall, commanding figure of a gentleman, wearing a gold-laced coat, on the breast of which a diamond star blazed and sparkled.

All in the room drew back, and Benrimo cried ecstatically:

"Praise be to God! Your highness does not come a moment too soon!"

When the men in the room heard this title, they sneaked off and attempted to hide behind the gentlemen who had followed close upon the first-comer.

"Moses, what is going on here?" asked the duke, for it was no less a person.

Benrimo dropped his sword in affright, for it suddenly became clear to him what a situation he was in.

"Your highness," said the old man, in embarrassment, looking at the Jews behind the officers—"your highness must excuse us, we were fencing for amusement."

"But Moses," returned the duke, incredulously, "you just said that I did not come a moment too soon."

"Did I say that? Then your highness must ascribe it to my wish of having such a connoisseur of fencing as witness to our performance. But will not your highness be seated?"

"No, thanks; but what," continued the duke, with unusual obstinacy, "what do all these people here and in the street want of you?"

"Those—ah——" cried Benrimo, confusedly scratching his head, "oh—they came to offer their congratulations, as the day is my birthday."

"Moses, Moses, you must have grown imbecile! Do people come in the evening to offer birthday wishes? Or think you that I have such a bad memory for my friends, that I do not remember your birthday, like mine, is in autumn, and not in spring."

"I humbly implore your highness to let this matter rest; kindly believe what I have spoken to be true, and allow me again to express my joy at seeing you, and to ask to what happy chance I owe the honor of your visit."

"I am on a visit to my castle on the Rhine; last night the conversation turned on you, my Moses, and these gentlemen"—the duke indicated his companions—"expressed a desire to make your acquaintance. So we made a little trip to Immenfeld."

Moses did not answer immediately; after a pause, he said in an embarrassed way:

"Will it please your highness to take your humble servant with you?"

What, Moses! What say you?" cried the duke, greatly rejoiced; "you want to go with me, old friend? You want to go away from here, despite that the whole Jewish population of the place congratulated you as early as to-day for your birthday in the autumn, an honor which was never done me?" A smile accompanied the duke's last words.

"Yes, your highness," said Moses, with an answering smile at the duke's remark, "yes, I wish to leave this place, although I have enjoyed a great many benefits here. There is such a thing as wearying, even at good things."

Count Hugo, and you, baron," said the duke, turning to two of his companions who stood nearest him, "escort Benrimo to my carriage, for he is not very fleet of foot."

The two gentlemen smilingly hastened to perform the duke's behest, and the Jews of Immenfeld enjoyed the rare spectacle of seeing the man whom they had not only anathematized, but even accused of kidnapping, lifted into the carriage by a count and a baron.

But the Jews of Immenfeld did not know what they had lost in the "Spaniard" until a few days after Benrimo's departure, when a courier arrived at the president's house with a message from the duke. As the message was written in German, the courier read it aloud. It was as follows:

"To My Jewish Subjects in Immenfeld,—You are a band of outlaws and rowdies. I would have had a tower built for each of you; had my Moses demanded it. You treated him shamefully, and yet you now owe it to his intercession that I do not have every one of you whipped out of the country. As punishment, I make over to you the chagrin you must feel, at not having known what golden eggs the goose could lay whom you were about to slay, when fortunately arrived

"Your duke,

"FRANCIS XII. OF WIMMERSTELN."

CHAPTER XII.

A CONVENT.

THE convent of "St. Francis" was situated in a dreary ravine among the mountains. The monks of this convent belonged to the order of Franciscan Friars, a clerical order, which not only required its members to take a vow of poverty, but so stretched this vow to its utmost limits that their pertinacious begging rendered the region about them as barren as locusts are wont to make a blossoming tract of land. But these Franciscan Friars were a worse plague than the locusts, for the latter at some time or other forsook the region they had invaded, while the monks never did so; neither storm nor rain could drive them from where they had established themselves, and they understood how to make every one around them subservient to their purposes. To render their poverty very apparent, they went barefoot summer and winter. Their one garment consisted of a long brown habit, the hood of which was drawn closely around their eyes; the only ornament was a rude rope tied about their waists, a cross and rosary dangling from the ends. Dirt constituted not a small part of their equipment. When the monks of the Convent of St. Francis were out on a begging tour, they would receive a dry crust of bread with many thanks and blessings, and would consume it with the greatest apparent satisfaction, while behind the walls of their convent they feasted on dainties Lucullus would not have disdained. Although the monks of the Convent of St. Francis still continued to beg, it was said of them that their convent was the richest in the country, and the peasants round about fiercely hated the hypocritical parasites. But no; there was one monk whom they did not hate. This exception was Father Anselmo. Very much in contrast to the other monks, Father Anselmo was not at all corpulent. Sobriety and intelligence had established their thrones on his forehead. Wherever the long, thin figure of Father Anselmo was seen, people hastened to greet him and implore his blessing.

All the harm inflicted on the surrounding country by the monks was overbalanced by Father Anselmo, for he was truly a man of God, a worker of miracles. Had Anselmo remained in the world, instead of secluding himself within the walls of a convent, he would have been the most celebrated physician of his time. Very often was Father Anselmo summoned to castles and palaces when the most skillful physicians had given up their distinguished patients' lives; and Father Anselmo gave relief after all had despaired of help.

For the convent, also, Anselmo was an invaluable acquisiton and treasure. The presents he received—often immense sums of money—all reverted to the convent, and greatly enriched it.

Anselmo practiced his glorious art not only for the relief of the rich but for the aid of the poorest peasant; and it gave him greater pleasure to preserve a poor laborer to his numerous family than to restore a tyrant, who had been at the brink of the grave, to his oppressed subjects.

But Anselmo had one weakness. He would impart his rich stores of knowledge to no person.

The superior of the convent had repeatedly importuned Anselmo to take an assistant, so that when he died the convent would not lose its fame; but Father Anselmo rejected every proposal and every offer, with the remark that he had found neither within nor without the walls of the convent any one who was worthy to inherit the crumbs of wisdom he had so painfully picked up and become his scholar. The superior was forced to content himself with this, but he already shuddered at the thought of the learned Anselmo's death, for then the great source of revenue to the convent would cease to flow.

The porter's bell of the convent sounded. It was already quite dusk, and the porter, a lay brother, greatly wondering who it might be that demanded admittance to the convent so late in the day, hastened to the door and slipped back the heavy bolts which barred it.

"Blessed be the Father, the S—— The devil! Baron Witzleb!" cried the porter, surprised at sight of the nobleman. "What brings you here?"

"Good-evening, Christian," returned Kuno of Witzleb. "Well, won't you let me in? Your position here as porter seems to agree with you well; the brown habit becomes you charmingly; but your nose has grown a little ruddier, and you are more dirty than usual. Well, how fares it altogether?"

While uttering these words Kuno entered the reception-room. Christian answered the last question:

"Not very well, gracious sir; those cursed priests have not made me butler as yet."

"That is a proof of their penetration, Christian, for that would be setting the cat to mind the cream."

"Oh, I wish the devil would take them all."

"Christian, Christian," cried Kuno, laughing. "it seems that neither this sacred spot nor the holy fathers have cured you of your habit of swearing and wickedness."

"Those," cried Christian, contemptuously: "they curse like troopers. Listen, gracious sir," and Christian approached his mouth to the baron's ear; "you must see and hear these priests within their own convent walls; truly our band in the city is an assemblage of saints in comparison."

Kuno smiled knowingly, then said:

"Christian, go and announce my arrival to the superior."

"I don't think I can venture to do so; the worthy superior is just at supper."

"Sheepshead, for that very reason you must announce me."

Christian glided through several corridors, entered the room of Father Ignatius, the superior, and greeted him:

"Blessed be Jesus Christ."

"Confounded fool!" roared the worthy superior, his mouth full of chicken, "why do you disturb me?"

"I beg the worthy prior's pardon," returned Christian, derisively, "I forgot that we are in Lent, and that you were just partaking of lenten food." The fat prior's face grew purple with rage, but Christian knew what oil to pour on the troubled waters. He did not wait for the prior to regain his breath, but quickly said: "Kuno of Witzleb has come with the Jewish money he promised to your reverence."

The prior's face lighted up with pleasure; his anger was forgotten.

"Quick, you fool, clear off the table; bring in boiled fish and oatmeal porridge, and then invite the baron to come hither."

Christian took up the dishes, and had already reached the door, when Father Ignatius called after him: "I give you a dispensation for to-day; you may eat all the chicken I have left."

When the lenten dishes were placed on the table, Kuno was conducted to the room. He bowed and allowed Father Ignatius to bless him. When the holy father assigned him a place at the table, the baron candidly said: "Excuse me, reverend father, but I feel no desire for such food."

"My son, my son," said the prior in an admonitory tone, "remember we are in Lent. I hope that you do not transgress Christ's commandment, and prefer meat to these frugal dishes."

"Reverend father, what do you think," cried Kuno, indignantly, "does your reverence take me to be such a bad Christian?"

"No, no; God forbid my son; but it is duty for us to

guide Christians to the right path. But what news do you bring?"

"Reverend father, I come to fulfill a vow I have made to the convent. I wish to donate three thousand florins to it, if such a gift seems not too small to your reverence."

The prior's little eyes, which were almost smothered in fat, glittered as he replied: "My son, it does not beseem us to reject alms offered by a pious Christian. I accept the generous offer."

"Apply it to the diffusion of Christianity, reverend father; for this purpose I took it away from the Jews in the city. As they are too obstinate to allow themselves to be baptized, they must at least give their money so that others may be baptized."

The prior placed his hands over his well-fed stomach, twirled his thumbs, and looked upward as if transfigured.

A long pause ensued; then the baron began: "Your reverence has probably already heard what a misfortune has befallen my family, the only child of Count Weiden has been stolen by gypsies."

"I think, my son, that you told me this some time ago."

"Yes, your reverence, but you are always so taken up by holy and sacred matters, that I thought you had forgotten this worldly affair."

"That would have been the case, my son, if the child had fallen into the hands of God, or of good Christians; but into the hands of heathens, idolatrous gypsies, O Jesus! O holy Jesus!"

"Yes, yes, your reverence; that is just what hurt me most," said Kuno, drying his eyes; "your reverence knows this. But the Lord has enlightened me, he has instructed me in a dream to procure another soul for the one that is lost, and to bring it to you, reverend father, for further guidance to the feet of the lamb, our sweet Lord Jesus,"

"You are a truly devout Christian, my son, and the blessing of God will rest upon you."

"Amen, reverend father, amen! I have performed my part of the task, and come to place the accomplishment of it into your anointed hands."

"You did well, my son, very well; where is the child who is to wear the crown of Christianity instead of the one who is stolen?"

"In the carriage, your reverence, which I left at the entrance of the ravine. After I have received your permission, I will bring the boy here, with the help of two brothers," returned Kuno, completely changing his tone, as the comedy which he and the prior were acting began to weary him, and the latter signed that there was now no fear of eavesdroppers.

The prior also changed his manner, and arising from his chair, he said:

"Is the money in your carriage, also, baron?"

"Yes, Father Ignatius; it is good money, which you may without fear send to any mint, or invest in some profitable undertaking."

"Have you brought some of the other kind?" asked the prior.

"No, not to-day; we have discovered a new market for it, and I think we had rather cease here awhile, as the whole district is flooded with it, and the peasants have grown so distrustful that they even examine good money with critical eyes, as I had opportunity to observe on my journey here."

"But you will let us have a percentage of your gainings elsewhere?" asked the prior.

"Certainly, certainly; consider the three thousand florins as part. Another thing; never let Christian suspect that you and I are confederates; and in future, give the counterfeit money only to those monks who are too stupid to know the difference, or to such as you can safely depend on. But, in particular, do not draw Father Anselmo into our game; he looks upon some things far too seriously, and recognizes such a counterfeit coin from afar."

"Do not trouble yourself, baron; I have always been very careful, and intend to remain so. But let us go for the Jewish boy."

"Ah, yes; it is well that you remind me of him; he is a splendid boy, intelligent, wide awake, and will in some future time do honor to his bringing up. I intend great things from him; no less than———"

"Than what, baron?"

"Never mind, your reverence; we will speak about that later on. But I will tell you what you are to do with the boy. Teach him everything that can be imparted to him here. If possible, try to infuse some love of Christianity into him; but in any case, make a man of him, with whom something can be done."

"To begin with, we will of course give him holy baptism," said the superior, smilingly.

"By no means," cried Kuno, hotly; "for God's sake do not force the boy to anything, else all our exertions will be in vain. The boy's character is such that, with kindness, you may move him to any action; by compulsion, however, you will never attain anything. He is exceedingly anxious to learn, but should you try to force him to study, he will not desire to know anything. When he will feel so much love for Christianity as to ask for baptism, you may give it him, but no sooner. You are well aware what you and I think of religion.

"With Father Anselmo, also," continued Kuno, "you must be very careful in this matter. He will soon enough be anxious to instruct the boy, for so far I have found no one who could resist the influence of this glorious child; but you must place difficulties in the way, and then Anselmo will be all the more set upon teaching him. But now, your reverence, call two brothers to my aid, that I may bring the lost sheep into the fold," said Kuno, falling into his former sanctimonious tone.

The prior applied a silver whistle to his lips. At his

call Christian appeared and received the requisite instructions. An hour later the porter's bell of the convent again sounded, and Kuno of Witzleb entered, followed by two monks bearing a struggling human figure, the head of which was enveloped in a thick sack.

The struggling figure was brought into the convent refectory, and the sack taken from its head.

"The holy Virgin protect me!" ejaculated Christian as the lamp light fell on the countenance of the sobbing boy; "why, that is Joseph Bonafit, from the Jews' lane in Immen——"

A resounding box on the ear, dealt by the baron's bony hand, stopped all further disclosures Christian was disposed to make.

CHAPTER XIII.
A PROPHECY.

In every great city there are parks and pleasure grounds where the residents may take refuge from the dust and noise of the crowded streets. The same city which was in one part defaced by Rubbish lane, was in another part ornamented by a large and beautiful park, full of leafy arbors, grassy lawns, and sparkling fountains.

Whoever sought quiet, and yet did not wish wholly to withdraw from the world's bustle, could find recreation in these beautiful walks, or did he possess a carriage, might recline in it at ease and look on the gay throngs at their pleasuring. But whoever sought pleasure in solitude, found countless delightful retreats in the many arbors and grottoes of the park.

"Here, Frederick, stop the carriage here; I will get out and repair to a grassy bank behind yonder trees, which has become a favorite with me, and dream away an hour there."

The carriage stopped instantly.

A servant in the ducal livery leaped down, opened the coach door, and assisted an elegantly dressed gentleman, who had but one leg, to descend.

"Shall I accompany you, gracious sir?" asked the servant.

"No, thanks," returned the gentleman, whom our readers doubtless have already recognized; "just give me that cloak, for although it is already pretty warm, it is rather chilly for old folks."

"Shall I remain within call?" asked the coachman.

"You may walk the horses up and down this avenue and await me at this spot," said Benrimo, while the servant threw a light cloak over his splendid, gold-embroidered dress, thus hiding a number of orders which glittered on his breast. The latter now assumed his crutches and was soon lost to view in the shrubbery of the park.

"Come on, comrades, come on; let us penetrate into the thicket, and arrange a game," shouted the clear though feeble voice of a boy, and a group of youths, clad in the uniform of the ducal military school, came wantonly pushing their way though the crowd of promenaders in the walk.

Although all appeared to be much older than the one who called, the latter was evidently the leader, for the rest closely followed him. In him, also, we recognize an acquaintance, the descendant of the Weidens, no other than young Baron Egmont.

His uncle's predictions did not seem to have been verified, for the results of a Spartan education were by no means observable in the young cadet. The youths, our Egmont at their head, behaved and deported themselves, not like pupils of a patrician institution, but like street boys. Thus Egmont, winking slyly at his comrades, tripped a corpulent gentleman, and as the latter in falling grasped a lady's dress and tore it from the waist, the whole group laughed uproariously, and vanished behind the trees.

"Egmont, Egmont!" said one of the older cadets, "I am afraid we have made a pretty mess of it. I wish I had stayed at home and not gone out again against our tutor's command. If you would but leave off playing tricks, which can only aggravate our situation."

"Pshaw, Henry the Raven, cease your croaking; we want to have a jollification," cried Egmont; "and even if we are locked up for several hours, all the better; we have nothing to study then."

Henry, surnamed the Raven, on account of his gloomy prophecies, was silent, and followed his comrades, who stormed on with Egmont at their head.

After the cadets had for awhile committed all sorts of mischief, such as trampling on flowers, aiming stones at birds, or strewing sand on the clothes of some unsuspecting promenader, they began to weary of this sport, and heaped reproaches on Egmont, who had promised them great pleasures. All sank down ill-humoredly on the grass, only Egmont remained standing, in a reflecting mood; his influence on his comrades was in danger of being lost, if he could not discover something new to please them.

"What a pity," began Egmont, "that Jews are excluded from this walk; what splendid fun we could make of them."

"Look out for some sport, Egmont, else we will go home and surrender ourselves in a body to the tutor."

Egmont vanished; the boys amused themselves for awhile, and had almost forgotten him, when he came back treading cautiously and signing them to do likewise. The group of cadets now glided noiselessly after their leader until the latter halted before a grotto. They pressed forward to the entrance, and with difficulty suppressed a cry of surprise, so beautiful was the picture presented to their view.

The little daylight that penetrated into the grotto dimly illuminated the figure of a lady, who was sitting on a stone bench, with head drooped in fatigue or sorrow. She was attired wholly in black, and long golden curls fell gracefully on her shoulders. Her hands, clasped in her lap, gleamed like alabaster against the black folds of her dress. Artists' hands had never chiseled a more perfect statue of Grief!

Egmont broke the spell which held the boys inthralled, by a frivolous remark, for he had no appreciation of the beautiful:

"See, that is the Witch of Endor; who shall be King Saul, and ask his fate of her?"

"Egmont, I don't suppose you want to play a trick on this poor lady who is so overcome with grief?" said Henry the Raven.

"Certainly; what does the sorrow of another concern me, if I can only amuse myself and redeem my promise to you? Moreover, I think the beautiful lady is asleep, and as it is cold in the grotto she might catch cold if I do not rouse her."

"Shame, Egmont," again began the Raven, "does it beseem young officers to insult a lady? The instant I see you disturb the lady, I shall go away."

"Go to the devil, Raven, and leave us in peace," cried Egmont, almost aloud.

Henry turned away, without uttering a word, and departed.

"Now, attention," cried Egmont; and stooping down, he crept into the grotto and up to the lady's feet, where he suddenly erected himself. But the lady did not observe him.

Egmont now drew his sword (the cadets carried small swords) and—the boys at the entrance drew back in affright—lightly tapped the lady's shoulder with it. The latter uttered a cry of terror and started up in revery from her seat, thus revealing a beautiful countenance to the group of boys at the entrance. On catching sight of the cadets, she smiled sorrowfully, and turning to Egmont, said, in a silvery voice: "Ah! young man, you startled and almost frightened me." Upon this, she prepared to leave the grotto, but Egmont barred her way, and the boys collected around him.

"Nay, beautiful witch," cried Egmont, "you cannot

leave this spot ere you have prophesied. I am King Saul, and these are my halberdiers!"

"Pshaw! children; desist!" said the lady, coloring up, faintly; "do not be naughty."

"Witch of the grotto, you dare to call us children!" cried Egmont, seizing the lady's hand. The latter hastily withdrew it, and hurled Egmont back into the grotto, at which his comrades burst into loud laughter, without, however, allowing the lady to pass out. Egmont's face was distorted with rage, as we have seen it once before at the swamp. Regaining his feet, he again approached the lady and said:

"Do you think that I will suffer such an insult? Know that I am an officer and a nobleman, and will allow no woman to throw me down!"

"Shame on you!" said the lady, her lips trembling with rage and displeasure; "you not only disgrace the school to which you belong, but the ducal uniform you wear! The duty of every one who carries a sword, be he only a cadet, is to protect a lady, not to insult her! Clear the way, boys, or it will fare badly with you!"

But not one of the insolent fellows stirred.

"There is but one way, my lady," said Egmont, mockingly, "and that is to tell us our fortune. I am Baron Egmont, of Weiden, and my word holds good."

The lady uttered a low cry and started back. This, Egmont attributed to the effect which the mention of his name and station had produced. But the lady quickly recovered her self-possession, and, stepping forward, said:

"Very well, Baron Egmont, of Weiden, as you insist upon it, I will utter a prophecy: Your escutcheon, Baron Egmont, of Weiden, will be trampled upon by the hangman, as was that of your uncle, Baron Witzleb!"

The boys at the entrance of the grotto silently gave way, and the lady stepped forth. Egmont stood for a few moments like one stunned, then, giving vent to a howl of rage, he rushed after the lady with uplifted sword, and would have certainly thrust it into her back, had not a firm hand grasped his wrist. He glanced up in surprise, and saw the angry face of Benrimo, whom he immediately recognized, as he had seen him at the castle.

He forgot the lady, who was leaning against a tree, pale and trembling, and cried:

"Come on, comrades! here is a Jew in this forbidden place."

Several of the more courageous of his comrades ventured forth from the shrubbery, and one even asked, in a threatening tone, how a Jew could possess the impudence, not only to enter a forbidden part of the park, but insult one of his royal highness's cadets.

Benrimo released Egmont, and quietly unbuttoned his cloak. When the boys saw his gold-embroidered uniform and the orders on his breast, they began to feel rather ill at ease, and tremblingly put their hands to their caps to perform the military salute, while Egmont stood like one fallen from the clouds.

"Go," said Benrimo, "go; your punishment will reach you soon enough. And you, young serpent," he continued, turning to Egmont, "you will not disgrace the ducal uniform much longer."

Then the old gentleman turned to the lady, who had witnessed the whole occurrence:

"You seem to be greatly agitated; allow me to escort you until we reach a public walk."

"Thanks, sir," answered the lady, gratefully; "but I see that it is difficult for you to walk, and I will here await my servant, who escorts me to this grotto every day, for here I can dwell on my sorrows in peace. Permit me, however, to inquire the name of the knightly nobleman to whom I owe my rescue."

"That man is neither a nobleman nor a knight," returned Benrimo, smilingly, "but an old Jew who is fortunate enough to be in the good graces of his royal highness."

"Ah, you are Benrimo, the friend of our gracious sovereign," returned the lady, agreeably surprised; "then allow me to press your hand, and accompany you back to the grotto."

The lady took Benrimo's hand, offered him a seat, and sat down beside him on the stone bench.

"It is now my duty," began the lady, "to acquaint you with my name. I am the Countess of Weiden."

"Good God!" cried Benrimo, "you are the lady——"

"Yes, I am the lady who has had the misfortune to lose her child in such a horrible manner," interrupted the countess, and her glorious blue eyes were suffused with tears.

"You are, then, the relative of the young baron who insulted you so infamously to-day."

"Alas, yes; I am his aunt, and he is the sole heir of my fortune, in case—in case my little angel is not found again."

"Did you not know the young baron?"

"No, I never saw him before. We have no intercourse with the family, in order not to excite the duke's displeasure."

"My lady, did you not say that this boy is sole heir to your fortune and the title of your husband?"

"I said so, and as my husband is an aged man, he perhaps will soon possess what does not belong to him."

"Are you certain, my lady, that your child was stolen by gypsies?"

"Yes—that is to say, I was told so. Oh, perhaps I alone am to blame, for I neglected the poor little boy," and the countess began to weep softly.

"I am heartily sorry to renew your pain," said Benrimo, "but it is not curiosity that impels me to ask you for the particulars."

"Oh, I know that well; there is not a single person in the city who does not pity my unfortunate case; only my relative, the Baroness of Weiden, has not expressed one word of regret."

"I believe you," muttered Benrimo, "and I can imagine the reason."

The countess did not hear this remark; she began again:

"My husband and I had been to a ball given by a friend. When we returned we found the servants in the most terrible consternation, the nurse under the influence of a narcotic, and our poor darling child gone. All researches on our part were fruitless. All we could discover was that the nurse had walked with the child in the garden, and had there met a gypsy woman who told her her fortune, and on *her* suspicion now rests."

"What became of the nurse?"

"The count delivered her into the hands of justice, for he suspected that she knew more of the child's disappearance than she confessed. She was about to be put to the torture, although I protested violently against it, when she deprived herself of life. Now the mystery is darker than ever."

"Was the gypsy captured?"

"No, she has never been seen since."

"Were gypsies encamped in the neighborhood at the time the child was stolen?"

"No, nowhere."

Benrimo threw back his cloak; it seemed as if he felt too warm even in the cool grotto. He remained lost in thought for awhile, gesticulated with his hand, stroked his beard, and at last said:

"Countess, I must urgently beg you to leave this country for a time."

The countess, to whom the old man's gestures had seemed very strange, now looked at him in surprise, nay, even in anxiety, and asked:

"Do you mean this, Mr. Benrimo?"

"I seriously mean it, gracious lady."

"But why?"

"Because your life is in danger."

"My life! Pardon me, sir, but I think——"

"You think that I talk foolishly; do not be afraid to say so, my lady. But take my word for it, your child has not been stolen by gypsies—for the present I can say no more. But again I urgently beg of you to leave this country, and tell no one where you are going."

"Are you a prophet that you see the shadows of coming events?"

Benrimo thought of the conversation he had had with Joseph, and sighed. He was about to answer, when the lady's servant entered to get his mistress, whom he brought to the grotto every day, where she offered up a sacrifice of tears to her child.

She gave her hand to Benrimo (who gallantly, after the manner of the French, pressed a kiss on it) and said, heartily:

"Mr. Benrimo, if you will honor us by a visit, I shall be very happy to receive you."

"Gracious countess, if you desire ever to see your child again, take the advice I have given you," said Benrimo, instead of replying to the invitation of the countess.

CHAPTER XIV.

THE FIRST STEP TOWARD RUIN.

The duke was sitting in his private room, the one which he called his pouting-place, and opposite him sat his friend Benrimo, who had been invested with the title "interpreter" since his return to court; for in that age, court etiquette and the prejudices of the people, would not allow the conferring of titles and offices on Jews, the Gentiles deeming that they alone had a right to such. Consequently, the duke had been obliged to create a new office, with which to invest his friend.

It was still very early in the morning, and the duke was apparently in a bad humor, for he looked very gloomy, and repeatedly shook his gray head.

"It is strange," began his royal highness, "how one mangy sheep may infect the whole flock. Such ill-mannered jests and sports—nay, I may say, crimes, have never before been perpetrated in my military school; Egmont of Weiden, instead of being improved by the strict discipline, has demoralized my other cadets. An end must be put to this."

"Yes, indeed, the boy will cause your highness many vexations, and when he will have grown to be a man your highness will have an implacable enemy in him," said Benrimo.

"Yes, he comes of a bad family; his paternal ancestors were good and noble, but the connection with the Witzlebs was fatal to the race. A pity that the Countess of Weiden has become childless; a strong young branch would have grown on an old trunk. You've heard the story, Moses?"

"Yes, your highness has told it me before," returned Moses, in an indifferent tone of voice; "it is very strange; the wicked all remain, while the good are taken away."

"According to this, we also will have to do away with ourselves pretty soon, if we wish to be counted among the good ones," remarked the duke, a light smile dispelling the gloom on his countenance.

"I did not think of that, your highness; I thought only of my poor pupil, who disappeared as suddenly and tracklessly as the little count; I allude to Joseph Bonafit. In him I would have reared a support to every throne, an object of pride to every prince."

"Have you heard nothing whatever of him?"

"Nothing, your highness; the poor boy must have been carried off by some enemy of mine, who, perhaps, had found out how dear Joseph had become to me."

"Think you so?" asked the duke, watchfully. "I, too, have had this thought, and I will now confess it; my suspicion is, that the Jews of Immenfeld put the boy out of the way, and then accused you of being his kidnapper, in order to get rid of you."

"Heaven forbid, your highness; will you never learn that a Jew is incapable of such a crime or deed? No, no! the Jews of Immenfeld have erred, but they are far from being wicked. Nay, it is to be ascribed just to their exaggerated piety, their fear of God, resulting in fanaticism, that I was not well liked among them."

"Has your messenger brought no tidings from there?"

"No, your highness; all I heard was that Joseph's mother had recovered from her severe illness, and again goes out about her daily employments. She seems to be somewhat resigned to her fate and comforted, for she says that she has had a vision that her son lives. I think, however that she has received certainty of this from another source."

"Could you not do something for the poor woman?" asked the duke.

"I could not, your highness, she would not accept it from me; but if the gift were sent in your name, it might be welcome," returned Benrimo, hastily making use of this good opportunity.

"Then I will grant her a pension of two hundred florins a year, if you will take in charge the paying of it."

"Most gladly, your highness."

"Then consider it settled." After a pause the duke continued:

"This conversation has somewhat dispersed my bad humor."

"But why does your highness permit your temper to be disturbed by such a rogue as this Egmont is?"

"It is not that, Moses, at least not that alone. See, what I have here!"

The duke handed Moses a handful of shining silver coins. The latter looked at them for awhile, then returned them to the duke with a questioning look.

"That is counterfeit money, Moses," said the duke; "my whole country is flooded with it, and still my police cannot discover the place where it is coined. Is not that sufficient to put me in a bad humor?"

"Excuse me, your highness, I somewhat doubt the excellence of your police force."

"I also, Moses,"

"All the worse; what can become of a country in which the police is good for nothing?"

"Or in which the rogues are too wary to be caught. Do you know, Moses, these counterfeiters can be none else than Jews; only they are shrewd enough to evade the hands of justice."

"Your highness speaks so only to make my humor suit yours," returned Benrimo, in a grieved tone; "everything bad must perforce proceed from the Jews."

"Well, well, do not excite yourself, my friend; this time I intended nothing but a jest. No, it is not the Jews, although they may have some part in the game; the main body of counterfeiters are in a region totally devoid of Jews. The coin was first discovered in the mountains, there where the Convent of St. Francis is situated, and from thence, apparently, it has spread over the whole country."

Benrimo remarked:

"May not the monks of the Convent of St. Francis be the counterfeiters? They are almost, if not quite, as cunning as the Jews."

The duke noted the retaliation and smiled without returning an answer. Had either known how closely they approached the truth, there would have been an end of the counterfeit money.

"Now, come, Moses, accompany me," said the duke, rising. "I will show this detestable boy the consequence of disgracing my colors and my name."

* * * * * *

In the great courtyard of this military school about a hundred youths were stationed in rank and file. Among them were boys who had hardly outgrown childhood and youths who were near man's estate. Immovably they stood, with arms reversed and a painful expectation expressed on every countenance. Even the officers and teachers walked about uneasily, and conversed with each other in whispers. A great event was impending, but what it was to be only the guilty knew.

The duke had sent his adjutant with the command to station all classes in the courtyard, and to cover the flag with crape and the drums with black cloth, as at a funeral. The commanding officer had posted a guard at the gate, for the purpose of announcing the duke's arrival.

Suddenly the trampling of horses was heard, the guard signed, and the duke, followed by his suite, galloped into the yard. A small basket-carriage brought up the rear. In it sat Benrimo, attired in a uniform which was distinguished by its foreign fashion and rich decorations.

The drums beat a salute, the flag was lowered, and the cadets presented arms. The duke's face was very gloomy, and though all the officers at his side returned the salute, he made no motion to do so.

An anxious shudder passed through the ranks; the officers grew pale at the ominous sign that the duke did not salute his own colors. When the salutations were at an end, the duke ordered an ensign to the front, and said, in a loud, angry tone:

"Away with the flag! It would disgrace it to wave longer over a people who have dishonored it! It shall not be borne before you, nor salute me, until the guilty are punished and the honor of my corps of cadets is restored without a blemish; until the wonted discipline and order reign again supreme among youths, of whom almost all bear old, honorable names."

Tears glittered in the eyes of many youths, who were innocent of any fault, and on whom this dreadful punishment fell undeservedly. To be forbidden to bear a flag was a humiliation deeply felt by all.

"Egmont of Weiden to the front!" thundered the duke.

The youth, thus summoned, slowly crept from the ranks, and advanced to the duke's horse. The feelings which animated him were far from being consoling.

The duke, casting a glance of marked contempt at the boy, turned to the cadets, and said:

"You see here the descendant of an old, noble family,

a boy whose father was a brave man, and a man of honor; all of you know this boy's name. He yesterday not only disgraced this, but dishonored the sword which his sovereign had conferred on him. Had he been guilty of a boyish prank, I would have forgiven him; but, not only did he insult an unprotected lady, not only did he strike her—yes, gentlemen, strike her—with the sword which, on his admittance here, he swore to wield only for protection and right; he would have murdered her, had not a stronger hand opportunely intervened. I would have placed him before a court-martial, but I do not want to inflict such disgrace on honorable men as to order them to sit in judgment of such a wretch. I will expel him from the ranks to which he has lost all right of belonging. Provost, advance!"

One of the duke's suite rode forward, dismounted and approached Egmont, who could hardly keep his feet, and was whimpering:

"Mercy, mercy!"

"Provost, relieve the boy of his sword!" commanded the duke.

A moment later, Egmont's sword fell with a crash to the ground.

"Provost," the duke went on to command, "cut the buttons which bear the arms of his sovereign off the malefactor's coat."

Another moment, and Egmont was devoid of all military decorations; not a button was left him.

"Drummers, advance!" again commanded the duke.

The drummers advanced.

"Drum this villain out of the regiment."

Deadened and mournfully, as at a funeral march, the drums rolled, and to their sound the boy who had just received such a severe but just punishment, crept out of the gate, thrust forth from a profession which honor considers its greatest good.

Arrived at the street, Egmont turned and spat contemptuously on the pavement.

"This disgrace shall be repaid tenfold, base tyrant," said he to himself; "and be it ever so far in the future! Nor will I forget to serve out well my beloved aunt and the old Jew."

A mocking laughter aroused Egmont from his amiable thoughts. He looked up and saw a young man who was about nineteen years of age, and very elegantly dressed, but had a wild expression in his eyes. His figure was tall and slender, and beneath his nose a mustache had just begun to make its appearance. Through a knot-hole in the gate he had witnessed the whole proceeding, and when Egmont crept forth, had noticed his gestures and overheard his half-whispered words.

When Egmont, disagreeably surprised by his laughter, looked sullenly at the young man, the latter suddenly grew serious, and approaching close to Egmont, tapped him familiarly on the shoulder, and said:

"Never mind, my boy; there are substitutes for the buttons, and the world is large enough not to be obliged to be dependent on an old tyrant."

"But I am dishonored, disgraced for life," said Egmont, grinding his teeth, and contemplating his buttonless coat.

"Pshaw! You only think so now; I thought so, too, when I was expelled from the high-school; yet I've come to disregard it by this time. What you are now actually in fear of is doubtless a sound thrashing from your father."

"Nonsense!" cried Egmont, contemptuously; "my father is dead; I have only a mother."

"You are more fortunate than I, I have neither father nor mother any more; nor do I regret it, for their joy and pride in me would not be great."

At these last words the young man's face had become serious, even mournful; but the good impulse quickly forsook him, and he said lightly:

"What will your mother say, when she hears of your—misfortune, my boy?"

"She may say anything she likes, for all I care," returned Egmont, sullenly; "she can't give me anything, for she is poor."

"I thought you were a noble, as only such are admitted into the military school."

"That is just my misfortune; they make such a fuss about this nobility, one must not sin, turn neither to the right nor left. If some plebeian wretch had committed such a harmless jest not a hair of his head would have been harmed."

"What crime was it for which you were so disgracefully expelled?" asked the young man.

Egmont related the events of the preceding day, and added that the Jew who sat in the carriage in the courtyard was chiefly to blame for this misfortune.

"Very well," began the stranger again, after a pause of reflection; "you have sworn vengeance on all in there; I will help you to carry it out, particularly toward the Jew."

"How?" asked Egmont, his face clearing.

"You know," said the young man, "that the idol of the Jews is the golden calf; that is to say, money is all they strive for and adore." Now the tempter bent down to Egmont's ear. "Take away their money, and you deprive them at the same time of life."

Egmont started back.

He had grown paler than usual.

"Steal?" asked he aloud, "steal? No, a Weiden does not steal!"

Again the stranger broke into mocking laughter; then he said:

"Look at your coat, my boy; regard it well, and tell me how a Baron of Weiden ought to look."

Egmont stamped his foot and clinched his hand, but, as we already know, he was wanting in courage, and the stranger was too strong for him.

"Don't be a fool," said the latter; "do you want to go to your home, most likely an old, ruinous barrack, which you call a castle, and where even the swine-herds will point you out to each other; for think you that your disgrace will remain a secret? Do you want to mope there, and listen daily to your mother's laments and reproaches? Or do you want to be a gay and free man, elegantly dressed, your pockets full of money,"—here the stranger jingled the coins in his pocket,—"move in merry, gentlemanly society, which last is most to be considered, and have the prospect of avenging yourself on those who have so grossly insulted you?"

Thus spoke the tempter, and Egmont hearkened to his words.

Yes, it was even as the stranger said. At home, revilings and shame, want and grief awaited him; it could not get to be worse than that here.

But once again his guardian angel approached him, and he thought, perhaps for the first time in his life, of his mother.

"No, no, leave me; I will do nothing to add more disgrace to my name; I will not become a thief. I am young; I may grow better."

"Little fool! who told you to become a thief? Have I, perhaps, said so?"

"Not literally, but you gave me to understand as much."

"Because you did not understand me; just come with me and you will see that there is as great a difference between the trade I and my comrades ply and stealing, as there is between an expelled cadet and an old Jewish officer."

At these derisive remarks Egmont's face again grew dark, and he turned angrily away.

The stranger saw that he had gone too far, and accordingly began in another strain:

"Come, young gentleman, don't be a fool and take my jest in bad part; come with me; you can leave us at any time if you don't like our company."

"But my mother?"

"Pshaw! what does your mother concern me; have you not sense enough to write to her and quiet her as to your absence? Tell her you have left the military school, in order to go to college and study medicine or ply some other vocation."

"Well, for my part," and Egmont put his hand into the outstretched hand of the stranger, "I will try it; but"—he hesitated again—"what is your name?"

"I am called Devil's Fred," was the reply.

And they went from thence, the tempter and his victim, Devil's Fred and the young Baron of Weiden. The first step toward ruin is taken—when will the last be attained?

CHAPTER XV.
A VISITOR IN IMMENFELD.

THE Jewish community of Immenfeld again harbored a guest. The lesson they had in regard to the Spaniard several years ago had tended to increase rather than diminish their hospitality, all the more as it had proved to them in such a painful manner that birds might be judged of by their feathers, but travelers not by their lost legs.

Every stranger who, after Benrimo had left the village, made a halt there, was considered as though he were a prince, traveling *incognito*, and was received in the most hospitable, friendly and cordial manner; however, none turned out to be a duke's friend in disguise.

It was about the same time when Baron Egmont had followed the tempter into the path of destruction, that a traveler presented himself at the dwelling of the president of the Immenfeld congregation. The stranger looked so dignified and learned, applied such beautiful Hebrew verses to what he spoke, that the president felt quite loath to assign him a *plette* (billet) (our readers will remember that this signifies an order to a member of the congregation to give board and lodging over Saturday to any stranger), and determined to keep him at his own house.

When asked for his name, the stranger, like the "Spaniard," declared that he wished to keep it a secret, and the president's wife dubbed him Gallach (shaven one: the tonsorial application put at his investment as priest; a term often used for a Catholic priest, as the latter have a round piece on the crown shaven as a mark of their order), because she observed a round bald place on the back of his head. You perceive that the president's wife was never at a loss for a suitable nickname. However, her husband forbade her using this name, for the stranger had greatly impressed him; he assured his wife that he would discover the traveler's name on the morrow, when he would be called to the *Thora*, at divine service.

In direct contrast to the "Spaniard," the stranger was so pious that he would taste neither soup nor meat on Friday, and excused himself by saying that he never partook of the meat of an animal which had not been killed and dressed before his eyes. "This is truly a man of God," thought the president.

"This is truly a miserable man, to impute to me that I am not particular about having everything *Kosher*," thought the president's wife.

When, on the morrow, the stranger was called to the *Thora*, the president discovered no more than he had previously known. The name which the stranger gave was so insignificant, so common, that any one might bear it— *Yitzchak bar Yehudah*—and in Immenfeld alone there were at least five of the like name. But how impressively the stranger pronounced the blessing! He appeared to be greatly agitated, and, as the president noted, when he raised his eyes to Heaven, they were full of tears, and he lifted the *Thora* at least twelve inches from the desk.

"The man must have been wrecked at sea, or passed through some danger," soliloquized the president. "I'll see if he will pronounce the blessing for surmounted dangers."

But nothing of the kind occurred. The stranger thanked the president for having been found worthy of the honor to be called to the *Thora*, and after having bestowed no inconsiderable sum as a donation to the poor, repaired to the seat allotted to him.

On the congregation also the stranger had made an agreeable impression, and many forgot their devotions in observing him. After dinner the president, as was customary in every Jewish house, conversed with his guest about the *Thora* and its commentaries and other Jewish literature, and this gave occasion for a display of the stranger's great learning, which excited the president's most intense admiration.

When they had sufficiently exhausted these subjects, they turned to another, one highly interesting to the Jews of that age, the *Kabbalah* (a mysterious kind of science among some ancient rabbis, serving for the interpretation of the hidden and mysterious sense of Scripture). With due modesty the stranger confessed that he knew a little of it, and could, by means of various calculations and the use of the *Shem Hameforash* (the sacred, unpronounceable name of the Deity Eternal, *Jehovah*), clear up some subordinate mysteries.

The president was delighted, and entreated his guest to give him a proof of his learning. The stranger consented, but begged silence on the subject until the close of the Sabbath.

In the evening, when there was no cause why the stranger should not comply with his host's modest entreaty, the latter again referred to it. The stranger began:

"Ask me any question, and I will answer it in a brief time."

The president reflected for awhile, and then said:

"Tell me, Rabbi Fitzchak, what remarkable occurrence took place among the Jews of Immenfeld some time ago?"

The stranger drew a book from his *caftan*, read and

calculated, passed his left hand through his hair several times, vehemently pierced the air with the thumb of his right hand, closed his eyes as if transfigured, and at last said:

"Not long ago a Jew who had not yet become *bar-mitzvah* (confirmed) vanished in a remarkable manner from Immenfeld."

The president started from his seat and kissed the hem of the stranger's *caftan;* the latter, however, opposed this with all his strength.

"Rabbi," cried the president, transported with delight, "you are a genuine *Ba'al Shem* (master of the name of God—a cabalist).

"Now you can perhaps tell what the boy's name was, and how he looked?"

The stranger again performed the above described motions, and finally said:

"It is a name which one of our ancestors bore, a great name; it begins like the name of God with a *Yod*, and it does not beseem a cabalist to pronounce it."

"'Tis the work of God!" cried the awe-struck president.

"Proceed to question me," said Rabbi Yitzchak.

"What has become of the boy, rabbi."

The book was again consulted; then the rabbi raised his eyes to heaven and said:

"Signs are sent from the Lord, and miracles performed by him! The boy is in good hands, and will once go forth from the place which now shelters him for the joy and blessing of all Israel."

"May the place not be known, rabbi?"

"The Kabbalah envelops it in the deepest darkness, and the power of the greatest *cabalist* has its boundaries."

"May the mother be comforted by these tidings," said the president.

"Will the mother believe you?" returned the rabbi, watchfully.

"Rabbi, you will not fail to be my witness, if I entreat you for it."

"Gladly, gladly; lead me there, or, what is still better, tell me where the mother of this boy dwells, and I will go there alone. The woman probably saw me in the synagogue to-day, and I will not find it difficult to make her believe my tidings."

"Who, for God's sake, will not believe a man such as you are?" cried the president, raising his hands in wonder. Then, drawing his guest toward the window, he showed him the Widow Bonafit's house, which could be discerned from the others in the street by the circumstance that the faintest light proceeded from it. The president never thought that a man who could perform such wonders ought also to know where the Widow Bonafit dwelt. A few minutes later the famous rabbi, the president's guest, entered the low room of the Widow Bonafit.

"Blessed be he who cometh!" cried the widow, looking up from the book she had been reading by the faint lamplight.

"Blessed be the one whom he findeth!" returned the stranger, using the ancient Jewish formula for salutation. Both had spoken in the Hebrew language, which even the women of the time employed for greetings. Mrs. Bonafit had arisen, and now drew forth her best stool for the stranger. The latter attentively regarded the widow. Her slight figure was somewhat bent, her face was seamed with wrinkles, her eyes were dim and the eyelids inflamed.

"That is not the mother he described to me," said the stranger to himself; "but her eyes are swollen with weeping, her face crossed with wrinkles from passionate longing for her dear lost one, and her figure bent by the heavy load of grief."

"What does the strange gentleman bring?" asked the widow.

"As you have blessed my coming," returned the stranger, "it shall be so. I bring peace to your house, joy to your heart."

"God grant it! for it is long, worthy sir, since either sojourned here."

"I bring you tidings from——"

"From whom—from whom?" said Mrs. Bonafit, seized by such a violent trembling that she was forced to cling to the table for support.

"Even from him you think dead. He lives, and is as happy as he can be without his mother, and hopes to see her again, although not till the lapse of a few years."

The poor mother was weeping. Her praises and thanks to God, who had preserved her son, were so pathetic that the stranger was forced to turn away his face an instant.

But the news was too good—the poor creature could not credit it, and doubts soon smothered her joy.

"Oh, sir!" entreated the widow, wringing her hands, "do not deceive me—for God's sake do not. If you have, perchance, come to offer hollow comfort to a poor widow, of whose loss you have heard, oh, then, it would have been far better had you refrained from coming; for it would be dreadful, it would break my heart, were your tidings deception; it would bring my heavy head to the grave, had your good heart led you to tell me an untruth."

"Compose yourself, good mother of a brave son. I have fortunately brought proofs of the truth of my assertion."

The stranger drew a folded paper from his *caftan* and handed it to the widow, who, in her feverish haste to open it, partly tore it. Oh, these must be the familiar Hebrew characters of her son, for she sinks, half crying, half laughing, on a chair, holds the paper near the dim light, and essays to read it with her weak eyes.

The paper contained a few lines, of the following purport:

"MY DEAR, GOOD MOTHER,—I am well and happy, for I hope to gain what I have resolved upon. Do not grieve any more. At first, evil tidings appeared in store for me, but God has turned my sorrow to joy, my obscurity to light, and will continue to do so in the future. This is, perhaps, the only letter you will receive from me, until, at some future time, we will meet again. Rely upon it that your Joseph will ever keep his inheritance—the crown of a good name—as a diadem—bright, shining, and in luster. Your son, who, in imagination, kisses you. Your ever-loving JOSEPH."

The mother dropped the hand which held the letter, and asked:

"But why does not my Joseph come himself to his poor mother, who has grieved for him day and night? Why did he wait a whole year before he wrote to me?"

"We are ungrateful beings," said the stranger, sternly. "Ten minutes ago, news of your son made you ineffably happy, Mrs. Bonafit; now, a letter from him does not content you."

"Pardon, noble sir!" returned the widow, timidly; "you are right; but may I inquire where my Joseph is?"

"Did faithful Hannah ask what would become of her son Samuel, when God commanded her to bring him to the temple?"

"No, no, but——"

"No buts; your son is consecrated to a noble purpose; he is well, and in good hands; therefore, wait until it pleases God to send him back to you."

"Noble sir, you seem to know my boy well; consequently, he knows you, and his friend shall be mine. Will you not tell me whence you came, and whither you are going?"

"Does the cloud which the Lord sends say whence it came? and does the snow of winter tell whither it goes?" So answered the stranger, and arose from his seat.

Mrs. Bonafit did not venture to put any more questions; to her awe-struck senses, the stranger seemed a holy, a supernatural being, as he stood with arm upraised to heaven.

The stranger, looking steadily at the widow, who had involuntarily assumed an almost worshiping attitude, retreated slowly to the door, and vanished suddenly into the darkness.

Mrs. Bonafit read her son's letter again and yet again. The whole occurrence appeared to her like a dream, and she needed the rustling of the paper to convince her of the truth of this wondrous event. At last she arose, pressed a hearty kiss on the paper before placing it between the leaves of her prayer-book, and hastened out of the house, for her heart was too full, her joy too great, to keep all to herself.

The good woman well knew that the joy of the congregation would not be over great at these tidings; for, as we know, her son was not under the tongue of good report, and not very deep in their good graces; and then, the consistent people had shoved all the blame of the Spaniard's loss on him; for, reasoned they, had Joseph not disappeared, the Spaniard would be still among them, and sooner or later they would have discovered his worth. Only the president, whom we have learned to know as a quiet, sensible man, took the part of the poor widow, and to him she now hastened with the joyous news, which she knew would be gladly welcomed by him.

She found him in his room, where all the lights of the Sabbath lamps were lit, and a white cloth spread on the table. Mrs. Bonafit was surprised at these preparations, but her curiosity was not as great as her desire to impart her news, and she was about to speak, when the president began:

"God be with you, Mrs. Bonafit, you are a fortunate woman, that such a man has crossed your threshold. I know what you desire to tell me; I know all. But do you know who it is that brought you the glorious tidings?"

"No; but do you know it?"

"Certainly I do. Do you not see the Sabbath lamp lit, and the white cloth on the table? All these are in his honor. I entertain the stranger who visited you, it is my happiness to have him as a guest."

"Well, but who is he?" asked Mrs. Bonafit, burning with curiosity.

"He is a *Ba'al Shem!*" cried the president, reverently. Mrs. Bonafit sank on her knees in holy awe.

The Jews of Immenfeld were unfortunate in their guests; this time, also, they were on the wrong track.

CHAPTER XVI.
BA'AL SHEM AND FRANCISCAN FRIAR.

THAT a *Ba'al Shem* had come, that he had brought good tidings to Mrs. Bonafit, and that the man who had been the president's guest over the Sabbath was a *Ba'al Shem*—all these the Immenfeld Jews learned early the next morning, and not a few of them said, that although they had not been told who the stranger was, they had thought that only a *Ba'al Shem* could look as he did, and pronounce the blessing as he had done; in short, every one had something to say about the mysterious man. But how did their surprise increase when, on the following morning, this same mysterious man went from house to house, inquiring at each if its owner were a creditor of the Baroness of Weiden. When answered in the affirmative, he unbuckled a heavy belt of money, which he carried around his waist, and paid the note which had already been half given up as uncollectable, and not only did he pay the debt, but the interest also, in return for which he accepted the notes of the baroness.

When he had in this manner bought up all the debts, he inquired who were her creditors in other places, what mortgages there were, and the holders of them; then he left Immenfeld, after having promised the happy president that he would be his guest again on the coming Sabbath.

In Immenfeld, the Jews, as a matter of course, puzzled

their heads as to the cause of this strange conduct, and the president's home was fairly besieged by curious visitors, until he promised that he would ask the *Ba'al Shem* for his secret when he returned, as soon as he should have a good opportunity to do so.

The amount of interest that the Immenfeld congregation took in the *Ba'al Shem* may be calculated by the fact that those of them who during the week pursued their business avocations elsewhere, and generally returned to the village on Friday afternoon, returned this time on Thursday, and before proceeding home, went to the president's house, to inquire the latest news of the *Ba'al Shem*.

On Friday evening, just before commencement of Sabbath, our stranger again came to Immenfeld. A perfect ovation greeted the great man's return. The Sabbath was passed in peace and happiness, especially in the president's house, and when it was evening again, the worthy man took heart and said: "Excuse my presumption in asking you a question."

"Speak, my good man," returned the rabbi, in a condescending tone, "if it be in my power, I will gladly answer your question."

"What is your purpose, reverend rabbi, in buying up all the bonds of the baroness?" asked the president, full of curiosity, but rather timidly. "I do not ask out of pure love of asking," the president excused himself, "but to tell you, rabbi, that if it be a speculation of yours, the baroness does not possess one-fourth of what she owes."

"I thank you, my good man, but love of speculation did not impel me to do this; it has been done for the sanctification of the Name (that of God). My great Zohar (the great famous cabalistic book), shows me how to find out the enemies of Israel, and I found out that my people have no greater enemy than the baroness; accordingly I adopted this plan, in order to render this woman harmless now and in all time to come."

"But another thing, my dear president," continued the

stranger, rising from his seat, "I have intrusted my secret to you; you must keep silence, however, that you will reveal it to no one."

The president acquiesced in this, and to his credit be it here said, not a word of the *Ba'al Shem's* purpose became known to any member of his congregation.

The stranger continued:

"I will remain here to-morrow, but Monday, please God, I will go hence, as soon as the morning service is ended; but I hope and expect, that in regard to your own welfare, none of you will look after me, for danger lies in so doing."

"May God protect and preserve us," cried the president; "if it so be your will, reverend rabbi, we will no more look after you, than the people at the Cohanim (priests) while blessing them."

They went on to speak of different matters, when suddenly the stranger asked:

"Tell me, sir—my Fohar informed me that you had once a man here whom you excommunicated, a great and learned man."

The president looked at the *Ba'al Shem* in surprise.

"This also do you know, most reverend rabbi?"

"Yes, a higher art than mine revealed this to me."

"You probably know in what manner this man left us?"

"Certainly," returned the rabbi, lightly. An unprejudiced observer would have soon noticed that our *Ba'al Shem* knew nothing about it; but so well did he understand how to cross-examine the credulous president, that he drew from him all we already know about Benrimo, while all the time the worthy man fully believed that the stranger knew everything.

On Monday morning, when the service in the synagogue was ended, and most of the Jews were already going about their various vocations and employments, the stranger told his host that the time for his departure was at hand.

The president, as well as his wife, bowed his head to receive the great man's blessing, and thanked him for the honor he had done them in thinking them worthy to entertain such a noble and pious visitor.

Then the stranger left the house. The Jews' lane was quite deserted. Not for all the wealth of the Orient would man, woman or child have dared to look after the *Ba'al Shem* after he expressed the wish to the contrary.

The stranger turned in the direction of the graveyard, and ascended it. He looked closely at the tombstones and read the inscriptions on them. When he had arrived at a monument larger than the rest, and which had engraved on it two outstretched hands (the sign that a priest—Cohen—was buried there), while a large elm complety overshadowed it, the stranger passed behind it, where he was fully lost to view. After the lapse of five minutes a totally different figure emerged, apparently out of the ground. Although in size and age closely resembling the president's guest, this man who now came forth from behind the gravestone was clad in the habit and cowl of a Franciscan friar. A white rope was loosely tied about his waist, and a cross and rosary dangled from the ends. His face was perfectly smooth; there was not a trace of the long beard which the president's guest had worn.

A slight smile illuminating his features, the Franciscan friar turned to the village and said:

"This time, good people, you have harbored a genuine renegade."

Then he descended the graveyard on the other side, passed along the same road that Joseph Bonafit had taken on a certain eventful morning, and ascended the hill to the castle.

When he passed through the little gate into the courtyard, all whom he met sank on their knees before the lank, stern-looking monk and solicited his blessing, which he dispensed liberally enough. When the Franciscan entered the castle he remained standing for awhile, as if to recover breath. He pressed his hand on his heart, and muttered:

"At last, at last; the day has come on which I shall cry quits with you, serpent. Year after year have I looked for you, and at last I have found you." The monk went up a flight of broad, stone steps which led to the first story of the castle, and passed along the corridor until he came to a half-open door. He entered the room, in which he found a girl, who, as soon as she caught sight of him, sank on her knees, and implored the holy man's blessing.

"Is your mistress, the Baroness of Weiden, at home to any one?" asked the Franciscan.

"I'll go and ascertain, holy father," returned the girl, and vanished.

After a few minutes she returned, and desired the monk to follow her.

The Baroness of Weiden was sitting in the embrasure of the window, where we have seen her once before. When she caught sight of the monk, she arose hastily, and humbly advanced to the middle of the room.

"Praised be Jesus Christ," said the monk, in a deep voice.

The baroness started in terror; the words "forever and ever, amen," remained sticking in her throat, and she cast glances of mingled fright and suspicion at the monk's face, which was shaded by his cowl. Then the baroness uttered a dreadful shriek, and shrank back with the cry:

"God have mercy on me—Dr. Isaac Mundolfo!"

Pale and trembling in all her limbs she sank on a chair.

"You err, Agnes, Baroness of Weiden," said the monk, sternly; "the physician, Isaac Mundolfo, remained in the dungeons of the Inquisition; he who stands before you is the Franciscan monk, Father Auselmo, who has come, as such, to give his blessings. But, baroness," continued the monk, "you do not welcome me, do not offer me a seat? Is this the manner you treat the sons of the Church? You used to treat Dr. Mundolfo more politely."

The baroness did not answer; she could not answer. Her throat felt as if bound by bands of iron.

The monk went to the door, opened it, and called out: "My daughter, the baroness, is at home to no one. She is confessing." Then he closed the door, and bolted it.

Father Anselmo now took a chair, and seated himself opposite to the trembling baroness.

"Well, baroness," he began, "it is customary among business men that, when they wish to wind up their affairs, when they come to demand payment, they present a bill, on which a list of all the goods they have supplied or received is accurately marked down. All I have given and received is not marked on paper, like a merchant's bill, but it is graven in my head and heart, and you will see, Baroness of Weiden, that I have kept books well."

"But, Isaac—pshaw, Father Anselmo—what do you want of me? I have done you no harm, and I know not what induces you, who say you are a man of God, to force yourself into the presence of a lady, and terrify her with a flood of words of which she does not understand a syllable."

"Then, baroness," returned Father Anselmo, a mocking smile playing around his mouth, "then I have done well to bring my account, for you seem very forgetful. Very well, I will refresh your memory; should I make a mistake, have the kindness to correct it."

The baroness arose from her seat, and ran up and down the room, wringing her hands.

"Compose yourself, gracious lady; to arrange this account to our satisfaction you must be composed," observed Father Anselmo. "You must hear me, gracious lady, and the sooner we are done with it, the better for both of us."

The monk arose and led the faintly struggling baroness back to her chair, on which he forced her to sit down.

"About twenty years ago," began Father Anselmo, "there lived in Rome a young Jewish physician, by name Isaac Mundolfo. Although the Jews were prohibited from dwelling in the city, a particular edict had given permission to this young physician to reside where it pleased him; for young as this physician was, he surpassed in skill all the older physicians in Rome, and had been so fortunate as to cure even the Pope himself of a severe illness.

"The young and the old, the wealthy and the poor, contended for the favor of this Jewish doctor. He was often summoned when the last faint breath came from the sufferer's lips, as if it were in his power to banish death. This Jew was called the greatest man in the world.

"Mundolfo was ambitious. His ambition was to learn, to enrich his knowledge, daily and hourly, to make new inventions in the province of medicine and that of chemistry, which was just beginning to occupy the minds of men, in order to become more and more useful to his fellow-creatures.

"Then it happened to Mundolfo according to words in the second book of Moses, that '*a king arose in Egypt, who knew not Joseph.*' Thus it happened here also. A new Pope, who had never heard anything of Mundolfo, ascended the papal see. The Pope was constantly in fear of being poisoned by the Jesuits, and by no means enjoyed his life. His friends mentioned the name of Mundolfo to him; they described him as a performer of miracles, but neglected to say that he was a Jew.

"Mundolfo was summoned. He came in his carriage, profusely decorated with gold; was drawn by two beautiful Arabian horses. The Pope desired to assign him a post at his side; he was to scent from afar off the poison which his Holiness dreaded, and always have the antidote in readiness. For this purpose, he, as a matter of course, was to give up his immense practice, reject all who came to him for help, and turn a deaf ear to the entreaties of anxious mothers and grief-stricken children; and all this because an aged man feared the poison of his Christian brethren; a feeble, old man, who imagined himself to be the representative of God.

"Mundolfo did not hesitate long; the choice was not difficult for him; he had consecrated himself for humanity, and he would not forsake it. He rejected the Pope's proposal.

"To offend God is a sin, but to offend the 'Vicar of Christ' is a crime, punishable with death. Mundolfo was to discover this very soon. The Pope was informed that Mundolfo was a Jew. Had this Jew not been so popular, he would have been burned at the stake; but not even the Pope could venture upon such a hazardous enterprise.

"However, he revoked his predecessor's permission that Mundolfo could reside among Christians, and rendered his punishment more severe by commanding the physician to give up his carriage, and ordering him, who could come to princes and dukes unannounced, to wear a long *caftan*, and a cap with a red tassel, the badge of disgrace for all the Jews in Rome.

"Mundolfo accepted this punishment from an imbecile old man, with a contemptuous laugh, sold his carriage, and removed to the Ghetto.

"The Pope, however, had not punished the physician, but all his subjects, the foreign ambassadors, the wealthy and aristocratic strangers who resided in Rome, and all the Roman nobles, for Mundolfo proclaimed that he would now go to no patient, that they all must come to him.

"By this means he forced dainty aristocrats to come to the filthy, poor, remote streets of the Ghetto, to come for their health to a place which their feet had never trodden. This was his revenge, and it was complete. The Pope was almost forced to recall his foolish edict, but it was of no avail. Mundolfo remained in the Ghetto, and the aristocrats were still obliged to come to him, while he went on foot to the huts of the poor, and freely gave them his aid. Mundolfo had learned to know that knowledge places man far above kings and popes, nay, that it elevates him to be the real sovereign pontiff, for even the Pope had been forced to do homage to the man of science."

CHAPTER XVII.
A SETTLEMENT.

THE baroness, while apparently attentively listening to Father Anselmo's relation, sought for some means to escape hearing to the end what she already knew only too well. Father Anselmo remarked this, and said:

"The story bores you, baroness; but pray do not withdraw your attention, for the end is extremely interesting."

The baroness made a movement of impatience and was about to answer, but Father Anselmo prevented this. He began the second part of his tale.

"Mundolfo found happiness in the Ghetto of Rome. A beautiful and amiable woman became his wife, and in course of time a lovely little daughter was born unto him. For several happy years, Mundolfo enjoyed his good fortune and his triumph.

"But one day—baroness, pay close attention—a strange lady came to the physician's house. She held her dainty handkerchief before her mouth, for the peculiar odors of the Ghetto affected her unpleasantly. The physician immediately perceived that the lady was a foreigner, for the Roman nobles never insulted him so far as to declare, even without speech, that his place of residence was badly chosen as regarded their noses.

"The physician's supposition proved to be correct. The lady began to speak in very poor Italian, and was greatly delighted when the physician answered in good German. The lady gave her name as Agnes, Baroness of Weiden, and came on account of her sick husband. You grow pale, baroness. Bah! that is nothing. The story is old, and ought not to affect you any more." The monk interrupted his narration; but as the baroness did not answer him, he continued:

"However, the baroness did not come to the celebrated physician to seek alleviation for the sufferings of her husband—the high-born lady came to buy his death of the Jew. Yes! shriek, baroness, struggle against a fainting-fit! The accomplished, aristocratic lady asked for death of the physician, to whom all others came for life. 'Mundolfo is but a Jew, and all Jews can be bought.' Thus thought the noble lady; and thus, alas! a great many think.

"However, the Jew declined this offer, very decidedly, though the lady told him a pretty fable of a husband who was a monster and iniquity, who had squandered his vast patrimony of the fortune of his wife, who had sinned against morality in various ways, etc., but all was of no avail. The physician not only warmly abided by his decision, but admonished the baroness to give up her sinful undertaking, and promised to keep secret her disgraceful offer only on condition of her never attempting to jeopardize the life of her husband in any way.

"The lady departed, and Mundolfo took occasion to institute inquiries about the Baroness of Weiden and her husband. The noble lady had lied fearfully. Her husband was an honorable man, whose life she imbittered. The little fortune he had had she squandered by her extravagance and love of luxury; she herself had never been worth a penny, and was the descendant of a family whose ancestor had been executed for freebooting, and had left his heirs a heritage of which they ever strove to be worthy —the heritage of a notorious, if not infamous, reputation.

"Several months elapsed, and Mundolfo forgot his adventure with the lady. But one day one of his patients related to him that the Baron of Weiden was dangerously ill, and his fair wife would soon be free to woo another, richer husband.

"To the physician's mind it suddenly became clear what motive had driven the baroness to seek Mundolfo. The physician could not rest. He closely observed the hotel where the baron and his wife lodged. One day he saw the baroness leave the house, and without a moment's delay he entered it, and was conducted to the baron, who received him with great demonstrations of joy.

"One glance sufficed the practiced eye of the physician. His presentiment was only too well founded. The baron was being slowly poisoned. The physician examined the sick man, analyzed his medicines, and obtained convincing proofs of this fact. The crime had been committed, the patient was lost, he had but a few days more to live.

"As Mundolfo was taking leave of the baron, he heard a faint shriek behind him, and, on turning around, beheld the baroness, who was pale with fright, and clinging to a chair for support. Mundolfo retained his presence of mind, signed imperceptibly to the baroness, and retired to await her in the adjoining room.

"She entered. Her terror was gone. She stood before him a shameless murderess, and looked at him in an innocent, questioning manner.

"The physician stepped up close to her, and said, briefly: 'Madam, you have murdered your husband!'

"The lady recoiled; she had thought to deceive the sharp eyes of the doctor. She now had recourse to asseverations and vows of her innocence, and grew more and more violent, as she saw nothing but incredulity on the physician's face, and heard him utter the threat of denouncing her as a poisoner.

"In one corner of the room there was a *prie-dieu*, on which stood a crucifix.

"The baroness at last rushed to this, threw herself on the floor in a theatrical posture, and importuned the image of ebony and gold to reveal, by a miracle, her innocence of her husband's death.

"This play with religion so enraged the Jew that he

seized the cross, hurled it to the ground, and cried: 'Very well, madam; when this image of Christ arises from the ground, then I will believe you, but not before.'

"Mundolfo went home, fiercely resolved to denounce the fair prisoner on the next morning, but she forestalled him.

"That very night Mundolfo was torn from his bed by the *shirri* (constables) of the Pope, and thrown into the dungeons of the Inquisition, on an accusation of desecration of Christ.

"For a whole year Mundolfo languished in a damp cell, to which no ray of the blessed sun could penetrate. His feet and hands were loaded with heavy chains, and he was fettered to the wall by an iron band which passed around his waist.

"Mundolfo knew that all this was done at the Pope's instigation; that this cell would be his grave, did not a miracle liberate him.

"And the miracle came to pass.

"The Roman nobles came to the Pope to intercede for the unfortunate Jew, not because they pitied him, but because they were afraid of death, which they thought he could banish. But the Pope remained firm. He had got his enemy in his power, under the most plausible pretext, in which all Christendom must agree with him, and he would not let him go.

"But his Holiness became ill, very ill, indeed, and there were vague rumors of poisoning.

"One day, a cardinal, secretary to his Holiness, entered Mundolfo's prison, and announced to him that he could be free if he would become a Christian.

"Much is spoken of the martyrs of olden times. They are greatly admired. But Mundolfo was no martyr; he had a young wife and child at home. He had regarded science as his aim in life; he knew that a great many lives were sacrificed while he languished in prison. Mundolfo began to waver in his faith.

"The cardinal told him that his Holiness was seriously

ill, that he desired to have the desecrator of the cross for his doctor, but could not before Mundolfo had bowed down and worshiped what he had blasphemed. Light penetrated into Mundolfo's soul. It was a light of hell. This was the way to revenge himself on his enemy. If he became a Christian, not even the Pope could force him to be his doctor, did he not feel inclined to do so.

"And besides this, the unhappy man thought of his wife and child. This was the first time since his imprisonment that he had heard aught of them. The cardinal had told him that his wife and child were well, that they had promised the Pope that Mundolfo would allow himself to be baptized if he were set free, and that they would also renounce their faith for his.

"So Mundolfo was baptized in prison at his own request. The three drops of cold water did not touch his heart—the Franciscan monk, Father Anselmo, remained a Jew.

"The fetters fell. A carriage was waiting without the halls of the Inquisition. They did not even take time to cut off the new Christian's beard, which during his incarceration had grown down to his waist. Thus he was led into the sick-room of his Holiness. He asked the Pope if he were not afraid to be treated by his mortal enemy,

"'You are now a Christian, my son,' returned the Pope, 'and no Christian would dare to attack the life of the Vicar of Christ.'

"'And are the Jesuits, by whom your Holiness believes yourself to be poisoned, no Christians?'

"The Pope was silent. After a pause he asked:

"'Well, my son, what do you think of my case?'

"'I cannot say. I will not examine you before I have seen my wife and child.'

"All present in the sick-room looked at each other in confusion. Mundolfo was led out. He was informed that his wife had been imprisoned in a convent on the night of his arrest, that she had been forcibly baptized, and had died about two months previous to his liberation,

Her last words had been an imprecation on the cross, and for this reason she was not buried in consecrated ground. His child had also received holy baptism, and had then been adopted and taken to Germany by a German family, whose name was not even known.

"And all this was told to Mundolfo by the cardinal, the same holy man who a few hours previous had promised the prisoner to conduct him back to his wife and child.

"Mundolfo raved and swore, tore his hair and beard; he wished to go back to his prison, he wished his baptism to be revoked, he felt that the punishment for his apostasy had already begun—he felt that he was a lost man in this life and the life to come. But the baptism had taken place, and could not be recalled nor revoked.

"Mundolfo's art was dead to the Pope. He advanced to the bedside of his Holiness, and said, coldly and derisively:

"'Holy Father, you must die. To-morrow Jesus Christ will receive his representative in person.'

"Mundolfo had never done such a thing before. He had always had some word of comfort even for the dying. The miserable old man groaned and wept piteously; he did not wish to die. But Mundolfo sat cold and silent at his bedside, and only smiled contemptuously at the exertions of the other physicians, who sought in vain to detain the fleeing spirit. Mundolfo knew the remedy which could preserve the Pope's life, but he did not apply nor betray it. The next day the Vicar of Christ was dead.

"Mundolfo, now Anselmo, had only three purposes, to effect which he wished to live.

"The first was to find the woman who had made him unhappy for life; the second, to find his child in Germany, and the third, penance for his crime, apostasy.

"'With the latter I began,' Anselmo now proceeded to speak in the first person.

"I invented a new kind of penance, severer than any that sinner ever inflicted on himself. I remained

Christian in order to be reminded daily how heavily I had sinned, in order to render the punishment which my apostasy merits infinitely great in time to come, in order to abhor Christianity, while others pray for it. But I had not become a penitent who daily scourges his skin because he had abdicated his faith; I became one who daily martyrs his soul by practicing Christian ceremonies, while thinking and acting as Jew. At times the baptized Jew is overcome by an unconquerable longing for his brothers, for his religion. Then he throws off the cowl, creeps into the synagogue, and hears the Thorah read; and thus he expiates his sin more severely than sin ever was expiated before.

"The second purpose of my life, baroness, is now also accomplished," said Father Anselmo, rising; "after searching a long time in vain, I have at last found you; I have heard that you are no better now than you ever were; that you have again thrown Jews into a subterranean dungeon, only this time it was your dungeon, and not that of the Pope. It is time for all such things to cease. I came to avenge myself in punishing you."

The baroness had cowered lower and lower in her chair. She seemed perfectly lifeless. Father Anselmo drew a packet of papers from his habit.

"Here, baroness, are the bills of all you owe. I hereby give you notice of all of them; if every penny be not paid at the legally appointed time, you will leave this castle a beggar; I will give it to a Jew, and a Jew will reign in the ancestral hall of the Weidens. That is my sentence on you, baroness."

The baroness sprang up from her seat, and fell at the monk's feet; she importuned him, she entreated him to give her time, not to ruin her, not to undo her for her child's, her only child's sake.

"Did you, gracious baroness, have compassion on an only child?" asked Father Anselmo, mockingly.

"Oh, you are a noble man, a man of God; you are a priest," wailed the baroness, "forgive and forget. Do not make my child, my poor Egmont, unhappy; he has an honorable career before him; he is in the duke's military school."

"He *was* there, madam," returned Father Anselmo, quietly, "he is not there now; he was disgracefully expelled from the corps, and since then no one has heard anything of him."

"You lie, you lie, father!" cried the baroness, dreadfully agitated.

"No, I do not lie; here is the duke's general order, which has been printed and made public."

Father Anselmo handed a printed paper to the wretched woman. She seized it with trembling hands, cast an anxious glance at it, and sank with a loud shriek to the ground. Father Anselmo composedly walked past the prostrate figure, unbolted the door, stepped into the hall, and called out: "Come here, my daughter, the baroness has been greatly agitated by her confession."

* * * * * *

The Jews of Immenfeld were greatly surprised when about a month afterward the castle of the baroness was put up for sale at auction, and bought by a Franciscan monk for a person whose name did not transpire. The Immenfeld congregation held quite a little jubilee, for their tormentor was punished; and when the baroness, with some few possessions, rode from the castle on a rude wagon, no one knew whither she was bound, and no one cared.

CHAPTER XVIII.
HOME-SICK.

FATHER ANSELMO occupied the best cell in the Convent of Saint Francis. In truth, it could hardly be called a cell, so large and pleasant a room it was. And Father Anselmo had need of a large room, for his chemical and surgical instruments alone could not have been forced into a common cell, not to speak of his excellent library, and the skeletons and skulls which fairly lined the walls.

In the center of the room stood a large oaken table bearing a reading-lamp, which has just been lit as we enter, for it is evening.

Father Anselmo is not present, but despite this the room has an occupant, and the reading-lamp is serving the purpose it is intended for, to wit, reading.

At the table, his head supported by his hands, sits a curly-headed youth, zealously reading from a great Latin book. Paper lies near, and the reader holds a pen in his hand, with which from time to time he notes something down. Then he appears to be calculating what he has written; but as the result does not please him, he arises and fearlessly approaches one of the skeletons, turns it around, and counts the vertebræ of the spinal column from the neck downward.

His face is now turned our way, and we recognize an old acquaintance, changed but little, and that to his advantage; for although the habit fastened round the waist by a black girdle conceals his figure, exuberant health and extraordinary intelligence are plainly depicted on his countenance.

Yes, dear reader, the youth you see before you is Joseph Bonafit, who has now been in the convent somewhat longer than a year, and whose merry, sparkling black eyes prove that he is not at all badly off there.

Bonafit again sat down at the table, and again supported his head on his hands; then he suddenly closed his volume, and said:

"This is really a mystery to me, and I shall have to wait for its solution until Father Anselmo's return. Ah, good, kind Father Anselmo," Joseph continued to soliloquize, "how I long for him. I wonder what dear little mother said when she heard of me? How much I should like to see her again; but I must have patience. Heavens, if the Immenfeld Jews were to know where I am, their hair would stand on end. But perhaps it would not if they knew how I keep the Jewish rites in this Catholic convent.

These last words were suggested to Joseph by the entrance of another old acquaintance of ours, formerly Cobbler Christian of Immenfeld. He bore a waiter on which were a bowl of milk and some white bread.

"Praised be Jesus Christ!" said Christian, but received no answer to his salutation.

Christian, with a contemptuous movement, shoved the books and papers on the table to one side, set down his waiter, and said:

"Brother Joseph, here is your supper, and may you invite Christ to be your guest."

Joseph cast a contemptuous glance at the ex-cobbler, and said:

"Christian, did you invite Christ to be your guest, when you drank half of the prior's wine, and substituted water in its stead?"

"Sh—sh," whispered Christian, settling himself comfortably in a cushioned arm-chair opposite to Joseph.

"Sh—sh," he said again, "Brother Joseph, you must not speak anything you cannot justify; indeed, you ought not be permitted to speak at all to such holy men as I and the prior are."

Joseph laughed heartily at this connection of persons, but Christian did not seem to mind his merriment.

Joseph attacked his frugal supper with a good appetite, while Christian folded his hands over his greasy habit, elevated his nose, which was strongly inflamed by drink, to the ceiling, and seemed lost in admiration of a stuffed crocodile which hung there.

Suddenly he began:

"Now, Joseph, I should like to know how a person can live a whole year on nothing but bread-and-milk?"

"Why, you know that, Christian; just look at me and confess that bread-and-milk have agreed excellently with me; for I have eaten nothing else, excepting some radishes and fruit, since I came here."

"Yes, yes, I know that," returned Christian. "The holy fathers are fools to have permitted this. Not only have they received a Jew as inmate, not only have they refrained from baptizing him, they even allow him to eat what he likes, and leave what he dislikes. Well, I call that a real monastic training."

"Just like yours, Christian—just like yours. There the holy fathers take a drunkard into their cloister, and instead of subjecting him to a strict monastic discipline, they permit him to guzzle and drink as much as he wants to."

"Brother Joseph, you are very saucy."

"Thanks," returned Joseph, "but that does not improve the matter; the holy fathers knew very well that if they did not give me my way Father Anselmo would leave them and follow a call to Rome, where they seem to have some foreknowledge of his skill; and Father Anselmo is a gold mine to the convent."

"Rubbish and nonsense," returned the ex-cobbler, contemptuously; "there are other smart people in the world. For the rest, I really don't know what notion the crazy father has taken to you; at first he did not care about you at all."

"Yes, that is true; I did not even see him before I got so dangerously ill. But when my forcible abduction from home and my imprisonment here so affected my mind and body as to result in throwing me on a sick-bed, he came to see me. Even then he acted coldly and indifferently, prescribed the necessary medicines, and left me. But one day his eyes remained fixed on a sort of scapulary which you may remember having seen in Immenfeld—for all Jews wear it beneath their garments. See,—I mean this here,"—and Joseph drew from beneath his gown a small piece of stuff at whose forward end two woolen fringes were observable, and which is known to all Jews by the name *Arba-kanfoth* (four borders).

"Oh, yes; I know that the Jews wear it," returned Christian; "but what had this to do with Father Anselmo?"

"I cannot say, but from that day Father Anselmo's

manner to me changed, and you know that a father could not be better to me than he is."

"But I do not understand why the other fathers have no objections to Father Anselmo's taking you under his protection, and why they do not make some arrangements to have you baptized."

"Father Anselmo promised them that when my studies are completed he will not only himself instruct me in his religion, but will make me as good a Christian as he is. Now—as I heard from Father Anselmo himself—the holy fathers count on my becoming as learned as my teacher, and able at some future time to supply his place; therefore they grant me all reasonable liberties."

Christian was silent for a time, then he said:

"Brother Joseph——"

"Christian," the latter interrupted him in a vexed tone, " why do you persist in calling me *Brother* Joseph? You know that it vexes me."

"Because the old Joseph is dead, and I do not want you compared to him."

"Foolish man."

"You must not say that, Brother Joseph, I am no more foolish than any one, but they called me so in Immenfeld, and I don't mind being called so for memory's sake."

"Why, do you not like it here?" asked Joseph, in astonishment.

"No, not at all."

"I can't understand that. While in Immenfeld you had to work like a horse for dry bread, you live here like a lord, and yet you do not like it."

"No, you cannot comprehend that. Immenfeld is my native town; be it ever so humble, there is no place like home."

"Heaven knows that's true," sighed Joseph.

"Don't you feel so too? Do you not pine for your mother and for the little hut at home?"

"Indeed I do; but I have resolved to study and become a famous man before I return home."

"That is something else. I have no need to learn, I know enough," said Christian, so emphatically that Joseph smiled.

The ex-cobbler arose, walked around the table to Joseph's side, but bent down to his ear, and said:

"Joseph, I am going to run away; I can stand it here no longer; if you want to come along you may."

Joseph looked at the cobbler in surprise, and asked:

"Are you in earnest, Christian, or are you drunk?"

"I was never more sober, and never spoke more seriously in my life."

"But the holy fathers will not let you go, Christian; for, as you told me yourself, they treat you like a prisoner."

"That is just it. If I was at liberty to go where I pleased, I would not yearn so for Immenfeld. But I can stand this captivity no longer. I have prepared everything. When midnight mass is over I shall leave the convent, and we can journey toward our home."

The boy was rendered very anxious by the thought that, if Christian came to Immenfeld, he would betray his whereabouts, and he tried to dissuade the cobbler from his undertaking. However, he did not succeed, and Christian at last said:

"If you are bound not to let me go, you have only to betray me to the prior."

Joseph felt grieved by this, and told Christian so. The latter relented, and said:

"Well, yes, I know you will not betray me, else I would not have confided in you. But I was firmly convinced that you would go with me."

"No, not only can I not go with you, Christian, but I urgently pray you not to reveal my place of sojourn."

"Why, Joseph, are you crazy? Why not? Perhaps the Jews will come for you."

"That is just what I wish to avoid. They would hardly demand me back were they to know my whereabouts, and they would certainly consider me an apostate. You remember 'Spaniard'? Well, he was excommunicated for less serious reasons, and the same would anathematize me, were they to discover that I remained here voluntarily."

"Well, well, I can be silent, too," said Christian, holding out his hand to Joseph, who pressed it heartily. Then he took up the waiter with the remnants of the supper, and left the room.

Joseph remained sitting at the table in a very thoughtful mood. His thoughts flew over the space that lay between him and home, and he pictured his poor mother's joy if he were to appear suddenly before her, perhaps just as she was puzzling her head as to where her dear son could be. He almost repented not having consented to fly with Christian, and, once arrived at home, to place himself under Benrimo's protection, whom he believed to have much influence, and of whose departure from Immenfeld he knew nothing. A feeling of revenge against Witzleb also influenced him, for that it was he who had abducted him he had known a quarter of an hour after his capture.

These thoughts recalled to Joseph's mind the events of that night. He remembered how he had gone to his teacher to invite him to his *Bar-Mitzvah;* how his stay there had been prolonged till after midnight; how, on emerging from Benrimo's house, he had suddenly received a blow on the head which had rendered him senseless. On regaining his senses, he found himself in a coach, his feet and hands firmly bound, his mouth gagged, and opposite to him the hated Baron Witzleb, whose secret he had partly overheard, which fact, till now, had caused him nothing but suffering.

"Yes," he cried, suddenly, "yes, I will go home; I will fly with Christian. Home—hurrah! home to my dear, good mother!"

Joseph jumped up quickly to leave the room and look for Christian. His hand was already on the knob of the door, when he paused suddenly, and lowered his head. "And my resolutions," he said to himself, "my ambitious plans?" Joseph cast lingering glances on the shelves filled with books, on the surgical instruments, and even on the skeletons and skulls. "Alas!" he continued, mournfully, "ye are all so full of mysteries which I should like to fathom; ye still hold firmly to a world of wonders which the mouth of my master will reveal to me. And my master, whose heart is fondly set on me, shall I ungratefully leave him for the sake of a caprice, while he is full of joy at our prospective meeting? No; I shall remain and study. But my mother, my dear, good mother? Well, she also must wait until I can step up to her and say: 'Mother, dear, have you heard of the great, famous Bonafit? He is your son—he stands before you!' Yes, it shall be so."

Joseph's face grew bright again when he had taken this resolve; he even took up the Latin volume, and was about to resume his studies, when the convent bell tolled the hour of ten. Almost simultaneously the door-bell of the convent tinkled shrilly, and Joseph heard a well-known step on the stone stairs. He listened joyously. Now the steps had reached the corridor; they approached nearer and nearer. The boy sprang up so boisterously that the chair on which he had sat overturned with a crash. He rushed to the door, when it was opened from without, and Father Anselmo appeared on the threshold.

"Good-evening, my son," said he, stretching out his hands.

"Welcome, welcome, Rabbi Isaac," cried Joseph, throwing himself into the monk's arms, which held him closely. "Have you seen my dear, dear mother, rabbi—Father Anselmo?" The boy corrected himself, at a sign from the monk.

"Yes, my son; she is in good health, and sends you this kiss," and Father Anselmo pressed a kiss on Joseph's high, clear brow.

CHAPTER XIX.

BEHIND THE DOOR.

On the evening of Father Anselmo's return, the prior and the Baron of Witzleb sat eagerly conversing in the former's cell. Their topic must have been of great importance, for th   talked in whispers, to avoid all danger of their conversation being overheard. At last the prior said impatiently:

"Baron, you know that whispering is bad for my chest; do have the kindness to continue the conversation in your usual tone of voice; no one can possibly overhear us."

"Just as your reverence desires," answered Witzleb. "Speak louder, I will fall into your tone of voice."

"I have been puzzling my head for the last year what it is that you want to do with that Jewish boy, baron. The matter annoys me very much. Father Anselmo tyrannizes us all through this boy; he can eat and drink what he pleases, does not go to the chapel, never makes the sign of the cross; in short, he occupies an exceptional position here, one not at all suitable in a convent."

"Never mind, prior, this boy will yet become the pride and the making of this convent."

"I cannot comprehend in what manner."

"I can believe that; I refer to what I told you the evening I brought the boy hither. I intend to do great things by his aid."

"And may I not know anything of them?"

"No, reverend father; every player must try to retain a trump card for himself."

"But it is imposing a little too much on us, to encumber us with a Jewish boy, and then say we must not find out anything about him," returned the prior, peevishly.

"I did not say that; but I think it too soon to let the cat out of the bag.

"We two generally share our secrets," said the prior, almost threateningly.

The baron reflected a few moments, then said:

"Very well, your reverence, if you will swear on the crucifix to keep my secret inviolate, I will impart it to you."

"On one crucifix, baron; I will swear on all the crucifixes in the convent, a hundred times on each."

"That you are so willing to swear affects me disagreeably; for this reason I am afraid to intrust you with a secret which may cost you your head."

"Ugh, ugh!" said the prior, "then let the matter drop; I would rather not know it."

"But you will know it some time, although not till all my preparations are made, which will take some years."

The prior did not answer. He lowered his head, and the conflict between curiosity and fear could be plainly seen on his downcast face. At last the former gained the victory, and the prior began:

"It is all one in the end, whether a man dies earlier or later, as die he must at some time; and should this secret be the cause of my death, I will at least know for what I die. Impart it to me, baron; I swear never to reveal it."

"No, that is not sufficient guarantee for me any more. I must have other security."

"What shall that be?"

"You must put your reverend signature to a piece of writing setting forth that you are my accessory and accomplice. If we are caught, it must be in the same trap."

"Ahem, that is a confoundedly dangerous condition."

"Yes; but it is a confoundedly dangerous secret."

"Well, well, baron, I dare say you wish to lose your head as little as I, and as long as I am in possession of your secret, I may consider myself pretty safe. Go on, write, and I will sign."

"That will not take me long," said the baron, sitting down at the prior's desk. He was as good as his word, and soon had the following words written on a small piece of paper: "I voluntarily acknowledge myself to be an accomplice and accessory of Baron Kuno of Witzleb."

The very plainness of this statement made the prior hesitate again.

"The devil knows all you have ever done, baron, and I am to take half the guilt on myself? No, no, write something else. I will not sign that."

"Very well, said Kuno, preparing to tear the paper.

"Wait, wait a moment!" said the prior; and taking the paper he signed it.

Kuno took and folded it, put it in his bosom, sat down opposite to the prior, and said in a mysterious tone:

"Attention, your reverence, my words will astonish you. *I intend to become Duke of Wimmerstein.*"

The prior looked foolish; then, seizing Kuno's hand and feeling his pulse, he said quickly:

"You are feverish, Baron Witzleb, you ought to go to bed, and apply ice on your head."

Kuno smiled in a superior manner, and said:

"I knew it would surprise your reverence, but I am not feverish. I know what I say very well."

"That may be so; but I am far from comprehending you."

"Well, then, listen," said Kuno; "you know, or believe you know, that Duke Francis XII. has no direct heir. But he had a brother once, who, in his younger years, entered the French service, and went to the French colony in Canada, in America. He there fell in battle.

"On account of some little difficulties, I was obliged to leave the court and country of Duke Francis, and likewise went to Canada, but entered the English service there; consequently, I was opposed to the Prince of Wimmerstein.

"We had some Indians as allies, and these always secured the scalps of our fallen enemies. While prosecuting this hideous work, they came to the body of the prince, which was distinguished from the rest by the jewels and brilliant uniform on it.

"A dispute arose between the chiefs of two tribes as to whom the scalp of this distinguished white man rightfully belonged, and, as I was on good terms with both, they appointed me umpire.

"I had known the prince at court, and recognized him immediately.

"I took charge of the papers on him, and left the rest to the Indians, although I forbade their scalping him.

"That evening, when quietly settled in my tent, I examined the papers, and found, to my surprise, that the prince had been married, and that his young wife and infant boy resided in Quebec.

"At first I attached no importance whatever to my knowledge of this marriage, and I thought of nothing else than how best and soonest to communicate news of the prince to his wife.

"I took leave of my colonel and traveled to Quebec. I immediately called on the young widow and heard that she was ill and her life despaired of. I told her my name and gave her all the papers which were of no value to me.

"She was greatly surprised to find she was the wife of a prince; for her husband had kept his rank strictly secret.

"Then for the first time a project flashed across my brain, by which I could revenge myself in a brilliant manner on the duke. He was then absent from his country, and my plan was to take his brother's child to Germany, agitate a revolt in his favor, and have him proclaimed duke.

"I began operations by revealing as much of my plans as I thought necessary to the prince's wife. I bribed her physician to order a sea voyage for her, and conducted her and her infant to a vessel which was on the point of sailing for Europe. Of course I accompanied them. As I and the physician had foreseen, the lady died on the third day after we had set sail, and I remained sole possessor of her infant, a splendid child with black, curly hair. I took charge of the dead lady's papers, among which was a certificate of baptism of the young prince, and cared for him as much as was in my power.

"But the child also died during the voyage, and my beautiful plan apparently fell into the sea with him.

"But soon after I had reached Germany, I began to form other plans as to how I could procure another heir to the throne. But no one suited me until after the lapse of years I discovered Joseph Bonafit in the dungeon of my sister's castle, and found that he strongly resembled the little prince, as well as the latter's father. It is true that Joseph is a Jew, but baptism will speedily remedy that. When once this has been done, and the boy grown sensible enough to perceive what is to his advantage, he will be glad enough to act the pretender to the throne.

"Of course it is but natural that, if my plan succeeds, he will appoint me his guardian and regent; and, as I can unmask him at any time, he will be completely in my power. On my appearance at court, I will adopt such a disguise that no one will recognize me. When I am actually reigning duke on the part of my ward, I will richly endow this convent."

"That is all very well laid out, baron," said the prior, as Kuno ceased, "but it is only a phantom of the brain, and will hardly be realized."

"And why not?"

"Because great obstacles are in the way of your design being executed," returned the prior; "first of all, you cannot prove that the prince was married, as even his wife did not know his rank; further, it is much to be questioned, if the boy is adapted for a position so high as that of reigning duke, and then—and then, *no Jew shall reign and govern a Christian country, be it even a baptized one.*"

"Do not judge too hastily, your reverence; leave the accomplishment of my project to me, and all will be well."

"Yes, but——" the prior stopped suddenly, and bent in a listening attitude toward the door; then he signed to the baron, who tiptoed carefully to the door, and with a sudden movement opened it wide.

He recoiled in fear, for he beheld the confused and blushing face of Christian, who was crouching without the door, and had evidently been eavesdropping.

A long pause ensued. Then the baron began:

"Your reverence, are there any subterranean cells in this convent?"

"Yes, baron, very desirable ones indeed."

"I allude to such as are impenetrable to the light of day, and where all shrieks and screams never reach the ears of man."

"Oh, yes," returned the prior indifferently; "they are nothing but niches in the wall; but they are dreadfully unhealthy, and no one can live there long, for the water constantly stands a foot high in them, and very little air has access. In former times the nuns of the adjoining convent were imprisoned here when they had been unfaithful to their vows."

"Well, and now, your reverence, do they not imprison any nuns there?" asked Kuno, curiously.

"No, rarely; almost never," returned the prior, hesitatingly.

"Very well," said Kuno, arising and going to the door, which he opened. "It is the best way of guarding ourselves against eavesdroppers. Brother Christian must be made acquainted with the aspect of these cells this very night, and"—he continued in a whisper—"must never see the light of day again."

"Was he the eavesdropper?"

"Yes, I have not trusted this drunkard for a long time past, and would have liked to put him out of the way this good while; therefore I am not at all sorry that this has occurred to-day, as it affords me a chance to carry out my resolutions."

"Let us wait until after midnight mass; that is the best time," said the prior.

"Yes, then all are asleep. But how shall we get him down?"

"Leave that to me; I will leave my cell, and then Christian will enter it to drink the wine we have left. I will put an opiate in it. When he is asleep we will carry him down. As for the coming up, let him take care of that himself. I think he will have to give it up as a bad job."

The chapel bell now called the monks to midnight mass, and the prior and his guest arose to follow the summons.

It rather surprised the two conspirators that Christian was nowhere to be seen; but the prior whispered to the baron:

"The drunkard is doubtless in my cell drinking the wine we have left. May it agree with him, for it is the last he will ever drink."

When mass was over the monks retired to their respective cells, and the prior sent for Brother Christian. He was nowhere to be found.

Suddenly the door of the prior's cell was opened, and a lay-brother entered, holding in his hand a greasy habit and cowl, together with a rope and a rosary. He declared that he had found all these lying on the ground without the convent walls.

"That is Christian's habit," cried the prior and the baron simultaneously.

The lay-brother departed, in order to tell the news to the other monks who had not retired yet.

But the baron arose hastily, buckled on his sword, and put on his cap.

"Shall I order a horse to be saddled?" asked the prior.

"No; the rascal has no doubt fled to the mountains, and there a horse would be only in the way."

"If you will but catch him. We are lost else, for he has doubtless run away in order to reveal what he overheard," said the prior, clasping his trembling hands in terror.

"Rely entirely on me, your reverence. I warrant you Christian will not betray a syllable."

The baron hastily left the cell, and soon after the prior heard the convent door fall to with a loud crash.

CHAPTER XX.
THE CRIME IN THE DARK.

CHRISTIAN had executed his project; he had made his escape during mass. When he found himself without the convent walls he drew a breath of relief. The night air had never seemed so fresh and exhilarating to him before. He stretched his limbs like one who had long been standing in a cramped position.

"Ah," he said, in a half whisper, "I never thought that liberty was so pleasant, and could never understand that a day's imprisonment was considered a punishment, but now I understand it very well. But," the deserter interrupted his soliloquy, "it is time that I start, else the monks will get through their babbling and perhaps miss me, though that is hardly possible, as I am never wanted after midnight."

Christian took off his cowl, and all the vestments which would betray him as a monk. He had put on the clothes he had brought to the convent, under his habit, and, after cutting off a sturdy stick from a neighboring tree, he was equipped for his journey.

He had taken some bottles of wine from the convent, which he now tied up in a cloth, hung on the end of his stick, and put the stick over his shoulder. Then he started on his journey. The reader knows that the convent of St. Francis was situated in a ravine. Consequently, Christian had to walk up the mountain in order to gain the road to Immenfeld. It is true, he might have taken the easier way in the valley, where a good road lay, which also led to Immenfeld; but Christian had various good reasons for not choosing this way. First of all, it was a roundabout way; then, he might, perhaps, change his mind; and another province lay on yonder side of the mountain; at last, most important reason of all, the monks might discover his absence in time, and think it worth their while to pursue him, in which case he would be captured much more easily on an open road than in the mountains.

The foolish ex-cobbler never thought that the Baron of Witzleb, who was now in the convent, might not deem it advisable to let him escape, nor had he ever suspected that the baron had brought him to the convent because he knew too many of his secrets.

Nor did it at all trouble Christian that the baron had caught him listening; for, in the first place, he knew almost all the baron's secrets, and had never betrayed a word; and then, he had really heard nothing, for the heavy oaken door of the prior's cell closed far too well.

Christian walked up the mountain at a quick pace. Although the night air was very chill, the perspiration ran in streams from the wanderer's brow; for instinct taught him to take to the most impassable paths, and force his way through the densest shrubbery.

Had he once reached Immenfeld, calculated Christian, then, secrecy was no longer necessary; for there he was his own master, and, if questioned, would tell the baron that he had got tired of a convent life, would rather live in his little house, or go to the city and make merry with the baron's band there, of which the reader has already heard.

Christian was far on his way up the mountain when he heard the convent-bell toll the hour of two. He was astonished to think that he had not drunk for such a long while; he therefore halted, wiped his brow, untied the cloth, took out a bottle of wine, and almost emptied it.

Then the fugitive proceeded on his way, but was not so quick as before, for his head was somewhat heavy, and his feet were tired. Suddenly the moon arose, and Christian recoiled in terror. He had almost walked into the water, for he had reached the summit of the mounain, and there, surrounded by trees and shrubs, lay a smooth, glassy lake.

Much as the ex-cobbler's perception for the beauties of nature was blunted, yet the view before him was so enchanting that not even he could pass it by unnoticed.

"How beautiful, how beautiful!" murmured Christian, looking at the smooth surface of the water, in which the silvery moonlight was reflected, and across which the shadows of the willows on the bank were cast in a thousand fantastic shapes, while the nodding of the reeds, when the breezes whispered in them, resembled myriads of dancing little elves.

"This is just like an enchanted spot," said Christian. "I should not be at all surprised were the nymph of the water to come to me and say: 'Dear Christian, come down with me to my castle. I have numberless pocals of gold, from which you can drink as much wine as you please.'

"Aha!" Christian hemmed, to check the flow of his poetical thoughts, and, growing very prosaic, continued: "Talking of wine reminds me, I had better drink some first; the water-nymph might be somewhat long in coming." Christian looked about him for a seat, and soon descried the stump of a tree, on which he comfortably established himself, again untied his cloth, took out another bottle, waved it at the lake, and softly cried:

"Beautiful water-nymph, to your health!"

The sound of his own voice startled him; it seemed a desecration of peaceful nature. Gurgle, gurgle, gurgle—the bottle was empty, and Christian lifted his arm to throw it into the water, but, drawing it back again, he let the bottle fall into the grass.

"Such a thing might insult a water-nymph," he muttered, drunkenly. "The water-nymphs! But they are all dead, the holy priests killed them by cursing them. That must have been a beautiful time," he continued, "when water-nymphs and forest-elves lived their merry lives and had no church or priests to be afraid of. Now—

adays no one falls into the water unless he be thrown in, the water-nymph entices them no more to a watery grave. Yes, indeed, this is a splendid place to throw some one into the water. I don't believe that much would ever be heard about him."

No surprise must be felt at these poetic thoughts of Cobbler Christian, who did not even know how to read. The faith in water-nymphs and elves was deeply rooted in the people, and it is from this source that our poets have drawn their wealth of legends and fables.

Christian's head fell on his breast; he was lost in deep thought, which soon turned into profound slumber, and his snoring awoke the echoes of the forest.

Now the shrubbery was carefully pushed apart, and a face appeared at the aperture. Softly, softly, the whole figure forced its way through, and approached the sleeper, whose back was turned to it. The moon glided behind a cloud, as if anxious to avoid the coming scene.

"Accursed drunkard!" hissed the man, "you could not come in my way more opportunely. You will never overhear a secret of mine again."

Drawing a long rapier from his sheath, the man softly crept closer to the sleeper, taking heed of the rustle of every leaf, and pausing at every twig that cracked beneath his foot. Now he caught sight of the sleeper's face, which was turned to the lake; yes, it was he—most certainly it was he. If the moon would but show herself an instant, that one might be more sure in one's aim—ah! there she comes forth from the clouds; yes, it is Christian— mistake is impossible."

The murderer firmly clasps the hilt of his dagger; he prepares it for a thrust. With body bent forward, he breathlessly advances a step—another, and now a low cry escaped the murderer's lips, and he fell headlong on the ground with such force that his dagger flew from his hand and fell with a loud splash into the lake. The guardian spirit of drunkards had hovered here; the murderer had stumbled over the empty bottle which Christian had thrown into the grass. The latter started up with a cry of terror, for the dagger in its flight to the lake grazed him, and he found himself opposite his pursuer, who had regained his feet.

The baron—the reader has long since guessed that it is he—finding himself disarmed, calculated his chances against a man so strong as Christian, and who, besides, was armed with a good stick, and determined to get him into his power by good words and persuasion.

"Christian," said Witzleb, "why did you run away from the convent?"

"I did not like it there any more," sullenly returned Christian.

"And so you secretly escaped?"

"No, I did not do that; I can come and go at pleasure, and as it is hot work journeying by day, I went in the night-time."

"That was very foolish of you, Christian, very foolish indeed. The holy fathers think that you have run away; you had therefore better return with me to the convent, and leave it by day. Come, my friend, come."

"N-o," returned Christian, in a drawling tone; "I will not go back to the convent, all the less as you have taken the trouble to run after me.

Unconquerable rage boiled in the baron's breast, but he controlled himself, and said, persuasively:

"Christian, only anxiety for my faithful follower drove me after you, and I thank God that I have found you safe and well; therefore come back with me."

"No!" and with a cunning peculiar to drunkards, he continued: "Well, now you have found me, you may quietly return to the convent, since you know that nothing has happened to me."

The baron stamped his foot; his restraint was at an end.

"Will you go back with me or not?" he roared, in a tone of voice that woke the slumbering echoes, and made the little birds flutter uneasily in their nests.

"No, now I just will not."

The baron uttered a howl of rage and fell on Christian, who, not expecting this onslaught, was firmly pinioned, and could make no use of his stick. He accordingly let it drop, and embraced Kuno with his arms likewise. A fearful struggle now ensued. The combatants were well matched; neither brought the other down, and neither ventured to let go, for then the other would gain the advantage.

The grass round about was trampled down as if by horses' hoofs, the bushes and shrubs rustled and cracked beneath the steps of the combatants struggling for life and death, and yet neither fell. The baron forced Christian toward the lake without the latter having been able to prevent it. He recognized the baron's purpose, and gasped forth, the first words spoken since the beginning of the fearful combat:

"You must go down with me, baron; you must go down with me!"

The murderer perceived this very well, and tried to force Christian away from the water's edge all the more as he felt his powers diminishing.

Now the bottle which had foiled him once before that night, was again fatal to him. He stepped on it backward, and stumbling, fell on his back, while Christian fell on him, and pressed his knee on the baron's breast, so that the latter was obliged to loosen his hold.

But the reverence with which the lower classes regarded the aristocracy was so great, that Christian's fist, already lifted for a blow, did not descend on the baron's face; besides this, Christian was no murderer, he was a very good-natured man, and when he saw the master whom he had learned to respect laid low by him, his anger vanished like smoke, and still gasping, he said:

"There, baron, let us be friends. Get up; go to the convent, give my love to the holy fathers. Well, get up, baron."

The latter sprang to his feet like a flash of lightning,

flourished the bottle which he had picked up from the ground, high into the air and shattered it on the head of Christian, who sank with a low moan to the ground.

"There, now you will be silent, rascal," said the baron, kneeling down beside the lifeless body. "But to make the matter quite certain, we will confide him to the quiet waters of the lake," continued the baron, commencing to roll the lifeless body, which he could not lift, to the lake. Another push, another, and still another, and the waters parted with a splash, and closed gurglingly over the murdered man.

The baron washed his hands, and wiped the perspiration from his brow.

The day was dawning, the sun seemed in haste to reveal the scene of the crime just committed, for the eastern sky blushed rosy red. Suddenly the report of a gun broke the stillness, and this was answered by the barking of dogs.

The murderer turned and fled hastily down the mountain.

CHAPTER XXI.
THE SUN BRINGS THE CRIME TO LIGHT.

FATHER ANSELMO and his young friend and pupil sat up nearly the whole night conversing about the former's journey and its purpose.

"Was the Baroness of Weiden, who dwells in Immenfeld, the one whom you sought?" asked Joseph.

"Yes, my son, she is the woman who ruined me; I recognized her immediately."

"And is the purpose of your journey accomplished, father?"

"Perfectly; and I owe it to you, my son, that I have gained peace, at least in one direction, for it was you who first mentioned her name to me."

"That is not my desert, father."

"It is a dispensation of divine Providence, who visits the sins of the parents on the children and grandchildren, and to the third and fourth generations, as I have but lately clearly seen in the case of the baroness."

"In what manner, father? may I know in what manner?"

"Inasmuch as the son of that base woman has already proved himself unworthy of the name he bears."

Father Anselmo told the attentively listening boy all he knew of Baron Egmont, all that is already known to the reader. He added some exhortations to Joseph how wickedness is often punished betimes, and good rewarded; how an evil germ in the heart of a child, if not soon exterminated by good and rigid discipline, swells into a poisonous plant which destroys by its polluting breath all healthy sprouts that spring around it; how a bad bringing up lays the foundation for many a person's ruin, and the yielding to bad inclinations makes criminals even of children.

"Now, Father Anselmo," began Joseph, when his teacher had ended, "you have not yet told me what the punishment was which you went from here to inflict on the baroness."

"You shall hear it now, my son. The baroness has left the ancestral castle of her husband, and will never return there; for I have bought up all her debts, as I told you I would, before I started on my journey, when I heard from you how dreadfully embarrassed the noble lady's circumstances were."

"And who bought all these debts?"

"I, my son; and as a monk of our order is not allowed to be a possessor of any property, I had all the purchase deeds drawn up in another's name."

"But all this must have cost you a great deal of money," said Joseph, hesitatingly.

"Yes indeed; it required a neat little sum of money to satisfy all her creditors," returned Father Anselmo. "I know what is now tormenting your brain, my son."

"Well, what is it, Father Anselmo?"

"You would like to know where I got all the money—

I, a poor Franciscan friar, whose whole income belongs to the convent; this is what you would like to know, yet are afraid to ask. Am I not right?"

"You presumed it, Father Anselmo," answered Joseph, in some confusion.

"You need not be ashamed of your curiosity, my son, it is very pardonable in this case. Wait a moment and I will satisfy it."

Father Anselmo went to a skeleton which stood against the wall, and the single parts of which were hung in wire, as is the case in all artificially joined skeletons. He loosened one of the thigh-bones, and carried it to the table. He then proceeded to screw off the articular extremity of the bone, just as you would screw off the top of a needle-case, and showed to the wondering eyes of the boy a winding groove artfully carved within, into which the upper part fitted so exactly, that a person not initiated in the secret would never discover the trick. Father Anselmo inverted the bone, and a number of glittering stones, some as large as peas, and others small as pin-heads, fell from the cavity.

"Do you know what kind of stones these are, my son?" asked Father Anselmo of the wondering boy; "they are diamonds; and these tiny glass-like stones which you see here represent a value equal to that of the convent and its grounds."

Father Anselmo allowed Joseph's eyes to rest delightedly on the gleaming stones for awhile; then he replaced them in the cavity of the bone, screwed on the natural cover, and hung it in its place in the skeleton. Resuming his seat at the table, Father Anselmo said:

"All the hollow parts of this skeleton are nearly filled with precious stones, part of them diamonds, part emeralds, and the rest rubies. I prepared the skeleton in this manner during my residence in Rome; it contains the remnants of Dr. Isaac Mundolfo's vast fortune. At the time he was forced to retire to the Ghetto, he turned all his property into money, for which he bought precious stones. He had learned to know that no Jew, even be he a Mundolfo, and as famous, could rest safely in possession of his fortune. When, after my baptism, I was released from captivity, I found the skeleton uninjured in the attic of my house, where I had always kept it. All else that had been thought worth taking away was gone. But the plunderers had not known what to do with the skeleton; it was of too little value, as they thought.

"Now, attention, my son; when you leave this convent you shall take with you the contents of the skeleton, no matter whether I be dead or still alive. One part of its contents you shall employ to gain a position for yourself, and the other to find my child. Should you succeed in this last, I leave it to your generosity to give my daughter as much of the inheritance as you think right; I put all in your hands."

Joseph's face glowed with delight, not at the prospect of becoming a rich man, but at the unbounded confidence with which his teacher honored him, who was still but a child in years, at the thought that he was appointed to hold in trust an immense fortune, and that it was even left to him to give as much as he thought proper to the child of Anselmo, whom the latter most certainly loved dearly. The boy's breast heaved high with noble pride, and he stammered:

"My dear, honored teacher, how shall I make myself worthy of the great trust you have reposed in me?"

"You have already proved yourself worthy of it, my son; you are discreet and faithful, not like a boy, but like a man. You have God and warm love for your mother in your heart, and can therefore commit no wrong. Great burdens will be rolled on your shoulders, but you will be the man to bear them; and it is but to spur you on, to inspire you with high resolves and their accomplishment, that I have intrusted you with all my secrets, my religion, my journey, and, most important of all, that of the skeleton. But now, my son, retire to rest for a few hours; the day is dawning, and the convent bell will soon toll for early mass. I shall perform my morning prayers according to the Jewish ritual ere I repair to the chapel for mass."

Joseph retired to his cell, which was close to Father Anselmo's room, and threw himself on his hard couch. He was just falling into a light slumber, when the bell for early mass aroused him. His thoughts dwelt on what Father Anselmo had intrusted him with that night; he erected the most beautiful air-castles; he imagined how happy he would be when he led Anselmo's child to him. It was strange that Joseph always thought of Father Anselmo's daughter as a half-grown girl, although he repeatedly told himself that many, many years had passed since she had been taken away from her father, and that perhaps many more would elapse ere she was restored to him, if the latter should ever be the case at all. Yet it was the same with Father Anselmo. He thought of his daughter, who might now be a married woman, as the little child from whom he had been parted.

"Study, study, that is the main thing," said Joseph to himself, always recurring to his favorite theme; "I must try to learn all Father Anselmo can teach me, then I shall see the world at my feet. But if I lie here making plans I shall get no sleep, and shall be too tired all day to study as I ought to."

The boy turned his face to the wall and closed his tired eyes.

He was again awakened from his half sleep, and this time by a violent ringing of the convent door-bell. Joseph knew not why, but the sound of the bell seemed fearful and anxious to him; all the more, as its shrill peal did not subside, but called desperately again and again. Soon after Joseph heard hasty steps approaching Father Anselmo's door, and the latter was torn open. Some words were uttered, Father Anselmo departed hastily, but soon came back, knocked at the door of Joseph's cell, and called him:

"Joseph, my son, get up, quick; there is a great need of making haste!"

Joseph leaped from his bed and opened the door.

"Come, Joseph, you are to accompany me; all dispatch is required: a great crime has apparently been committed."

Joseph put on his habit as quickly as could be, and left his cell. Father Anselmo handed him a case containing bandages and instruments, and hastened, as fast as his feet would carry him, down the stone stairs. Joseph put no questions; he knew they were going to some sick person, for, lately, his teacher always took him along when the distance was not too great; the prior would not permit Joseph to go far from the convent. When they arrived in the courtyard, the two donkeys, which were always kept saddled for cases of emergency, were already standing there, and a young fellow in the livery of a hunter was holding a horse by the bridle.

"Where is the wounded man?" asked Father Anselmo of the latter.

"In the Forest Inn, on the mountain," was the answer.

"Very well, let us start," cried Father Anselmo; and the three mounted their beasts.

After a hard ride of about an hour, the Forest Inn came in sight. All this time not a word had been spoken. Although Joseph would have liked to know to whom and for what purpose Father Anselmo had been summoned in such haste, he restrained his curiosity and waited for the clearing-up of this mystery.

A number of hunters and peasants anxiously expecting the arrival of the father, were collected in front of the Forest Inn, which crowned the summit of the mountains, in one of whose ravines the Convent of Saint Francis lay.

The landlord of the inn came out hastily, assisted Father Anselmo to dismount, and, without speaking a word, conducted him up the creaking wooden stairs to the second story. His hand was already on the door-knob, when Father Anselmo laid a restraining hold on his arm, and asked:

"So you really do not know the man?"

"No, your reverence; he seems to be a perfect stranger in these parts; to judge by his dress, he is a laborer."

The landlord opened the door, and all entered.

On the poor bed an immovable figure lay stretched out, the head so enveloped and covered by wet cloths that the face could not be discerned.

Father Anselmo approached the bed, and carefully raised the cloths. He started back and uttered a low cry. Joseph, who believed that the dreadful appearance of the wounded man had elicited the father's low cry, took courage, and also approached the bed. He also uttered a low cry, and started back.

"Do you know him?" asked Father Anselmo.

"It is Christian," returned Joseph, with pale lips; "how comes he here, and in such a condition?"

"God knows," returned Father Anselmo, preparing to examine the shattered head of the lifeless man.

It must here be remembered that neither Father Anselmo nor Joseph had been informed of poor Christian's disappearance; nor could the monks of the convent suspect who the wounded man was, as he was not clad in monastic garb, but in his ordinary clothes.

"There is life in him still," said Father Anselmo, continuing his examination; "we must try to restore him to consciousness, if but for two minutes, so that he may reveal to us the name of his murderer."

"Is that all you hope to attain?" asked Joseph, sorrowfully; "is there no prospect of recovery?"

"Not the least; and I doubt if he will be able to speak a word, and tell us who it was that put him in this terrible state.

"My good friend," said Father Anselmo, turning to the landlord, "I beg you to leave us, for what we have to do with the wounded man may be too much for your nerves."

The landlord was glad to be released, and hurried from the room.

"Who could it be that put this poor devil into such a state?" asked Father Anselmo, in a low tone, while he poured out a few drops of some fluid into a spoon, and administered them to the heavily breathing man.

"I have a dreadful suspicion, Father Anselmo," whispered Joseph; "a suspicion which almost becomes a certainty, when I reflect how much it lay in the interest of a certain person to put this man out of the way."

"Who could have had such an interest in this poor drunkard?" asked Father Anselmo, without removing his eyes from Christian's pale countenance, while his hand pressed the sick man's pulse.

"A man whose secret was known to this poor drunkard; a man whom not only I, but all who know him, must believe capable of such a deed."

"Do I know him?" asked Father Anselmo.

"Yes, father, it is Baron Kuno, of Witzleb."

"*It was he! it was he!*" cried a weak voice from the bed.

Christian had opened his eyes, and was looking at Father Anselmo. He had regained his senses; he had denounced his murderer.

CHAPTER XXII.

A DEATH-BED.

FATHER ANSELMO looked at Joseph in surprise. The boy had guessed aright; this penetration and acuteness greatly pleased him.

"Where and how did this happen?" asked Father Anselmo of Christian.

But the light of reason had again vanished in darkness; the sick man's eyes were half closed, and his labored breathing gave the only sign of life.

"Do not let him die yet," whispered Joseph; "he must be more explicit in his revelations."

"That is not necessary, as we know the murderer; the man who found the poor fellow will tell us the particulars, and we shall probably discover in the convent how Christian came in this dress to the place where he was murdered. It is sinful, and does not beseem our noble profession, to call back the fleeing spirit for the sake of mere curiosity."

"But it is not curiosity, father," cried Joseph, anxiously, "indeed it is not curiosity; this man will take with him into the grave a secret which has imbittered my days, and probably cost him his life."

"That is another thing; why did you not tell me this before, my son?"

"An oath binds me to secrecy. I dare not tell any one what I know, and should poor Christian regain his senses, I do not see how I am to draw from him what he knows, without violating my oath."

The wounded man now grew restless, and tossed about on the bed. Father Anselmo again poured some drops down his throat, but without any visible result. It is true, Christian began to talk again, but it was in wild, disconnected sentences, and his voice grew weaker and weaker, until it sank to a whisper, while his words grew fewer, and the pauses between them longer.

Father Anselmo suddenly signed to Joseph to come nearer.

"At the moment of death, the light of reason often flickers up again," he whispered. Joseph and Father Anselmo bent their faces closer to that of Christian. The latter muttered:

"Have you the child, baron? The carriage must return to-day—just—give it—to me. Yes, yes—the countess will weep—away—with the child—to the—Jew's lane—the child—to the—Jew's lane—the city is large—there it will—be least looked for—just give—it to—P——

Here the muttering suddenly ceased, the wounded man uttered a piercing cry, raised his hand to his head, stretched his body, and was dead.

Father Anselmo closed the ex-cobbler's eyes and said to Joseph:

"Well, have these last words any reference to your secret, or were they but the wanderings of a delirious brain?"

"I believe," returned Joseph, thoughtfully, "I believe that they have reference to what I know, and though I have not learned much, still I am a great deal nearer to the discovery of the secret."

"And you do not want to impart to me what you know of the secret which has probably cost this man his life?"

"Excuse me, father, but do not require this of me."

"You are afraid for yourself, should you betray anything?"

"No, my most honored teacher, you ought to be convinced that I would risk even my life to please you; but do not forget that an oath binds me, and I hold it sacred."

"God bless you, my son!" said Father Anselmo, greatly rejoiced; "you have a true idea of honor, and I see that my secrets will rest safely in your bosom. But let us go down now, and inquire into the particulars of this murder. The man must have received the fatal blow, and then been thrown or have fallen into the water, for his garments are dripping wet."

Several hunters and peasants sat in the tap-room of the inn, anxiously awaiting the physician's report. Although the tidings he brought had been generally expected, still all countenances grew pale, for a murder is an occurrence which makes all men shudder.

On being questioned, the hunters now related how, at dawn of day, they had approached the forest lake, and their dogs, barking violently, had rushed into the reeds of the banks and drawn ashore the body of the wounded man, who had lain with his feet in the water and his head and body among the reeds.

Father Anselmo observed that the police justice of the

district ought to be informed of the murder, and was told that this had been done early in the morning, and that the officers were momentarily expected. The landlord inquired whether the murdered man had confessed, and received absolution and the consolation of the church from his reverence.

Father Anselmo returned neither an affirmative nor negative reply. He simply said that he had done all it was in his power to do for the man, which statement Joseph understood as it was meant; while the landlord, who was a strict Catholic, interpreted it to his complete satisfaction.

When the officers arrived, they gathered all the details of the murder, and finally asked if any one knew who the murderer was. Father Anselmo did not hesitate a moment, and denounced Baron Kuno, of Witzleb.

As Father Anselmo believed that the baron was still in the convent, preparations were made to arrest him; but he was not found there, nor could he be found anywhere.

The prior did not deny that Witzleb had been in the convent till midnight, and that on hearing of Christian's flight he had gone away with the clearly expressed design of searching for him, but he had not since returned to the convent.

Kuno, of Witzleb, remained lost; no one ever saw him again.

Only once, about a year after the murder, Father Anselmo, on passing the prior's cell, believed he heard the baron's voice within. He opened the door and discovered that he had been deceived. The man who sat opposite the prior had hair white as snow, and a long white beard reaching almost to the waist. He wore the habit of the Dominicans, an order who had a convent not far off, and whose members often came to visit the monks of St. Francis.

But let us take up the thread of our story again.

As there was no more work either for the priest or the physician in the inn, Father Anselmo and his pupil rode back to the convent. Each was so lost in thought that no conversation passed between them.

When they had reached the convent, told their news, and heard in return of Christian's flight, they retired to their respective cells, and there sought the rest they were so much in need of.

Evening found teacher and pupil together again, and the subject of their conversation was the murder of Christian. Joseph now called to mind what Father Anselmo's arrival had caused him wholly to forget—that Christian had told him how much he wished to return to Immenfeld. Thoughts of Immenfeld brought Benrimo to his mind, and he asked his teacher if he had heard any tidings of him. His surprise was almost as great as that of the Jews had once been, when he heard that the duke had carried off Benrimo in his carriage.

"I know that the good old man was anxious about me," said Joseph; "all the more as I was the innocent cause of his last quarrel with the congregation. I think it will be best to let him know that I am well and contented, as I did my mother."

"I would not do that," returned Father Anselmo, after reflecting for a time. "I wish to keep the place of your sojourn as secret as possible. It does not suit my plans to let every one know what has become of you; and only reluctantly I gave my consent to your wish of writing to your mother. Danger lies in this even for me, for how very easily could the monks find out to what religion I formerly belonged, all the more as I was not at all reserved in my conversation with the baroness. It is therefore better to leave things as they are."

Joseph Bonafit unhesitatingly submitted in this, as he did in all matters, to his beloved teacher.

"When I return to the world," said Joseph, later on, "it will be my first endeavor to find the mother of that child, of whom you heard without any interference on my part. 'In the Jew's lane of the city, with a certain P——,' said the dying man. That is not much to guide me, but it is more than you discovered in your search for your child, and as you have not yet given up hope of finding her, I am all the more sanguine. I do not know how it is," continued Joseph, "but it appears to me as if this secret must have some relation to me, or to one whom I know and love, and I have always considered my discovery of a part of it as a dispensation of God. I wish, oh, how I wish I could tell you more! but my oath, my oath!"

"Do not allow yourself to be carried away either by your wish to satisfy my curiosity or the desire to have my counsel in the matter. Moreover, you could not tell me much more than I heard from Christian, for I do not believe that you know the main facts of the secret, and the minor particulars would not interest me. Therefore, let us drop this unsatisfactory subject, and resume our studies."

Father Anselmo instructed, and Joseph Bonafit eagerly learned, storing every day a fund of knowledge. The ambitious boy devoured all books; no subject was too difficult for him, no problem made too great a demand on his industry; he never for one moment lost sight of his purpose—to enter the world as one of the learned men of his time. Father Anselmo managed to procure all the works which appeared from time to time, and which corrected old theories, or explained new phenomena.

Thus occupied by studies, the time passed quickly away; the only change in their daily life was when the teacher took his pupil with him to some patient, so that the young student might learn by practice, what he knew already theoretically. All to whom Father Anselmo came knew his pupil, loved and honored him, for such rare industry could not remain unobserved, and all were happy at the thought that Father Anselmo had a successor as worthy and skillful as himself.

CHAPTER XXIII.

AFTER FIVE YEARS.

"THE measure of time is triple. The future approaches slowly, the present speeds away like an arrow from the bow, and the past is an immovable wall."

To the young, time passes all too slowly; their restless blood is impatient for what is to come; they have not learned to economize with life; the short span that lies before them seems inexhaustible to them; they have not yet learned to measure it. The little past that lies behind them has been spent in unconsciousness of self, and what small part they remember is enveloped in mist and clouds. To him who commences a journey the way before him appears infinitely long; after having gone a little way, he will have a scale to measure by, and as he proceeds onward his progress will seem faster and faster.

After this little dissertation the young reader will not think of crying, "Oh, what a long time!" when we tell him that between this and the last chapter five years have elapsed—five years have sunk into the ocean of eternity.

Yes, Joseph Bonafit has been eight years in the convent; for when we left him, in the last chapter, he had been there three years, and we now see him again; he is a handsome young man of twenty-one years. Tall, broad-shouldered, of noble appearance and gait; the lower part of his face shaded by a short, dark beard; the brow, back of which an immense treasure of knowledge lies concealed, high and clear; his eyes unfathomable and shining, mirroring a pure soul—thus Joseph Bonafit now presents himself to us, prepared to begin his struggle, not only with life, but with all evil and the vicissitudes of the world.

Although Witzleb had not reappeared since he had been accused of the murder of Christian, he still seemed to influence Joseph's fate in the convent, for no obstacles were placed in the way of the latter's inclinations and wishes, and he was not forced to attend the convent chapel nor take part in the service.

Joseph was in his twenty-second year, when one day Father Anselmo was summoned to the prior's cell. When he arrived there, the Dominican friar, of whom we have once before spoken, was sitting opposite to the worthy prior. The latter began:

"Brother Anselmo, how is your pupil?"

"Thanks for your inquiry," returned Anselmo, "he is passably well. For the rest, he is already an excellent physician, as your reverence must have heard from all the people around, for they do not ask for me any more, when they think they can have Joseph."

"Yes, yes," said the prior, interrupting Anselmo. "I know all about that; but has he made as much progress in religious instruction?"

"Since your reverence, I think it was last year, commissioned me to instruct the youth in our holy religion, I have studied with him day and night. He now knows as much as any monk, and I will send him to your reverence to be examined."

Father Anselmo purposely said this last, for he knew that there was no greater ignoramus in the convent than the prior, although he pretended to be very learned, and loved people to think he was so.

Father Anselmo was soon convinced that he had acted wisely, for the prior said:

"I have full confidence in you, Brother Anselmo, and know that you are able to initiate your pupil into the sacred doctrines of our most holy religion. I know your piety so well that I am fully convinced your pupil can but follow in your footsteps. Therefore, an examination by me is not at all requisite."

"At the time the boy became my pupil, I declared to your reverence that your purpose—that of making a good physician of him—would never be accomplished did you force him to become a Christian ere he himself desired it. Neither the convent nor Christianity has sustained a loss by your compliance with my request. While, then, his baptism would have been a forcible act, and perhaps have filled the boy's heart with aversion to our religion, it is now the voluntary request of the man, brings joy to our Saviour, and does honor to the convent."

"Brother Anselmo, do you mean to say that the young man wishes to become a Christian, and has himself asked for baptism?" asked the prior, in suspense.

"That is just what I meant to say, your reverence; and had I not now been summoned hither, I would have come of my own accord to ask, in Joseph's name, that he may be taken into the bosom of the only true and holy church of salvation."

The Dominican friar, who had all this time seemed quite an indifferent auditor, could not refrain from a murmur of applause; while the prior, raising his eyes and folding his hands, ejaculated a prayer of thanks to the Holy Virgin.

Neither of them observed the derisive smile on Father Anselmo's countenance.

After a pause, the prior asked:

"Brother Anselmo, when do you think that the holy ceremony shall take place?"

"When your reverence pleases."

"Well, the sooner the better. The assumption of the Holy Virgin will be a fortnight from Sunday, and we will fix it for that day. In the meanwhile we will publish the tidings of this blessed news," said the prior, quite enthusiastically.

"Hold, your reverence—that must not be. Your reverence forgets that no one knows we have so long sheltered a Jew, and that it is a Jew who heals the peasants round about. Your reverence must also be aware that he will then ever be considered a baptized Jew, and as such never gain the confidence of Christians."

"That may be, Brother Anselmo, but we have given up the idea of keeping Joseph here. Two equally good physicians are too much for one convent to keep. You,

Brother Anselmo, are still robust; therefore I have promised this worthy Dominican friar that he may take Joseph with him to his convent. Later on, when it will please God and the saints to take you away, Joseph can return here."

Anselmo grew pale at the prior's words, but he soon collected himself, and answered, composedly:

"Your reverence has but to command, and is always wise enough to order the right thing. But I should now like to bring this joyous and glorious news to my pupil."

"By all means, worthy brother, go, and the Lord be with you," said the prior, and Anselmo departed. The door had hardly closed behind him, when the Dominican friar sprang to it, and pushed the bolt forward.

"Make yourself comfortable, dear Witzleb," said the prior, filling two glasses with sparkling wine from a decanter; "you must feel dreadfully warm in that beard and wig."

The friar took off his beard and wig, also his nose, which he laid on the table, and now the police could have easily found Baron Witzleb, the murderer of Christian, for there he sat as large as life in the prior's cell.

"Matters are better than we thought," said the prior; "why, the boy fairly begs to be baptized."

"This must be ascribed chiefly to Father Anselmo's zeal," returned Witzleb, who, like all others, had a proper respect for Father Anselmo.

"But it is to be questioned whether the young man will enter so readily upon the second part of your plan."

"That he will, and soon enough; you must not forget that the boy is of Jewish descent. Power and money are the constant aim of his race, and then, what young man would refuse a position such as I can offer him?"

"This one perhaps, for he has been educated by Father Anselmo, a man who does not know what ambition is."

"Offer a duchy to the old friar, and see whether he will reject it," returned Witzleb, contemptuously.

"How do you mean to begin?" asked the prior, after a short pause.

"After Joseph has been baptized, I will introduce myself to him in my character as a Dominican friar, for I dare not risk showing my real self to him, and prove to him, by the documents I have in my possession, that he is heir to the duke, and was only intrusted to the care of the old Jewess in Immenfeld. One easily believes something so agreeable."

"Well, supposing he does not consent, despite all this?"

"What then? Really, I have not thought of that at all; in that case, of course, all these years would have been wasted, and I should be obliged to begin afresh."

"Yes," said the prior, peevishly, "then we would have boarded and instructed a Jew eight years, and all for nothing."

"Not for nothing, prior; you have gained your end, and led a stray soul to the feet of the Lord Jesus."

The prior laughed bitterly, and said:

"Truly, 'twould be dearly bought, even not counting the danger to which we expose ourselves should Joseph reveal our project to the duke. Then, another thing, do you not think Father Anselmo would recognize his pupil even on the duke's throne?"

"I will provide against this. I shall take the young man with me under pretense of introducing him into a Dominican convent. You, as I well know, do not permit your monks to pass beyond this province, so there is no danger that Father Anselmo will ever meet Joseph. Very little news of the world penetrates to this convent, and even should Father Anselmo hear of a pretender to the crown, he will never dream that it is Joseph."

"But he is often summoned to the city to visit aristocratic patients, and he might see and recognize Joseph."

"Do you think a monk exists who would not like to

see his convent enriched? Is not Father Anselmo a monk?"

"That does not ease my mind in the least," said the prior, in a discontented tone.

"Well then," cried Witzleb, impatiently; "as soon as we see that Father Anselmo knows too much, we will do with him as with Christian."

"But in that case our convent loses an immense income."

"Which the young duke will replace seven-fold."

"Still I must repeat my former question," said the prior, with unusual obstinacy; "suppose Joseph does not agree to your proposal?"

"That is hardly to be imagined."

"Still, if it should be the case?"

"Well, then he shall be put into one of the cells we once destined for Christian; he will not blab much there."

"But what becomes of your heir to the throne then, baron?"

"Then? Why, then I must look for another?"

"Are these to be found so easily?"

"Oh, they are plentiful."

"Well, then I wonder you took the trouble to steal a Jewish boy, and have burdened us with him for so long a time."

"You do not understand; I have before told you that this boy closely resembles the duke's lost brother."

"And why did you delay so long to play your trump-card?"

"For three reasons. First, I desired the boy to leave off his Jewish speech, jargon and gestures; second, I wanted him to become a Christian; third, eight years ago the duke was still young and strong; now, that he is old and feeble, he will listen more easily to the story of an heir."

"Well, well, I leave all in your hands, Witzleb; let us drink again, to the success of your scheme," said the prior, filling his and the baron's glass; "to the crown pretender!"

CHAPTER XXIV.
AN INTERRUPTED JOY.

When Father Anselmo returned to his cell his face bore an expression of undisguised, intense hate.

Joseph was not there, so Father Anselmo had time to think over the piece of news he was to impart to him. He sat down in the arm-chair before his table and soliloquized:

"Thus all things are perishable and transitory; it seems but yesterday that I took the boy to be my scholar, and now our parting is imminent. Well, praise be to God, I have done all in my power for him. When his fame will penetrate to my solitary cell, I shall be richly rewarded for all my work and trouble. But now I must devise some project by which to withdraw the young man, not only from the danger of being baptized, but from all pursuit by the prior. Perhaps it would have been better had Joseph made his escape shortly after his arrival here, and denounced Witzleb as a kidnapper; but the boy's ardent desire for knowledge was greater than his wish for liberty. Later on, my selfishness contributed no small share to his staying here, for I could not bear the thought of parting from him. Now, however, all such considerations must retire to the background; he must go away, and if it be only to escape the stings of conscience that torture me."

Father Anselmo fell into a deep reverie as to the ways and means by which Joseph could escape the danger that threatened him, and just seemed to have found the right thing by the satisfied look his face assumed, when the door opened and Joseph Bonafit entered. He hastened to his teacher and affectionately pressed his hand.

"What news, Father Anselmo?" asked the young man, dropping into a chair lightly and gracefully, despite the cumbersome garment he wore.

"I have nothing very agreeable to impart."

"Ah, but there is something?"

"Yes, and the sooner you know it, the better for both of us. While you were absent I was summoned to the prior's cell, and he asked me if you were prepared to become a Christian."

"Of course you answered in the negative," said Joseph, as if this answer were quite self-evident.

"You are mistaken, my son, I have averted the catastrophe as long as I could; I knew that it would break in on us at some time, and as it has come in a time when you need fear it no longer, I thought it best to look it in the face. You must go out in the world and employ your learning and skill for the good of your fellow-beings; you must go hence to fill your tasks, that of finding my child and clearing up the mystery of Christian's confession; the sooner you go the better."

"I acquiesce; much as I grieve to leave you, my dear, good teacher, I will go away, I will escape this very day, if you think it necessary," cried Joseph, starting from his seat.

"No, my son," said Father Anselmo, gently pushing back Joseph into his seat, "that is not my intention, and nothing would be gained by it. The monks must voluntarily let you go forever, else you will always live in fear of pursuit, besides having drawn the hate of the priesthood on yourself; and I know what that is, especially toward a Jew. Furthermore, I have a presentiment, that that Witzleb who brought you here is not so lost sight of as they would fain have it believed; indeed, I think that he still exercises considerable influence on your life. He, above all, must be kept in ignorance of our proceedings; for, as you well know, he does not scruple at a murder."

"If you wish to act against your enemies and those of Israel you must work in the dark, as they do; nor must you step forth into the light until you have your adversaries in your power. But, in particular, be careful not to raise the anger of the church, for then no hiding or fleeing is of avail; her arm stretches afar, and her eyes penetrate the dark. You see, therefore, that you must part in peace, not only from the monks, but from the Dominican friar, who seems to have quite another end in view than occasional visits to the prior."

"Then, according to your opinion, I had better be baptized," said Joseph, who had grown pale, in an anxious tone.

"Did I say that, short-sighted boy? Is that all you understand from my words?"

"But how then shall I depart from here in peace?"

"As a dead man," said Father Anselmo, composedly.

Without answering a word, Joseph looked at his teacher in surprise, nay, in anxiety; his look was returned by a smiling glance. However, when Father Anselmo saw bright drops of sweat appear on Joseph's brow, he arose, and caressingly stroking the young man's curly locks, said:

"Do not be terrified, my son; I have considered well, and think this way the best. We will discuss the particulars another time."

"Are you quite well, Father Anselmo?" asked Joseph, anxiously, in a hesitating tone.

"Quite, my son, quite."

"Perhaps the prospect of our parting has agitated you?"

"Although I am deeply grieved at losing you, I have gone through worse calamities. I know what you think, my Joseph; you think I talk a little oddly. Do not let this discompose you; although I am baptized, I confidently hope to ward off and frustrate the designs of that wicked Baron Witzleb."

"Then you meant something else when you told me I must die?"

Instead of an answer to this question, Father Anselmo asked:

"Do you trust in me, Joseph?"

"How can you ask, Father Anselmo.

"Very well, submit yourself to my care."

"So be it," said Joseph, stretching out his hand to Father Anselmo, who pressed it affectionately.

"Now, Joseph, hasten down to the prior and tell him how rejoiced you are to find yourself at the goal of your wishes."

"But that is not my opinion."

"Certainly it is, and you speak the truth when you say it; you do not tell him that to be baptized is the desire of your heart; if he understands it so, 'tis not our fault."

"But he will examine me in the catechism."

"No, he will not, for he does not know it himself. I have bragged so much about your knowledge that you must rest assured he will not ask a single question, for fear that you may discover his ignorance. I am now going down to the village to buy what I think necessary for seasoning the holy water for the baptismal ceremony."

Father Anselmo went to the village and made several purchases. On his homeward way he filled his sack (all Franciscan friars carried sacks) with large stones. When, panting under his burden, he came to the convent door, the porter asked him what it was that he was carrying.

"Oh, 'tis a penance I have imposed on myself," answered Father Anselmo, "because my profession does not leave me time to go about and beg bread and vegetables for our convent."

"A remarkably pious man," muttered the porter, as Father Anselmo ascended the stairs, staggering under his burden.

The next fourteen days saw the quiet convent turned into a busy, bustling place. The whole house was cleaned and scrubbed, the chapel was painted, and the images of the saints received a new coat of varnish; in short, the convent gained an appearance so splendid, the like of which it had not worn since its erection.

A cell, in which he was to prepare himself for the great hour of baptism, was assigned to the proselyte, and he was conducted to it by the prior himself. However, he was not very lonely there, for whenever a monk returned from his begging excursion he hastened to Joseph's cell, and there conversed with him on pious and godly subjects.

The monks had always murmured at the sojourn of a heretic in their convent; but they had been told that he was Baron Witzleb's protege, and as this nobleman was very liberal in gifts to their treasury, they could raise no remonstrances. After Christian's murder and the baron's disappearance, the influence of the prior, whom they feared, and of Anselmo, whom they reverenced, was powerful enough to keep them silent. To the peasants in the neighborhood they never betrayed anything that passed within their convent walls, for their own safety's sake. Their joy was great when they heard of Joseph's request, and all hastened to congratulate him on his resolve. On the Saturday which preceded the Sunday for which the baptism was appointed, Father Anselmo and the young proselyte visited the prior, by whom they were received with extreme unction, the worthy superior even going so far as to bless the Jew.

For the last fortnight Father Anselmo had not been able to avoid taking Joseph to mass with him, and the monks had all been enchanted by the young man's air of devotion.

The prior alluded to this, and praised Joseph's zeal, which praise was modestly disclaimed by the young man.

"Anticipation of the morrow, and probably the excitement of preparing for it, have somewhat agitated the young man," said Father Anselmo; "he is not as well as I should like to see him."

"It is indeed a solemn act in which the young man is about to take part," said the prior, with great pathos.

"I feel that it is so," answered Joseph, "and, your reverence, let me assure you that I rejoice greatly at the prospect of my liberation from bondage."

"Very well expressed, my son, very well indeed," cried

the prior, who, as a matter of course, misconstrued Joseph's words; "yes, erring mankind without the pale of Christianity may well be compared to captives confined in the dark. You will not forget, my son, that it was this convent that made a man and a Christian of you."

"No, your reverence, I will never forget that Father Anselmo made a man of me, and that you also desired to make a Christian of me."

Thus the conversation went on, Joseph, in his light, youthful spirits, always giving such answers as the prior could interpret to his own liking, while Father Anselmo understood them as they were meant.

The prior dismissed them shortly before midnight, after having again given the young proselyte his blessing.

It was about four o'clock in the morning when a hasty step descending to the lower story awoke the convent cook. He opened his door, and saw before him the pale, anxious face of Father Anselmo, who begged him for God's sake to kindle a fire as quickly as could be, and cook some tea for the young proselyte, who had been taken violently sick.

If a flash of lightning had struck the convent, its inmates could not have been more terrified than when, before repairing to early mass, they heard the unwelcome news of Joseph's illness. The prior, at other times so sleepy and slow, bounded up the stairs, two at a time, to Joseph Bonafit's cell.

Father Anselmo sat, pale and depressed, beside the young man's bed. Joseph was tossing about in a high fever, and when the prior entered he called him a great donkey.

"What has happened to him, Father Anselmo?" cried the prior; "how is it possible that the young man sickened so suddenly?"

"Probably the excitement he has lately undergone is chiefly to blame," said Anselmo, sadly.

"Do you think he will recover sufficiently to be able to go through the holy ceremony?"

"It may be, if the fever will subside, but I hardly believe that will be the case. It has set in so violently that I cannot but think it is the precursor of a severe illness."

"Let us hope for the best," said the prior, sorrowfully, and took his departure, as the delirious young man incessantly called out: "Take the big donkey away—take him away!"

It was quite early when the Dominican monk made his appearance, and was met by the crushing tidings. He hurried to the sick-room, which was darkened by shades at the window. These the Dominican tore away, and stepped up to the bed. It required but one look to convince him that the prior's words had been only too true. The sick man's eyes were wide open and staring vacantly into the distance, his cheeks were scarlet, and his lips parched and dry. The Dominican tried another test; he seized the young man's hand, but dropped it immediately, for it burned like fire.

Dubiously shaking his head, and without speaking a word, the Dominican left the room.

The door had hardly closed behind him, when Father Anselmo arose, and saying, "He was the one least easy to deceive," he poured a few drops from a small glass into a spoon, and infused them into Joseph's mouth. After but five minutes the vivid color disappeared from Joseph's face, his hands sank quietly down, his eyes regained expression, and he asked, smilingly:

"How is the matter going on, Father Anselmo?"

"Famously," returned the latter, in a whisper. "My invention is invaluable; keep the recipe of it, you may be in need of it some time."

"Still, it has somewhat exhausted me," said Joseph, languidly. His eyes closed wearily, and he fell into a deep sleep.

CHAPTER XXV.

THE CHURCH OUTWITTED.

THE Sunday which the monks of the Convent of St. Francis had expected to be the day of festivity and rejoicing, passed in dullness and sorrow; and when evening arrived the patient was no better than he had been in the morning. The Dominican friar seemed most affected by this calamitous event. He sat gloomily brooding in his cell, receiving the same unrefreshing reports.

The prior sought to comfort him in various ways, and said:

"Do not let this sad accident affect you so much; the boy is not dead yet. How often do not people who have fever recover from it? Father Anselmo can do wonders, and here, where his heart is in the case, he will do all **in** his power, you may depend upon it."

"It's all very well for you to talk—you do not lose a duchy if this boy dies," cried Witzleb, peevishly.

"As **if it** had been in your possession already—as if you had **only** to stretch out your hands for it!"

"**Yes,** yes; I was as sure of it as if **it had** already been in my grasp. My schemes were admirably laid. With the remnants of the fortune I made by the manufacture of counterfeit money I have bought a house in the city and furnished it; I have appeared in society in the *role* of a foreigner; I have for the last three years studied the English language, and now all, all for nothing."

"But you have two other irons in the fire, baron."

"Will you kindly mention these," returned the baron, sarcastically.

"As you still have the house in the Jew's lane, and as it is provided with all necessary implements, you can have recourse to counterfeiting again. That is one plan. And then, did you not tell me that you are heir to a large estate?"

"The latter is true; but since I have busied myself

with my great project, I have completely neglected my little boy."

"Well, then all you have to do is, to look after the little count again."

"You talk like a silly child, prior; goodness knows how long it will still be until the old count dies, and then all I will get is the ready money; the immense estates pass to my sister's son, who has not been heard of for the last eight years. Besides, I think that the duke will ask the emperor to cut off the entail, as he is not very favorably disposed toward Egmont of Weiden."

"Where is the Count of Weiden with his wife now?" asked the prior.

"Somewhere in Italy; he has been traveling there for the last eight years."

"That is vexatious; you do not know where he is at present?"

"No, I wish I did; I would soon put an end to this matter, but I think fear of my sister, the Baroness of Weiden, has caused his flight."

"And where is she?"

"God knows. At the time a monk bought up all her debts, she left the castle, went to the city, and disappeared, leaving no trace of her whereabouts. You see, all things conspire against me, and were the old count to die this very day, I would gain nothing by it while my nephew remained lost. All I could claim would be the few paltry dollars that are offered as a reward to the finder of the little count; that is, if I could bring myself to give him up."

"Where is the child of the Countess of Weiden?" asked the prior, watchfully.

Witzleb was on his guard, and answered:

"I held the Jews in check with it, as long as I kept my weapon shop in the Jew's lane. But these are trivial matters, let us drop the disagreeable subject."

"But one thing more, baron. Should you be in need

of money again, will you have recourse to your counterfeiting?"

"Why, you know that we cannot compete with the new brand. Had we not been bunglers compared to this people, we would never have given up the business."

"Join this band, Witzleb; when one cannot be first, one must be contented to be second."

"That is impossible; no one knows who belong to this band. Their money is to be found everywhere, but neither of them nor their leader can the least trace be discovered."

"That is very unfortunate; but still, I do not think that you will long remain in want of money; I just happen to call to mind that you once forced quite a neat little sum from the Jews in the city. Could not this be repeated?"

"God or the devil has inspired you with this thought," cried Witzleb, joyously jumping up from his chair. "Yes, this shall be repeated. I must have money, whether Joseph lives or dies; yes, yes, the Jews shall furnish me with money, in case I am compelled to search for a new pretender."

At this moment the door of the cell was opened, and Father Anselmo entered sadly.

"Well, father?" cried the prior and the Dominican simultaneously.

"I am very sorry not to be the bearer of more pleasant tidings; but our poor Joseph has the small-pox."

Both men uttered a shriek of dread. The prior's face grew distorted, and he sank back moaning into his chair.

But he suddenly sprang up, seized Father Anselmo by the shoulders and pushed him toward the door, crying:

"Go away, go away, father, you are infecting the whole convent. Go up to your patient and do not come down again. Hasten, hasten!" and he thrust Father Anselmo out of the cell, and slammed the door behind him; then he sat down in his chair again, trembling in all his limbs.

"And it is you whom we have to thank for all this,"

he cried, wrathfully to the baron; "what a thing to happen in our convent!"

Although Witzleb was likewise greatly shaken by the dreadful news, he retained his coolness and temper, and essayed to quiet the prior, in which, however, he did not succeed, as the prior's discomposure was augmented by the lamentations of the monks in the corridors, who had been informed by Father Anselmo of the nature of Joseph's illness, and were beside themselves with fear of contagion.

When Witzleb saw that his soothing words produced no effect, he arose and prepared to go away, which act brought down on him another flood of reproaches and curses; the prior screaming that now, after bringing so much misfortune to the convent, he went quietly away, and left the poor monks to remain and bear their chances of catching the dreadful disease.

Witzleb quietly suffered all this, and went away full of malicious joy, that the accident which caused him so much sorrow, equally, though in another manner, grieved the monks also. That night and the following day were passed by the monks in fear and dread. Those of them whose cells were in the same story with that of Anselmo, had removed down-stairs, and were quartered two and three in one cell. All tremblingly awaited what the future would bring forth. Thus another day passed without any news from the sick-room. That evening the prior was sitting in his cell, letting his rosary glide through his trembling hands, when he heard a soft footfall without his door. He recognized the step, and started up to bolt his door, but he was too late, and Father Anselmo entered.

"Away, away!" cried the prior. "Who called you hither, Father Anselmo?"

Anselmo approached the prior, who retreated until he was stopped short by the wall.

"Most reverend prior," said Anselmo, when he had got

the prior to a stand-still, "the patient has asked for holy baptism."

"Then baptize him in the dev—in the Lord's name!"

"Your reverence, it is the beautiful, nay, the agreeable task of the superior to perform this holy ceremony."

"You are a meritorious man, Father Anselmo," said the prior, his teeth chattering, audibly; "the convent owes you an acknowledgment. I convey my rights and honors on you; baptize the sick man in my name."

"That is too much happiness for me, your reverence; I cannot accept it, indeed——"

"Accept it, accept it, Father Anselmo, for God's sake!"

"If your reverence commands it, I am bound to obey; but I require witnesses; will your reverence be one?"

"No, no!" cried the prior, beginning to tremble again; "ask Father Martin, or Father Andrew: they are very old, and it cannot hurt them—no, no; I meant to say, the honor belongs to them. But now go, Father Anselmo; go, for God's sake; else the young man may die without baptism, and go straight to hell!"

Father Anselmo doubtless felt the truth of this, for he turned and left the room. He had already opened the door, when he once more turned back, causing the fat prior to make a backward leap which would have done credit to an agile school-boy.

"But if the two monks refuse to be witnesses, your reverence?"

"Then baptize him without witnesses," cried the prior, quite beside himself; "then the Father, Son, and Holy Ghost will be witnesses!"

Father Anselmo departed, and slipped up the stone stairs, while the prior washed himself with vinegar. When Father Anselmo entered his cell, the young man, whose illness caused so much terror to the monks, sat at the table, consuming bread and milk with a very good appetite. His laughing face and speaking eyes gave token that he expected to hear some delectable account from his teacher.

Father Anselmo sat down, and, forcibly restraining his inclination to laugh, told Joseph his conversation with the prior, which sent off the young man into such fits of laughter that Anselmo was obliged to admonish him to quiet his merriment.

The night advanced, and Father Anselmo gave the young man many good counsels—how, when he had entered the world, to avoid all snares and temptations. Joseph expressed a wish to visit his mother, but Father Anselmo strongly and decidedly objected, and plainly proved to Joseph that for the present he durst not betray himself; that, as he had waited thus long, he must, for his own welfare and for that of all who loved him, wait awhile longer.

When, according to Father Anselmo's calculation, midnight mass was about over, he arose in order to play out the last scenes in this comedy. As he divined that the prior now kept his cell locked, he concealed himself in one of the niches in the corridor, and here awaited the prior's return from the chapel. The latter uttered a piercing cry as Anselmo suddenly appeared before him.

"What are you here for again? What do you want, Father Anselmo?"

"The dying man wants extreme unction, or the last sacrament, your reverence."

"Well, give it him, give it him," stammered the prior, "and leave me in peace!"

"But your reverence knows that one alone cannot administer the holy sacrament. I need two assistants, for if I hold the host, I cannot hold the bell and the candles."

The prior hesitated a moment, for the administering of the sacrament to the dying is one of the most solemn ceremonies of the Catholic church, and Father Anselmo grew pale with fear lest the prior might overcome his terror and enter the sick-room. But the prior's terror was greater than his piety: Anselmo's fear was unfounded.

"I'll tell you what it is, Father Anselmo," began the

prior; "on the whole, the dying man is but a baptized Jew, and therefore has no claim on all the privileges of the Church; besides, I shall procure a dispensation from the bishop afterward; leave off the lights, carry the host in the dark, and ring the bell yourself."

"But, your reverence——"

"I know very well, that I can rely on you, Father Anselmo; you will not speak of this to any one. I know that what we are about to do is not quite right, but I cannot risk the danger of infecting the whole convent. No, no, good father, go, and be assured of my gratitude." The prior slipped into his cell and bolted the door.

Shortly after, the monks heard the peal of the bell from the sick-room resound through the corridors. All sprang from their beds and fell on their knees, but not one opened the door of his cell. Each one rejoiced that he was not the one selected to administer the holy sacrament to the dying man.

Toward morning the death-bell in the chapel tolled for the new Christian who had given such great promise, and rang a knell to the bright hopes the monks had placed in him.

In Father Anselmo's room, teacher and pupil sat conversing eagerly. They had not even taken the precaution of locking the door, for they were very sure that no one would disturb them.

"You see, my son, that I have schemed the matter well, and that it has succeeded admirably. By midnight to-morrow you will leave the convent, and enter the world as a new-born child, so to say; for here you will be dead and buried. Do not forget my teachings, and remain faithful to your God and to yourself.

"It is true that I became an apostate to my faith, but you know why, and God knows it too. When the day will come on which my penance is at an end, I may perhaps turn to the mercy of God. I committed a mistake, and could not render it undone. Therefore, take heed of the first step in the wrong path, for it leads to destruction.

"Now, bend your head that I may give you my blessing; though it is the blessing of a renegade; God, who knows what is passing in my heart, will set it down to your account, and fulfill it."

CHAPTER XXVI.
THE BURIAL.

On the following day, when Father Anselmo went down-stairs to speak to the prior in regard to the arrangements for his pupil's burial, he was not admitted, as he had very well foreseen.

The prior called out, that he would write all directions on a piece of paper which he would slip out beneath the door. This he accordingly did, and Father Anselmo repaired to the village and ordered a coffin, which was brought to the convent toward evening.

On his homeward way Anselmo passed the graveyard of the convent, and saw two monks engaged in digging a grave; he requested one of them to help him to carry up the coffin when it should arrive, and then assist him in carrying it down with its mournful burden.

The monk, leaning on his spade, explained to Father Anselmo that the prior had that morning forbidden any of the monks to take part in the new convert's funeral, in order not to render the danger of infection still greater. However, Father Anselmo was at liberty to procure as much aid as he needed from the village, and the convent would bear the expense.

Anselmo was satisfied thereat, but exhorted the monks to assemble in the chapel toward midnight, and read masses for the soul of the dead man. To this the monks readily and gladly expressed their acquiescence, and Father Anselmo repaired to his cell.

"Now, my Joseph," said he, closing the door and bolting it, "I shall give you the treasure we once spoke of, and you shall change your clothes."

Anselmo took his skeleton apart, unscrewed bone after bone, and poured the glittering contents on the table. Then he put the skeleton together again, and, after laying aside several of the least valuable gems, sewed all the rest into a leather belt, which he fastened around Joseph's waist under his habit.

Joseph submitted entirely to his teacher's directions, not even a word of thanks passed his lips; for whenever he opened his mouth Anselmo signed him to be silent, for fear some eavesdropper might be on the guard.

When Father Anselmo had done fastening on the belt, he pulled forth a complete peasant's suit from the mattress which constituted his bed, and Joseph prepared to invest himself with it. An ejaculation of glad surprise escaped Anselmo's lips when he caught sight of the young man in this unaccustomed garb.

The long, loose habit which Joseph had always worn since his arrival in the convent had completely concealed his fine figure, which was now set off to the best advantage by the closelyfitting peasant's suit. The little fur cap, thrown jauntily on his head, became the young man excellently, and he looked the *beau ideal* of manly beauty. As there was no mirror in the room, Father Anselmo told Joseph to look at himself in a dish of clear water. The image which there met the young man's view so surprised him that he started back in affright. He did not recognize himself.

Passionately embracing his teacher, Joseph stammered forth his thanks, while his tears of joy fell into the gray beard of the old man, whose eyes also grew moist.

"Oh, Father Anselmo! oh, my dear Rabbi Isaac Mundolfo, how can I ever, ever prove my gratitude to you?" said the young man.

"By always walking in the way of the Lord, Joseph: by never tiring to do good deeds, by remaining a good Jew, and by employing the art I have taught you, that noblest art, by means of which you can release men from the bonds of illness, for the benefit of all, Jews, Gentiles, and the whole human family; further, my dear boy, by ever trying to prevent evil and by encouraging good, by lending your aid to the poor, by drying the widow's tears and calming the orphan's cries. My son, I have set upon you to work out my expiation. The benefits you will perform for mankind may perhaps mitigate my crime in the eyes of the Almighty, and He will not set it down so heavily to my account, as it is I who have given you the skill to heal the sick. God knows I harbored no selfish thoughts in imparting my science to you; I did not work for a reward; I do not want to be pointed out as your master, for my ambition lies buried in the dungeon of Rome.

"When, in the practice of your profession, two patients summon you at the same time, one of them rich and willing to compensate you generously, the other poor and unable to pay you for your services, hasten first to the latter, for it may be that a large family depends upon the strength of his arm, while the rich man can procure as many physicians as he pleases.

"You will not recognize how far I have advanced in the knowledge of medicine, my Joseph, until you will have the opportunity of making comparisons. I have disclosed to you numberless secrets which are hidden in impenetrable darkness to the most prominent physicians of our century. I have taught you to know poisons that can kill a man in a moment of time, and whose existence no other living physician suspects.

"But apply these poisons only as remedies, only as antidotes to other poisons. Be a physician such as I have been, as I am. I once committed a great mistake, and I bear the punishment of it to the present day. I could have saved my mortal enemy, the Pope; the remedy was within reach of my hand; I did not do it. This was murder, for God did not let me discover this poison in order to kill with it, but to apply it for healing purposes. I acted against his will; it is true I did not poison, but neither did I heal. I should have forgotten and forgiven; in me, the man, not the physician, had been outraged, and science ranks higher than man; it is of godlike nature.

"Should you, my son, ever be similarly situated, spare yourself all future stings of conscience by letting the physician in you speak, and not the man. Live as I wish that I had lived, and you will richly reward me for all I have done for you."

When night had set in, and Joseph had lit the lamp, Father Anselmo repaired down-stairs to get the coffin which had been brought to the convent. With great difficulty he prevailed upon a novice to assist him in carrying the coffin up to the corridor on which his cell lay. Arrived here, the novice was seized with a panic of fear, and almost fell down-stairs in his haste to escape.

Father Anselmo had told the novice that he had succeeded in finding a peasant who was ignorant of what sickness Joseph had died of, and would assist in the the latter's burial.

When Father Anselmo had dragged the coffin into his room, Joseph helped him to screw off the cover. They then proceeded to dress the skeleton, which had contained the diamonds, in Joseph's habit, and carefully placed it in the coffin.

"I brought some stones with me," said Father Anselmo; "for I did not know but that the monks might be courageous enough to carry the coffin to the grave; and in that case I would have been obliged to make it heavier. Now, however, this is not necessary."

"Then, Father Anselmo," said Joseph, "it would not be necessary to bury this valuable skeleton. We could just as well consign the empty coffin to the earth."

"No," returned Father Anselmo; "in this act I am guided by two motives: One is a sort of duty that I owe to this skeleton, which once belonged to a human being. Although it was denied a resting-place in the earth, it served what will seem a nobler purpose to every thinking man. But I desecrated it; I made use of this skeleton for profane purposes, and now wish to repair my wrong by giving it the rest in the grave it has till now been forced to relinquish. My other motive is, to make a discovery of this fictitious burial almost impossible. It is often the case that graves are emptied of their contents after the lapse of but one decade, and thus it may be with this coffin. The discovery of an empty coffin would be of evil consequences for me, were I still alive; and were I dead, my name, which is reverenced like that of a saint in the country round about, would be covered by shame and infamy."

Joseph did not find fault with his teacher's anxiety to preserve his good name in the community whose religion he did not admire, for it is all that clings to a man who had once had a glorious future in prospect. "Better is a good name than precious ointment." (See Ecclesiastes.)

When the bell of the chapel rang for the midnight mass, the two friends waited until all the monks had repaired thither, before they shouldered their sad burden. Slowly they descended the stone stairs, for it was in truth a dead body they bore to the last resting-place it had so long been denied.

Joseph could not refrain from smiling at the comical and strange position he indulged in. It was certainly somewhat of a novelty that had never occurred before, a man to be a mourner at his *own* funeral, and, so to say, carry himself to his own sepulcher.

Arrived at the cemetery, they lowered the coffin into the grave that had been dug for it, and shoveled the earth on it until a stately mound marked the place. Then Anselmo threw away his spade, and passionately embraced Joseph.

"Farewell, my son," cried he, "farewell, and do not forget your teacher."

The good man's voice failed him; it was choked by tears.

Joseph with difficulty suppressed his sobs, and embraced his teacher again and again, until the latter forced him away and pointed toward the open gate of the churchyard, which led to the forest beyond.

At this moment the sound of the organ in the chapel died away, and the moon glided from behind a bank of clouds.

Joseph silently and fervently pressed the old man's hand, waved his cap, and disappeared on the other side of the churchyard wall.

Thoughtfully leaning on his spade, Father Anselmo followed him with his eyes.

"Thus everything passeth away," said he to himself, "What difference does it make to me, that I have not actually buried Joseph here to-night. It is after all but a short delay, to-day or later on. He is lost to me as he is to the world who believe him dead and concealed beneath this mound.

"Yes, yes, Anselmo, you have dreamed a dream again; for a few years you had some one to love, some one for whom you desired to live; now your hours of penance begin again; you have this night buried your dream—buried it with this spade. Hope that it may have been your last dream, and that your waking will be a pleasant one."

The monks were returning from mass. Their way led past the churchyard, and when they beheld Father Anselmo standing by the newly made grave, their fear subsided, "for what was covered by the earth could not be contagious any longer." Many stepped up to the grave and counted off their rosaries for the convert, who shortly before his death hastened to become a member of the only church of salvation.

In the meanwhile Joseph briskly stepped up the mountain path, in order to reach the other side before dawn of day. He felt like one newly endowed with life: at last he was out in the world, at last he was a man dependent on his own resources, a man who could enter upon his struggle with the world. His breath came freely and joyously, he would have shouted out his joy, had not thoughts of his dear, now so solitary, teacher restrained him; his poor teacher, who was now again alone with his torn heart: his teacher who had been more than a father to him, and had given him an inheritance on than which a royal prince could not have a greater. Still, Joseph did not think of his wealth in money, only in so far as it would serve his purposes. It was the thought of the wealth of knowledge stored in his brain and mind, and which he had accumulated by untiring zeal and industry, that made his heart swell with pride and exultation. Now, when he thought of the eight years, of which he had passed many a night depriving himself of sleep in order to pick up, grain by grain, the treasures of knowledge; now, when he surveyed the time spent, it seemed to him like a few days, and that which, while it lay before him, had appeared insurmountable, he now thought of as having been acquired easily and without exertion.

Joseph's thoughts were suddenly checked by the sound of footsteps. He quickly sprang to one side and concealed himself behind a tree. The footsteps came nearer, and soon the figure of a man emerged into the moonlight.

"Heavens!" softly muttered Joseph, as the stranger unsuspectingly passed by, "that is Baron Kuno of Witzleb. In his hand he has a long white beard, and he is carrying the habit of the Dominican friar, whom I have so often seen in the convent. Ah, it is always well to know one's enemy; friend Witzleb, I stand in quite another position toward you than once did little Joseph of the Jews' lane!"

CHAPTER XXVII.
AN AGREEABLE RECOGNITION.

WE are in the city again, and in front of a neatly painted house on Wolf street. The house is decorated with a little sign, on which may be seen in black letters:

"MADAME AGNES, FORTUNE-TELLER."

At the moment the bell beneath the sign was pulled the door would suddenly fly open. This seemingly magical performance was a great surprise to all comers, although it was but the work of a little mechanical contrivance, and instead of pulling the bell, as the visitor believed he did, he pulled open the door.

This was quite in keeping with the character of the place, for it has but meet to be received in an unusual and startling manner on the very threshold of a magician. Many shuddered and started back in amazement when the door was opened for them so suddenly, by the invisible spirit of Madame Agnes, as they imagined. The door, instead of opening into a hall, as is usually the case, led into a neatly furnished room, the floor of which was covered by matting, the walls hung with pictures—some bad wood-carvings—mostly mythological subjects and Biblical scenes.

Several old-fashioned chairs were ranged along the walls, firmly fastened to the floor. Beside each chair there was a kind of knob on the wall, which was generally considered nothing but decoration.

Did any one sit down on any of these chairs, he was suddenly startled by the call, Mr. ———, as the same may be, apparently proceeding from the wall close beside him. On turning around, the waiting person saw no one, of course, nor could he know that the knob on the wall beside him was the outlet of a speaking-tube.

At the same time, an open door became suddenly visible, and a voice again invited him to enter. All these contrivances had conduced to give Madame Agnes such a reputation for skill, that members of the highest aristocracy came to her from time to time, to have their future cleared up by her prophetic sight as a seer.

Madame Agnes knew everybody, called everybody by name, whether they were born in the city or came from foreign countries. Let us follow one of Madame Agnes' visitors, and discover what she knows.

A deeply veiled lady stepped from her carriage at the corner of Wolf street, and ordered her coachman to await her there. The lady walked slowly down the street until she arrived at the little house we have described. Her hand already touched the bell-knob when, suddenly drawing it back, she pressed it on her heart, and murmured:

"What will I hear? Oh, God! what will I hear?"

The lady turned from the door in an irresolute manner, and was about to retrace her way to the carriage, when she heard a firm, manly step approaching. Quickly resolved, she pulled the bell, the door flew open, and the lady was in the anteroom. She turned around to close the door, but uttered a faint shriek as she beheld in the doorway the figure of a man, whose face was partially covered by a black mask.

"My God!" murmured the lady. "The Black Mask, what does he want here?"

The man with the mask sat down on one of the chairs, and silently waved the lady to another. She unhesitatingly obeyed the motion of his hand, and likewise sat down on one of the chairs.

Suddenly a voice resounded close beside her:

"Countess of Weiden, you are entreated to enter."

The lady started in affright, and drew back her heavy veil. Secrecy was no longer possible.

Did the Black Mask desire it, he could now glance into a face which, though no longer young, was still indescribably beautiful. It was a real madonna face, framed by thick golden curls, and the figure which now disappeared behind the opened door was slender and infinitely graceful.

When the Countess of Weiden entered the room to which she had been bidden, she beheld a remarkable, strange-looking female figure seated at a table which was covered by skulls and all sorts of astrological instruments. Long white curls fell from her temples to the table before which she sat; her eyes were concealed by green spectacles, and a minute little beard quivered on her chin. While her head was covered by a turban, the neck of her black silk dress was adorned by a wide, lady's collar, reaching almost to her shoulders. Her hands were incased in black gloves.

"Welcome, Countess of Weiden; long, long ago my

prophetic spirit whispered to me that you would return from a foreign land; long, long have I waited for your coming, for the stars have given me an injunction regarding you."

"Wise woman," returned the countess, with trembling lips, "I come——"

"You came to ask about Hugo of Weiden, your first and only born."

"Yes, even so, Madame Agnes, and as you are so wise as to have known me without ever having seen me, I hope that——"

"It is vain to hope, gracious lady; one of us can simulate compassion for a tortured heart; your little boy is dead, countess."

A heart-rending cry escaped the poor lady, and covering her face with her hands she fell sobbing into a chair.

The fortune-teller cast a look of derison at the bowed form of the sobbing countess; then she said slowly, as if each word were a dagger stroke:

"The house of Weiden is one accursed; it is dying out fast; all glory is departing from it; ere the sun will have thrice completed his course the Count of Weiden will be a dead man."

"Oh, all merciful Father in Heaven!" cried the countess. "Cease, Madame Agnes, cease."

"Where there is a wound, there is a remedy," said the fortune-teller, in a monotonous voice.

A ray of hope enlivened the pale face of the countess.

"Yes, countess, the stars have told me that a woman from the East will come to you, a woman who, though she cannot detain the fleeting spirit of the count, can protect you against the evil that darkly looms up and threatens you."

"Does misfortune threaten me also?" asked the lady.

"All who belong to the house of Weiden are doomed."

"Oh, my God, my God!"

"But it is written in the stars that this woman may be

your guardian angel, this woman who is coming from the East."

"But where, my God, where shall I find her?"

"She will come to you herself, poor and begging humbly for alms. Draw her to your heart. Keep her near your person, closely follow her advice, let no stranger step between you and her, and your life will be protected, the stars will have no power over you."

"When will this woman come?" asked the countess, anxiously.

"After three days, six days or nine days, at dusk of day."

"And concerning my child? Have you no comfort to give me?"

"None; the fire that is extinguished, its dead embers cannot be fanned to flame again."

The lady heaved a deep sigh; then, arising, she pressed some gold into the fortune-teller's hand, and quitted the room.

When she entered the anteroom, the man in the mask, who had apparently awaited her return, arose and followed her to the street; the trembling countess accelerated her steps.

She was within calling distance of her carriage when the Black Mask suddenly stepped before her and barred her progress.

"Countess," said he, in a melodious voice, "the woman has lied; your child is living; you will see it again."

"Sir, you know?"

"I know more than yonder woman, who is an impostor; have patience and wait; I myself will restore your child to you."

"But, sir, who are you; why this mysterious disguise which all in the city know and fear?"

"None but the wicked need fear me," returned the Mask.

"Oh, I know that well; the Black Mask is always mentioned with awe, for he does wonders, he keeps even death at bay; but he does not show his face, and this renders him an object of fear."

"Ask those who confided in me if I betrayed their trust; ask the sick man tossing on his bed if my mask seem not brighter to him than the most beautiful face?"

"Yes, yes, I know that, your name has justly grown famous in a remarkably short time.

"Why then did you not ask my aid for your husband? 'Tis now longer than a year that I have resided in this city, 'tis one-half a year that every one knows me and my reputation."

"The count himself despairs of his life; it is old age that prostrates him."

"Still you went to yonder impostor for advice, as if science was rubbish, and impostors seers."

"Pardon me, sir, you are right; but I am so utterly alone, and without a friend. Formerly, when the duke was stronger, he often invited my husband and me to court, and was a good friend to me. But now, I am indeed utterly forsaken."

The lady's voice trembled.

"Let me be your friend, countess; for to protect you is one of the chief aims of my life."

"By what name shall I call you, sir; by what token know that you are my friend?"

"Call me the Black Mask, as all the world call me, and allow me to approach your husband's sick-bed, if but for once; then I will give you proof of my friendship."

The lady was about to answer, but the Black Mask had left her side and entered one of the by-streets. With a heart full of conflicting emotions, yet a blessed feeling of hope pervading her, the lady entered her carriage.

When the Countess of Weiden had left the room of the fortune-teller, the latter slid back a little panel in the wall, and applied her eyes to the opening. She recoiled in terror.

"My God! the Black Mask!" she cried, in despair; "how comes he here? Oh, this portends misfortune!"

She drew a relieved breath as she saw the Black Mask leave her house directly after the countess.

"That is one who appears to be dabbling in my trade," muttered Madame Agnes, resuming her seat at the table. "His name is in every one's mouth. Well, he is welcome to all my customers; I'll soon have done with all this foolery." She started slightly, for the spring that opened the door creaked, and she knew that another customer had come.

She arose quickly in order to look through the spy-hole at the person who had come to consult her wisdom.

But the visitor seemed to be in a great hurry, for the sibyl had not made a step toward her post of observation, when the door flew open, and a somewhat tipsy young man burst into the room.

Madame Agnes drew back, greatly frightened, for she had quite an abhorrence for drunkards.

"Hallo, old witch!" cried the comer, boisterously, "you shall tell me my fortune, for times are bad, and still one must live. Therefore tell me how much money there is in your box, so that we may remain good friends."

The woman had fearfully retreated behind a table, and groped about under it, apparently looking for something.

The young man observed this, and darted forward at the old woman, striving to get hold of her; but she, with a fleetness that belied her years, sped to the wall, and, bracing herself against it, pointed a dagger at her assailant. The young man paused for a moment; then, suddenly springing forward, he seized the old woman's arm and twisted it so violently that the joints cracked, and the weapon fell to the floor. Now a struggle began, whose issue could not long remain doubtful; the young man wondered at the strength of his antagonist who made it so hard for him to gain a victory. In addition to this, he was vexed that a woman could resist him so long, while her incessant cries for help increased his rage.

At last she seemed yielding; but, suddenly gathering her strength for a last onslaught, she seized his hair with her long, bony fingers. O, wonder! it remained in her hands. The fortune-teller shrieked louder than ever, and cried:

"Egmont, Egmont, my son, robbing his own mother?"

The person thus addressed immediately loosened his hold, and started back in astonishment, while the fortune-teller slowly and painfully tottered to a seat. With her right hand she tore turban and wig off her head, and mother and son confronted each other.

"Ha, ha!" cried Egmont, "my honored mother, the proud Baroness of Weiden, a fortune-teller and a witch!"

"Curses on you, ungrateful son that you are! The Baron of Weiden has become a robber, has attempted to rob his own mother!" shrieked the magician.

CHAPTER XXVIII.
THE OUTLAWS.

A NUMBER of young men were sitting round a table in the bar-room of the Lamb. The appearance of most of them evinced a sort of reduced elegance. Their fine attire was quite out of keeping with the tone of their conversation, and contrasted glaringly with their unkempt locks and neglected beards.

The tavern of the Lamb by no means merited the name it bore, for, instead of lambs, it sheltered wolves, who lived on the spoils they unlawfully wrested from their fellow-beings.

The Lamb was generally known in the city as the resort of thieves and assembly burglars. When a daring burglary was committed, when counterfeit money was put into circulation, when any one was stabbed in an affray, the police generally went to the Lamb for the malefactor and misdoer, and were rarely disappointed in their search.

Formerly the tavern had not been so notorious, although it was well known that all sorts of suspicious characters congregated there; but since several years the most daring and cunningly contrived depredatory excursions issued from here, and still none of the rogues could be captured, so well was all arranged, so excellently conducted. Although the police were well aware that an organized band of robbers held their headquarters at the Lamb, and though they often arrested men on suspicion, it could never be shown that such a band was actually in existence. There was a rumor in circulation to the purport that it was a young man of twenty-one who had organized this band, who planned their burglaries, and reigned like a king over the criminals in the city; but the police laughed at the nonsense, for they had never forced a confession to this effect from any prisoner, even by means of the torture.

Well, a company of young men sat around the table in the bar-room of the Lamb, drinking and talking.

The subject of their conversation was the Black Mask. About a year ago this mysterious person had come to the city, bought a house in one of the best streets, and established himself as a physician.

The police allowed his wearing the mask, and it was even maintained that the doctor's sign on the door was but a blind, and that the Black Mask was, in fact, a secret agent of the police—for who else would dare to go about in broad daylight with a mask on his face? The young men around the table expressed various opinions regarding the Black Mask, who was an object of awe to these lawless, rascally fellows, who shunned the daylight as much as possible.

"It is said that a fearful mark disfigures the upper part of his face, said a tall, lean young man, who was called Devil's Fred by his comrades. "Yes, yes," he continued, as his statement was greeted by derisive laughter; "for this reason he wears a mask."

"Stuff and nonsense!" returned a thick-set youth; "the man is neither more nor less than a detective; that is certain."

"But he practices as a physician, and has effected the most wonderful cures," said Devil's Fred again.

"What is the use of bothering our heads about a thing that doesn't concern us at all?" said the thick-set young man—who was known by the nick-name of Froggy—in a stentorian voice. "My only concern is where our captain may be. He ought to have been back long ago, and that with a full pocket."

"Sandwich," cried one of the company to the landlord, who was lounging lazily behind the bar, "go and see if Trumpcard is coming. He knows there is a meeting here to-night, and has only gone on a little business of his own. It is now ten o'clock, and he ought to have been back for some time."

The landlord, a large, corpulent man, muttered something to himself to the effect that it was all bosh, and decent people might be allowed to enjoy a little rest; but still he made his way from behind the bar and moved toward the door. At this moment the latter was suddenly torn open, and a young man with fair hair burst into the room.

"What has happened? What is the matter?" resounded from all sides. "Is some one pursuing you? Why, you have lost your beard and wig!"

The new-comer threw himself into a chair, and brought down his hands on the table with such force that the glasses and tumblers on it clinked dangerously.

"Silence!" he thundered, and in a moment the sound of a pin falling to the floor could have been distinctly heard.

"I've had a pretty fright," said the captain, after taking a hearty drink from his neighbor's glass.

"How so?" asked Froggy. "Did they nearly catch you?"

"No, no; they cannot catch Trumpcard so easily," returned the fair young man, complacently; "but I have seen my mother!"

"Your mother?" cried Devil's Fred, starting up from his chair.

The others seemed to receive this news quite coolly.

"Yes, yes; my mother. I was just about to wring her neck a little, when the touching recognition took place."

"This is very unfortunate; very unfortunate, indeed," returned Devil's Fred, thoughtfully.

"Why, what harm is there in that?" said Froggy; "we have all seen our mothers some time or other, and never made such a fuss about it."

"Come with me, Devil's Fred," said Trumpcard, rising and leading the way into a small adjoining room, which was furnished only with a few chairs and a worm-eaten table. One lamp on the table diffused such a faint light that the two could hardly distinguish each other. One after the other of those at the table in the bar-room arose, stepped into the hall, and there vanished.

"Listen, Devil's Fred," said Trumpcard, when both had seated themselves, "is it not a dreadful meeting, I, the Baron Egmont, a robber, attacking the Baroness of Weiden, my mother?"

"Yes, of course, it is not very agreeable; but how did you get out of the affair?"

"That was easier than you can imagine. Had I met my mother as still baroness, in all her former pride and haughtiness, the matter would have been much worse; but, just think, old Sibyl Agnes in Wolf street is my mother; she plays this pretty *role* in order to support herself."

"Strange, very strange."

"Yes, and a mother always remains a mother; for hardly had we done reproaching each other most bitterly, when she relented, and insisted on knowing my place of residence, as she says she has a great inheritance in prospect for me. Yes, she even wants to give up her business on account of seeing more particularly to my inheritance."

"Nonsense, you are always talking of this inheritance; I do not believe you ever will have a copper of it."

"Never mind that now, Devil's Fred. Tell me what has been going on here since my absence."

"Nothing of consequence, Egmont. That Black Mask becomes more and more an object of dread to our band, and I myself think that he is here solely on our account. Perhaps he has been summoned from England, which is famous for its detectives."

"Don't be fools," returned Egmont, the captain, peevishly. "I have never encountered him, but I desire nothing more than a little combat with him."

"Oh, you are always bragging, Egmont," returned Devil's Fred, "and you have not courage enough to assist at a burglary; at most you attack an old woman, who proves to be your mother."

Devil's Fred did not notice the evil glance Egmont cast at him; but the latter controlled himself, and said:

"Did you thrive so well ere I took command of the band? Did ever such faithfulness exist among you as since I am captain? What is the use of mechanically performed work without a scheme? I am the master; it is but just that the execution of my plans devolves upon you! But come, I suppose they are all assembled by this time, let us descend."

Egmont rose and left the room, followed by Devil's Fred.

On entering the bar-room, they beheld a little boy, with a basket of hot rolls which he was offering for sale. The boy was about ten years old, and his fair curls and straight features seemed to mark him of Christian descent, which, however, was contradicted by the jargon he spoke. Egmont, who naturally took the boy to be a Jew, could not refrain from pinching his ear. The boy with tears in his eyes, entreated the gentleman to let him alone, but this only incited Egmont to continue his cruelty, while he repeatedly cried:

"Jew, Jew."

Had Joseph Bonafit been present, he would have immediately known Trumpcard to be none other than Baron Egmont, by the way in which he pronounced this taunt.

The boy, when he perceived that his entreaties were fruitless, was overcome by rage, and trod on his persecutor's toes with his little feet, which were covered by heavily nailed shoes.

Egmont released the boy's ear and gave the poor child such a blow that he fell down senseless, while his rolls were scattered all over the floor. Egmont raised his foot to give the child another blow, but was restrained by Devil's Fred, who said:

"I think you have killed the child. Let us take him down-stairs. If he does not regain his senses we will bury him there."

"You, or that fat, lazy landlord may carry the child; I shall not soil my hands by touching the dirty Jewish rascal."

But Trumpcard suddenly stopped speaking, and grew dreadfully pale; his knees tottered, and his eyes seemed bursting from their sockets. Before him, as if suddenly risen from the ground, stood the Black Mask. Devil's Fred had also seen him, and escaped to the hall, where he vanished, as the rest had done before him. The eyes under the mask burned like glowing coals into the face of the youthful criminal.

"Egmont of Weiden," said the Black Mask, in a sonorous voice; "I know you. For the manner in which you treated the child, take this, and this."

The Black Mask gave the cowardly rogue two blows on the head, and leaving him standing like one petrified by terror, went to the bar, where, however, he saw no one, as the landlord had fled at the sight of the Black Mask.

He then picked up the lifeless child, wrapped him in his cloak, and left the inn.

Egmont remained motionless for a long time. He did not venture to look up, and it was not until Devil's Fred came to remind him, that he remembered the band were waiting for him down-stairs. Both stepped into the hall, pressed a knob, and the trap on which they stood slowly descended with them to the depths. They arrived in a brilliantly lighted vault, and as soon as they stepped from the trap it ascended with the rapidity of lightning.

The vault was of considerable extent, and resembled the magazine of some wealthy merchant. While bales and bales of goods were heaped up in one corner of the store-room, the other was occupied by a glass case containing the most valuable jewels. New and old weapons hung from the ceiling and on the walls, next to valuable paintings worth thousands of dollars. Edibles in abundance filled a safe which stood in a corner, while there was no lack of bottles of the rarest wine.

The vault was divided into two parts by a heavy velvet curtain, which perhaps once decorated the saloon of a wealthy prince.

When Egmont and Devil's Fred touched the bottom of the vault, they heard the sound of beating hammers and a peculiar hissing noise from beyond the curtain. The two entered the other part of the vault. Here two men stood at a small forge and melted metal, while three others were engaged in stamping it. Coins were heaped up on the floor in such profusion as if they were not of the least value. On benches ranged along the walls ten or twelve men were lazily lying smoking and talking. At a low whistle from Egmont the men ceased working, and all stepped into that part of the vault in front of the curtain. Here they seated themselves on the bales of goods and boxes which nearly filled up every space. Egmont and Devil's Fred remained standing.

"Comrades," began Egmont, "who of you know the Black Mask?"

"I, I," cried various voices.

"Comrades," cried Egmont, "the Black Mask must die."

A death-like silence ensued.

CHAPTER XXIX.

A CONSPIRACY.

"Do you hear?" cried Egmont, "the Black Mask must die!"

Still all remained silent.

"It almost seems as if you were afraid," continued Egmont.

"Yes, that is just it," one of them ventured to say.

"Why, do you know who the Black Mask is?" asked Egmont.

"I think he is the evil one himself," answered Froggy.

"Miserable cowards," cried Egmont, "the Black Mask is neither more nor less than a secret agent of the police, and if you will not put an end to him, he will do it to you."

"We do not believe that," returned one of them; "it is true that he is a mysterious personage, but he is very kind to poor people, and a police agent is not generally so."

"Besides," remarked another, "he can do most marvelous things. I do believe that he can make an amputated limb grow to the body again."

Egmont burst into a scornful laugh.

"You ought not to laugh, Trumpcard," broke in Devil's Fred; "do you know that he, like the Prophet Elijah, recalled to life the child of our comrade, Red John, after it had been dead two days, and was just about to be buried?"

"Nonsense!" cried Egmont, contemptuously; "nursery tales!"

"No, it is not a nursery tale. Just let me tell it to you. The child of Red John was suddenly seized by convulsions and died. No one, unless he was present at the time, can imagine how sorely the mother lamented her bright and blooming child's death. When the little corpse was placed in the coffin, the mother's grief for her son burst all bounds. Her shrieks could be heard three blocks off. Now the door was suddenly opened, and a man, the upper part of whose face was covered by a black mask, entered the room. All fell back in astonishment, even the bereaved mother momentarily forgot her grief; for at that time the Black Mask was still a stranger in the city. The Black Mask silently approached the little coffin, and attentively regarded the corpse. Suddenly he started and placed his hand on the body; then, turning around, he entreated all present to leave the room. His words remaining unheeded, he repeated his request in a loud, commanding voice, and all, even the mother left the room in great consternation. After the lapse of about ten minutes the Black Mask stepped into the hall and said to the mother, who was anxiously waiting there:

"'Go in, my good woman, your child lives.'

"And so it was, the child lived, and is alive this day."

"Yes, yes, Red John himself has told us this hundreds of times," cried all.

Egmont was very much crest-fallen; he had often heard of the wonderful, nay, miraculous cures made by the Black Mask, and, even before his encounter with the latter to-day, he entertained considerable awe for him. This awe was now greatly augmented, and being too fearful to attack him, he had wished to delegate this to his band; here, as we have seen, he met with an opposition, founded on fear.

The wonderful tale which Devil's Fred had just related only served to deject Egmont still more; for he, like the rest, ascribed the Black Mask's art to a supernatural source, and did not for one moment entertain the thought that the child had only been apparently dead. On the whole, the robbers did not have any cause to fear the Black Mask, for he had never laid any obstacles in their way. But the chastisement Egmont had that day received from that mysterious person, and the fact that the latter knew his name, which was unknown to all the band, with the single exception of Devil's Fred, seemed reasons enough for wishing him out of the way. Besides, the dread with which he inspired all who knew themselves not guiltless, was certainly no unimportant incentive.

"I shall pay," said Egmont, venturing upon a last attempt, "richly pay the one who will drive a knife into the impertinent rascal's heart."

"I believe you," cried Froggy, "but he is charmed; the knife would break like glass."

"Very well," said Egmont, convinced that he could not move any of his comrades to the venture, "then, for once in my life, I shall screw up my courage, and take charge of this matter myself."

The peal of a bell sounded from the wall. All listened in suspense. Egmont made a sign, and in a moment the lights were subdued by a large screen which was lowered from the ceiling of the vault. Simultaneously there was a sound of creaking and rustling, as when a clock is wound up.

"Who's there?" cried out Egmont.

"The Black Dog, with a new comrade," was the answer.

"Does the Black Dog know the password?"

"His hand against all, and all hands against him," came the answer.

"Can the Black Dog answer for the new comrade?" was now questioned.

"He can answer for him with his life; the new comrade was once his master."

"Well, then, he is welcome. In what profession was he the Black Dog's master?"

"He encroached upon the duke's rights, and took the liberty of stamping his own coins."

"Draw your swords, and raise the screen," cried Egmont; "if it proves to be an impostor, stab him, and do your work well."

The screen was raised, and a cry of astonishment and pleasure escaped from most of those present.

"Master Heberline, Master Heberline," resounded from all sides, and each hastened to shake hands with the stranger, who was standing beside a dark-bearded, dissipated-looking man.

"I knew you would be pleased to see your old master once more," cried the Black Dog; "it is a long time since he forsook us. But, where is our captain, that he may greet this old hero of our profession?"

But Egmont, the captain, was nowhere to be seen. Devil's Fred hurriedly made his way behind the curtain, and found Egmont crouching behind a bench, and making signals to him not to betray him. Egmont's situation was so comical, that Devil's Fred burst into a loud peal of laughter. The sound attracted all the company to the spot.

"The devil!" cried Master Heberline, throwing a look under the bench, "whom have we here?"

Unobserved by the others, Egmont placed his finger on his lips.

Heberline immediately understood him, and remained silent, although his face wore an expression of the most intense astonishment.

"This is our captain," cried Devil's Fred and the Black Dog; "he is a little nervous, but confoundedly cunning, and has such talent for organizing a company, and keeping a state in order, that he deserves to be a duke."

"Either God or the devil suggested this thought to you," muttered Heberline; then he signed to Egmont to come forth, which the latter accordingly did.

"Why did he steal away and hide here?" asked some.

"I by no means hid myself," cried Egmont, his face distorted with rage, "I wished to surprise Master Heberline, whom I knew long ago."

"Yes, that is so," said the latter; "and as proof of this, I entreat you, comrades, to leave us here, as we have much to say to each other after such a long separation. Go up-stairs, drink and eat as much as you please; I'll pay the bill."

When the two were alone, Heberline began:

"So it is here, and in such company, that I find you again! Truly you do honor to your name; you have developed into what you promised to be when a boy."

"At least I am no worse than my uncle, Kuno of Witzleb," returned Egmont, sullenly.

"Had you had but a drop in your veins of the blood of that Jewish boy, who, without any intention on his part, caused your removal to the city, you could have restored the degenerated family of Witzleb to their former pride and honor."

"Accursed be that Jew!" cried Egmont, furiously. "He alone is the cause of all my misfortunes. I have been looking for him all these years. I have no stronger desire than to lay my hands on him and deprive him of the breath of life."

"Do not excite yourself, nephew, do not," returned Witzleb—for it was he, as the reader has no doubt already divined. "He has long since escaped you forever, by paying the debt of nature, for he is dead and buried."

"I do not believe it, uncle!"

"You may believe me; I myself stood at his grave. But as to what regards your idea that he was the cause of all your misfortunes, I must contradict you, and defend him from your imputation. The only one to blame is your mother. She it was who, by her way of bringing you up, made you what you are—a robber, and perhaps even a murderer."

"Uncle, you are the most remarkable man I ever came across. While you yourself have been acknowledged a master-hand in this very profession, you take it upon yourself to moralize to me about it."

"My will was always good, my dear nephew, but my character was weak and not trained to firmness. When I committed my first error, I was left to myself and all the pangs of remorse. To deaden these, I sinned more and more; and you see before you what has become of the man who bears a name which once made kings and princes tremble. I once hoped to keep my manner of life a secret to my family, and especially to yourself. Had you restored its pristine honor to our name, I would, perhaps, for your sake, have attempted to tread in the path of the righteous again. However, neither you nor your mother did aught to make me wish to become a better man. But where is my amiable sister at present?"

"Do not speak of her," returned Egmont. "She did not do much toward upholding the family honor, either."

A pause ensued. Suddenly Witzleb peevishly shook his head, as if desirous to drive away all unpleasant memories, and said:

"On the whole, you have grown to be quite a passable young man, and, if you have the stuff for it in your head, may yet become a person of consequence."

"Uncle Kuno, if you wish me to execute some project which requires skill and cunning, I am the man for you," said Egmont, with great self-sufficiency.

"I should have preferred to hear you say, were you asked to execute some project which requires courage and daring, you are the man for it," returned Witzleb, sternly.

"Uncle Kuno," cried Egmont, angrily, "do not moralize—it does not become you. An owl is never more ridiculous than when mocking at other birds. Nor am I a boy any more, whom you can ill-treat as you once did. A hundred arms are mine at command, and if I so desire it, they will murder even the duke for me."

A look of hate and envy crept into Witzleb's eyes. He ground his teeth, and muttered: "Miserable reptile as you were, you are, and had I not such need of you I would soon put you out of the way." But aloud he said:

"Speaking of the duke reminds me that you have much cause to love him'

"Curse on him! I should have liked to revenge myself on him long ago, but I have never rightly known in what manner."

"Promise me that you will follow my advice, and your revenge on the duke shall not only be most satisfactory, but you will at the same time gain a position higher than any you can ever have dreamed of."

"A high position on the gallows, I suppose," returned Egmont, contemptuously.

"Foolish boy! do I not know what I speak? Of course there is some danger in the undertaking, but it is very well worth the trouble of trying; and if it succeeds, you and I are made men for life."

"Well, let me hear your plan."

"Not so fast, my son; you must promise to accept my conditions ere I proceed."

"I do not surrender myself to the enemy with pinioned hands."

"Impertinent fellow! would I confide in you if I were your enemy?"

"You know, dear uncle, that the members of our family have not much confidence in each other."

"That is true; but just trust me this once—you will not repent it," entreated Witzleb.

"No; I have already told you that I am no longer a child. First, you must tell me your plan, then I shall know if I can accept your conditions."

Witzleb reflected awhile, then he said:

"Very well, I agree."

Bending down, he whispered some words into the young man's ear. The latter started in surprise.

"That is impossible, uncle," said he, "clearly impossible, and may cost us both our heads."

"Coward! Supposing they convict you as a counterfeiter and the leader of a band of thieves, think you they will feed you on sweets?" asked Witzleb, contemptuously.

"That is something else; they cannot catch me so easily."

"But what has your profession profited you thus far? You have to encounter danger day by day, and your gains are but trifling. Rely entirely on me, my arrangements are made in a manner which makes failure impossible.

"Submit to my direction, and you will conquer. Here is my hand, give me yours."

"But both you and I are known at court," hesitatingly said Egmont, already half convinced.

"My whole life has been a masquerade," said Witzleb, "I will so disguise myself and you that your own mother would not recognize you. Is it a bargain, my son?"

Egmont hesitatingly put his hand into that of his uncle, and the compact between these two corrupted souls was sealed.

"Now, the first thing for you to do is to leave your comrades in such a manner that they will be quite unsuspicious of you. Then repair to an adjoining province, where I will meet you, and we will make our arrangements. Among other things, you must not forget to engage servants who do not know you."

"But what of my comrades?" asked Egmont, "perhaps they will recognize me."

"Leave all that to me;" Witzleb again bent down to Egmont's ear: "We shall denounce them; in barely two months they will all be hung."

Not one emotion of pity for the band that had been so faithful to him, and even trusted him with the leadership, agitated Egmont's breast. Quite the contrary; he nodded acquiescence.

"Yet another question, uncle; what brought you hither?"

"I will tell you. In the anticipation of finding a suitable man for my project, I bought and furnished a house. But I did not find such a man, and my finances being at a low ebb, I concluded to sell the house. On coming from the auctioneer, I accidentally met the Black Dog, who had once been one of my company. He brought me hither in order to appoint me leader of this band, as the men had grown tired of you."

Witzleb narrowly observed his nephew's face as he uttered these last words.

"By Heaven! the whole band shall be strung up; give

me your hand, uncle, I shall go with you," said Egmont, livid with rage.

CHAPTER XXX.

STRANGERS IN THE CITY.

One of the houses on Duke street, which was one of the most fashionable thoroughfares in the city, had long been uninhabited. As those who resided in this street were mostly of the aristocracy, and possessed the houses they dwelled in, and as strangers rarely came to the city, it was no wonder that when a house once became vacant it remained so for some time.

The neighbors had long been accustomed to seeing the shutters up and the grass growing luxuriantly from the cracks in the stone steps of the deserted house.

One morning—the worthy neighbors hardly trusted their eyes—the shutters were all down, the door, so long closed, stood wide open, and a number of workmen and charwomen bustled about in the house.

The upholsterers came and furnished the house most beautifully, a man from the coachmaker's came with two carriages and put them in the spacious stables; all was in readiness, but the occupant wanting.

But however longingly he was expected by the gossiping neighbors, he stayed away to try their patience.

At last their curiosity was to be satisfied; but in quite an unexpected manner. Large bills were posted all over the house, stating that all the costly furniture and the contents of the house were to be sold at auction on a certain day. That must be an eccentric man indeed, who spent thousands on a house and its furniture, only to sell it at auction. It was an unheard-of thing.

On the day appointed for the auction, all the rooms in the house were filled by inquisitive people. The very stairs were crowded, and mostly by the aristocratic people who resided in the neighborhood, and who curiously inspected the costly objects with which the house was crammed.

The arrival of the auctioneer was anxiously expected. He came and mounted the table; but it seemed as if the neighbors were doomed to be again disappointed; for hardly had the auctioneer attracted their attention, when a peremptory "Stop" was called out to him. A hunch-backed man, hobbling along by means of a stick, made his way through the crowd, to the table of the auctioneer. Arrived there, he doffed his three-cornered hat, and wiped the perspiration from his brow. His face could now be plainly seen. Long and straight black hair fell to his shoulders, framing a face of a copper color, such as had never before been seen on a human countenance in the city. The stranger's dress was also very remarkable. Instead of a coat, he had a large piece of cloth slung about his shoulders, and fastened around his waist by a girdle studded by pearls.

The small clothes which were visible beneath this piece of cloth were fashioned of yellow leather, and decorated with fringe at the sides. On his feet the stranger had cloth shoes embroidered with beads.

This foreign-looking individual signed to the auctioneer to descend from his elevated post, and, turning around, addressed the bystanders in a foreign accent, often mingling in strange words, which none present understood:

"I am greatly pleased to see such a numerous company here, but I have changed my mind about selling the house. A young friend of mine, whom I believed to have been shipwrecked, has, to my great joy, returned in safety, and he shall dwell here with me. I shall be greatly honored if you will favor me with a visit at some more appropriate time, and I assure you that I shall not be lacking in such hospitality toward you as is customary among my people in the far West."

"Ah, the hunchback is an Indian!" was whispered here and there, and the stranger was regarded even more attentively than before. But these people knew what was proper to do, and on being so plainly dismissed by the hunchback, hastened to leave the house. Many gave their cards to the red man, and the latter expressed his regret that he was not able to return the compliment, but added that his ward, who was better versed in the ways of fashionable life than he, would strive to make up for all his shortcomings. In a very few minutes the house was deserted, and the auctioneer dismissed.

About two hours subsequent to this event, a richly dressed young man, accompanied by five servants in livery, all on horseback, appeared at the end of the street. Arrived at the above-mentioned house, the cavalcade came to a halt; ere any of the servants had time to dismount, the door was opened, and the hunchbacked Indian hobbled out as fast as he could, knelt down, and lowered his head; the young man swung himself from his saddle, and allowed his foot to rest for a second on the back of the Indian.

With humbly lowered head, the latter extended his hand, and was about to lead the young man into the house, when both started back in terror, and the young man began to tremble so violently that he was obliged to lean on his horse for support. A man, the upper part of whose face was covered by a black mask, had passed between them. He did not seem to notice their terror, and passed quietly on; however, when he had walked some little way, he turned around, and carefully regarded the house before which the cavalcade had halted. The Indian and his young master had partially recovered from their terror; but, forgetful of all etiquette, they took hold of each other's hands, and, like frightened children, crept slowly up-stairs, and disappeared behind the door, which they closed and locked. The Black Mask approached the servants, who were engaged in unsaddling the horses, and, in a melodious voice, inquired about the rank of the two strangers; however, he received the same evasive answers that all previous inquiries had gained.

Dubiously shaking his head, the Black Mask passed on to a carriage which was waiting for him at the corner of the street. The coachman, reining in two splendid horses, in gold trappings, who were impatiently pawing the ground, sprang from the box and opened the carriage door for his master.

The Black Mask entered the carriage, the servant shut the door, and the vehicle set off at full speed. It rolled through squares and streets, through the Jew's quarter—where the Black Mask looked out of the windows and regarded everything with interest—and through the gate of the city, out into the country. To the right and left, the road was studded with beautiful villas, standing in miniature parks. At the gate of one of these villas, the coachman stopped his horses. The porter sprang from his lodge, opened the gate wide, and the carriage rolled up the path, which was bordered on each side by acacias. The coachman reined in his horses at the door of a charming little villa, almost hidden by clambering vines, leaped from his box, lifted the knocker, which was in the shape of a lion's head, and let it fall thrice against the door. The door was opened, and the coachman handed in a card.

About two minutes afterward, a lady appeared at the door. She was preceded by a servant in livery, who hastened to the carriage and assisted the Black Mask to alight. The latter approached the lady, and gallantly pressed a kiss on her hand.

"Welcome, doctor!" said the lady, evidently greatly pleased. "I have expected you for a long time past."

The Black Mask excused himself by saying that the very cold consent the lady had given to his request on the evening he had accompanied her to her carriage, had restrained his desire to come. During this conversation, they had entered the drawing-room, and the lady invited her visitor to a seat on the sofa beside her. If the reader has not already divined that the Black Mask is in the house of the Countess of Weiden, the question which he now puts to the lady about her husband, the Count of Weiden's, health will enlighten him as to the fact.

"Oh, sir," returned the Countess, drying her tears, my husband is in a very precarious condition; the physicians despair of his life!"

"Countess, you would render me happy did you allow me to see your husband, if but for a moment."

"It is my most heart-felt wish that you should see him, sir. If your wonderful skill, of which the whole city speaks, does not rescue my husband I shall soon be a widow."

"Be comforted, countess; as long as there is life, there is hope. Conduct me to your husband."

Both arose, and the lady led the way to her husband's apartment. Here the windows were so heavily draped that the doctor could not even distinguish the sick man's bed. He approached the window, and the next moment the rays of the evening sun illuminated the room to its furthest corners.

On a luxurious bed sat a middle-aged woman apparently of the peasant class. Hardly had the Black Mask allowed the sunlight admission, when she uttered a low cry, and hastily left the room.

"Who is this gentleman?" asked the count, in a faint voice.

"Who is that woman?" returned the Black Mask.

"This gentleman," said the countess, turning to her husband, "is a physician, who, during his short sojourn in this city, has gained great fame for his skill."

"Why are you masked? Since when does science wear a mask?" asked the count, in a querulous tone, and with all the arrogance peculiar to his class.

"Since time immemorial, science, and particularly of medicine, has worn a mask. Is not the recipe couched in language unintelligible to the layman? Were science shown in its actual form many would recoil in shuddering horror."

"What is your name, sir?" asked the count, in a peremptory tone.

"I am called the Black Mask," returned the doctor, attentively regarding the sick man's face.

"Can you give me health?" asked the count, in a voice full of ridicule and incredulity.

"Heavens," cried the countess, "you insult constantly the physician; that is not right, my husband."

"Perhaps not; but I should like to see the face of the man who comes to treat me," returned the count, moodily.

The Black Mask quietly sat down beside the sick man's bed and said.

"Imagine that the part of my face which I have covered is of such dreadful aspect as to terrify to death any one who sees it. Will that content you?"

"That is quite another matter," muttered the sick man, "but permit me another question. What is the motive in bestowing such marked attention?"

"Count, all your words are insulting, but it is my duty not to notice this. You do not know me, yet still I have made it the task of my life to find and restore to you your heir."

The countess, uttering a low cry, sank into a chair, while the count endeavored to raise himself in bed, but with many a groan was obliged to relinquish the attempt.

"But, sir, who are you that interest yourself for a totally strange family?" asked the count.

"I am the Black Mask; more I cannot tell you. Did not an oath bind me to secrecy, I would enlighten you as to the motives that guide me. But believe me that I already have a clew to the whereabouts of your heir."

"These are but empty words. My wife brought me the tidings that our son is dead. A famous fortune-teller told her so."

"And after this my mask is still in your way?" asked the Black Mask, in a slightly scornful tone; "you hesitate at being treated by a man in disguise, after giving full credence to the words of a vile impostor?"

"But the woman whom you call an impostor," returned the count, angrily, "not only told my wife all that had happened to her in the past, but prophesied something which has literally come true."

"And what is that?" asked the Black Mask, curiously.

"She said that a woman from the East would come to us and ask for shelter, and advised us to take the woman into our house; for only she could keep off a misfortune which hangs threateningly over the heads of those of the house of Weiden."

"And did this woman come?"

"She came after three days, as the sibyl had foretold. She speaks a strange language, and since she has taken up the position by my bed I feel much better."

"This is all very well, count, but, as you value your life, take no medicine from this woman; accept only what your wife hands to you; let her only be your nurse."

Full of astonishment, the count looked at the Black Mask. The old distrust expressed itself once more on his countenance, and he said:

"But, my dear sir, supposing I do not follow the advice you so generously give me?"

"Then you will never see your son again, count," briefly returned the Black Mask.

"And why not, sir? Your statements are contradictory," returned the count, in such a contemptuous tone of voice that the uncovered part of the Black Mask's face could be plainly seen to flush angrily.

He arose quickly and said:

"Because in that case the family vault of the Weidens will have opened to receive the last of that illustrious name ere the heir has been recovered."

A few minutes later the Black Mask's carriage bore him away from the house in which Fate, in the guise of the woman from the East, sat beside the dying count's bed.

CHAPTER XXXI.

A MYSTERIOUS TRIO.

In the Ghetto a splendid carriage had been observed as it rolled swiftly past. It rarely happened that such a grand turn-out passed through the Ghetto, but the owner of this carriage seemed to have a particular predilection for the Jews' quarter, and whenever he had occasion to leave the city he chose this road, always looking out of the window and narrowly regarding the ruinous houses and their inmates. Thus the Jews had had several opportunities to see the Black Mask, of whom so much was spoken in the city. However, far from being honored by this attention, the Jews disliked seeing the Black Mask's carriage in their part of the city. They knew that he was a great physician, but the fact that he concealed his face rendered them uneasy; for the poor, persecuted Jews scented a conspiracy against themselves in everything unusual, and very much feared that the Black Mask's predilection for the Ghetto portended a misfortune for them. Pinkus, the one-time president of the congregation, had stood at his door when the carriage rolled past, and was oppressed by thoughts similar to the above. The curiosity in regard to his neighbor's house, which had once caused so much unhappiness, troubled him no more; indeed, the house excited no one's curiosity, for it had been deserted this many a year. Doors and windows were closed and barricaded, and the house daily assumed a more ruinous appearance. Pinkus made a long face; something evidently troubled him, for it usually wore a very contented expression. This was doubtless observed by Sexton Wolf, who came up to Pinkus just as the carriage dashed past. Rubbing the sleeve of his calico jacket across his face, which action contributed not a little to increasing the shining appearance of said sleeve, he said to Pinkus:

"Well, Mr. Pinkus, what is the cause of your trouble? Has the carriage anything to do with it?"

"Partly, Wolf, partly. I was just thinking that we Jews are never left in peace. As soon as one *Gezerah* has passed another looms up. Suppose the man who left the Christian child in our care should turn up again. It is very probable, and then we would be ruined."

"You must not let that trouble you, Mr. Pinkus. God knows whether his ashes are not dispersed by the four winds of heaven. No one has seen him this many a long year."

"Yes, but the child causes me much anxiety."

"Have you heard nothing of him yet, Mr. Pinkus?"

"No, nothing; since that remarkable evening he has entirely disappeared."

"Don't take it in ill part, Mr. Pinkus, but indeed it was not right of you to send the child a-peddling with rolls."

"What was I to do? The boy is over nine years old, an age at which Jewish children are always set to work, and it would have been a shame to let him live on the charity of the congregation any longer. Moreover, the plan did not originate with me, the president desired it."

"Yes, yes, Mr. Pinkus,' said the sexton, in an important tone of voice, "if all could be of one thought. Times were different when you were president."

Pinkus was about to answer, when the sexton, with the cry, "*Shema Israel!*" recoiled in terror, and ran down the street as fast as his legs could carry him. Pinkus did not long remain in doubt as to the cause of the sexton's panic; but he lost all power to cry as well as to move.

Before him, as if arisen from the ground, stood a tall man attired in black, the upper part of his face covered by a black velvet mask. The mysterious figure signed to Pinkus to enter the house, and pushed him into the room, where the poor man, more dead than alive, fell on a chair, while the Black Mask remained standing before him.

"Well, Pinkus, my friend, how does the little boy who was confided to your care some years ago?" said he.

Pinkus shook from head to foot, opened and shut his

quivering lips, and at last ejaculated, in a hardly audible voice:

"Thanks for the inquiry, but I know of no child, the worthy gentleman has intrusted to me."

The Black Mask started; then he seemed to recollect something, and said in almost a friendly tone:

"Consider, my good Pinkus, consider. You may trust me. Tell me, what has become of the little boy?"

"I do not know anything of a little boy," sighed Pinkus. "I never knew anything about a little boy."

"Perhaps my mask confuses you. Do not let it disturb you; you may trust me. I am the same man who delivered the child to your care. As proof of this, I will confide to you that I charged a certain Master Heberline to collect the money for me, which was not given by the Jews till after the lapse of some time."

"I can remember nothing," stammered Pinkus, with a stubbornness born of despair. "I do not even remember such a name as Heberline."

The Black Mask stamped his feet impatiently, and cried in a voice which made Pinkus quake:

"You lie, Jew, and you know it. But your lies are of no avail; I have plenty of witnesses. Quick, show me the little boy, else your last hour is come. It is not advisable to do away with a Christian child, which has been received before a number of witnesses."

With these words the Black Mask drew a dagger from his breast, and seizing Pinkus by the throat, he aimed it at his heart. A groan from the tortured man was all the answer the Black Mask received.

"Will you confess, Jew!" cried he, grasping his victim still firmer, and planting his dagger close to the unfortunate man's body.

There was not much time to consider, Pinkus perceived, so he nodded convulsively. The Black Mask immediately loosened his hold.

"Oh, my God, my God!" groaned Pinkus, "how long, O Lord! shall we still be in *Galuth?*" (exile).

"Cease your whining, confess if you still have the boy, and let me see him."

"Oh, gracious sir, I had the boy until a few days ago, when he disappeared."

"You lie, Jew, you lie! You have hidden him somewhere."

"So may God help me in my utmost need, I do not know where the boy is. He went away from here a few days ago, and has not returned."

Had the stranger's face not been covered by a mask, it could have been seen that an expression of pleased surprise depicted itself on his countenance.

"That is worth one thousand florins more," muttered he; then he said, aloud: "You Jews have killed him and drank his blood! I came to get him to-day, and to reward you for the faithful accomplishment of your task. To my horror I find that you have done away with the child. 'Tis a bad business, and may cost every Jew's head in the city, be it man, woman or child."

"But we are guiltless, sir; the Lord knows, that we are guiltless; the boy ran away; there is Christian blood in his veins, and he has probably returned to those of his faith."

"Very well," said the Black Mask. "I shall procure my witnesses and confide this matter to a magistrate. He will pronounce judgment on you, if the mob has not previously hastened your departure from this world. Adieu, Pinkus."

"Mercy, mercy," howled Pinkus, falling on his knees and grasping the stranger's cloak.

The latter turned and said:

"You must not ask mercy of me, I have none to dispense."

"Oh, yes, gracious sir; oh, yes, you have yourself once before saved us from a great misfortune."

"I should like to do this again, but I know not in what manner. I require thousands of florins to make my witnesses hold their peace. If you are able to procure three thousand florins in about three days at most, I will see what I can do."

Now Pinkus had all this time suspected that the stranger's object was to extort money, and he was ready to promise any sacrifice on his part, and on that of the congregation, to avert an incalculable misfortune; all the more as he knew that the slightest accusation would gain strength by the fact of the boy's disappearance. But Pinkus was not president any more, and, therefore, could not agree to the stranger's demand. He explained this to the Black Mask, and the latter consented to come on the next day in order to hear the decision of the congregation. Then he left the unhappy Pinkus, who tore his hair and sat down on a foot-stool, rent his garments, as it is customary on the death of a relative, and regarded the calamity again pending on the inhabitants of the Ghetto.

We last saw the sexton flying down the street, impelled by terror of the Black Mask. He did not relax his speed until he came in sight of his house, which was situated in a cross street. Still breathing heavily, he ascended the steps, and, after fervently kissing the *Mezuza* fastened to the door-post, turned the knob and threw open the door. The cry the sexton now uttered would have made the hearer's hair stand on end. Indeed, the sexton's hair did not fail to do so, and his knees knocked against each other in an almost alarming manner. The reader must not laugh at him, for he certainly would have been just as terrified had he seen what Sexton Wolf beheld.

Sitting on a chair, and quietly turning over the leaves of a Hebrew book, sat the Black Mask. Wolf had made good speed; he knew that he was a runner; he had left the Black Mask at Pinkus' side, and now here he was; besides, while he himself was still quite out of breath, there the Black Mask sat quite composedly; and his breath seemed to come and go very easily. It was hard not to believe in miracles, and not to be afraid of masked individuals.

The Black Mask, on hearing the sexton's dreadful cry,

looked up and regarded the terrified man, who sank back into a chair near the door.

"Why did you shriek so, my good man?" asked the Black Mask, rising from his seat. "I am sorry to have been the cause of your terror; but I am here with no unfriendly intentions, and have been awaiting you this half an hour."

Good God, the matter grew worse and worse. The Black Mask had been there half an hour. Dreadful, dreadful! While he sat here, he was at the same time with Pinkus.

The Black Mask's words, far from pacifying the sexton, only terrified him the more. His tremors fairly shook the chair beneath him. This did not escape the stranger's observation, but he ascribed the tremors to a fever; and putting his hand in the pocket of his cloak, drew forth a small flask, and told the sexton to put forth his tongue. What could poor Wolf do other than put out his tongue? And he did it to such perfection that it hung out like that of a panting dog. The stranger poured a few drops from his flask upon it, and Wolf quickly drew back his tongue, while he made a wry face.

"There," said the Black Mask, "that will do you good; in five minutes the chills will have left you."

Then he resumed his seat, and continued:

"My good man, no doubt you will be surprised at the cause of my coming here."

The sexton essayed to nod; but as he had not as yet ceased to tremble, even this slight movement was unsuccessful.

"I wish to know how many Jews there are in the Ghetto, whose names begin with the letter P;" that is to say, only the names of *Ba'ale Battim*" (heads of families).

The Black Mask drew forth some tablets, and the sexton, opening and shutting his mouth several times quite in vain, at last began:

"'There—is—Per—Per—Peretz; then—Po—Po—Pol Pollack; then—Pin—Pink—ku—kus—Pinkus—and——"

"That will do, my good man," said the stranger; "your violent trembling impedes your speech. You probably have a list of the names of the members of the congregation. Will you be so kind as to let me see this?"

Glad to be able to escape from the object of his terror, if but for an instant, the sexton hastened as fast as his trembling limbs would permit, into the adjoining room, and soon returned with a book, which he deposited on the table.

The stranger began to copy this book, to the no small astonishment of the sexton; for, as a matter of course, the book was written in Hebrew characters.

When the Black Mask had finished, he arose, and saying, "Many thanks, my good man," took his departure.

For a time, the sexton did not dare to stir. When he at length arose and went to the table in order to close the book, which the stranger had left open, he found lying on it a gold coin of no inconsiderable value.

When he had recovered from his astonishment, and ascertained that the coin was by no means hot, he put it in his pocket, and ran straight to Pinkus. On reaching the corner of the street, he heard some one shout "Take care, there!" and on looking up, saw a carriage, from the window of which the Black Mask leaned forth. But when, about half a minute afterward, he reached the house of Pinkus, he saw the Black Mask, whose carriage he could still behold in the distance, step quietly forth into the street.

That evening it was known, not only in the Ghetto, but in half the city, that the Black Mask had been seen simultaneously in three parts of the Jews' quarter: in the house of Pinkus, in that of the sexton, and in his own carriage.

CHAPTER XXXII.

THE BLACK GLOVE.

Let us see what Pinkus did after the Black Mask left him. That very evening he made a call on the president and told him all the incidents of the Black Mask's visit and his demand. However, to all Pinkus' urgent entreaties that the president should summon a meeting of the congregation, the latter, who was of a quiet, phlegmatic disposition, returned the answer:

"We will wait awhile yet."

"But," cried Pinkus, "the man is coming for his money to-morrow forenoon."

"He will wait awhile," returned the president, with the greatest calmness.

"Oh, you do not know the man," cried Pinkus, in despair. "At the time of our last *Gazerah* you were at the *Yeshiba* (Rabbinical College). If the congregation were aware of what is in prospect for them, they would be as desperate as I am."

"The congregation will wait awhile also."

"Good God, with your everlasting waiting you will bring down destruction on all Israel."

"I will wait awhile with that, likewise."

Half dead with fright, Pinkus left the "waiting" president, and passed a most wretched night; for all he knew, the full measure of the stranger's wrath would descend on his head. A hundred times and more he bemoaned the unhappy fate which had wrested the scepter of his command over the congregation from him. How totally different to a placid man, who had no heart for the people under his guidance, would he have acted! Ah! little did he know what he was saying when, on the day its first misfortune broke in on the Ghetto, he wished that he were not president. Now the wish he had expressed in an evil hour was accomplished—accomplished to his detriment and that of the whole congregation.

The coming day was greeted by the unfortunate Pinkus as his last on earth. He arose betimes and taking his prayer-book and psalms to hand, read all that he could find that had any reference to a case like this. When he had finished, he got down from his shelves the books which contained the *Selichoth* (prayers for the ten penitential days), and selected from these the most fitting themes. When he had got through these, the day was pretty far advanced, yet still the dreaded stranger had not come; so Pinkus thought he had reason to believe that the fervor and strength of his prayers had banished him, and he accordingly looked about for even stronger exorcisms to keep the Black Mask at a safe distance.

He considered for awhile, and could think of nothing more forcible than the formula which is pronounced during a violent storm. Hardly, however, had the words escaped his lips, when a shadow fell across his book, and looking up, he beheld the Black Mask standing before him, as if in truth sent there by the lightning.

Pinkus wanted to cry out, but his voice failed him; he wanted to rise, but his limbs were powerless to obey the impulse; he could only think what a blunder he had made to recite a prayer which was intended for thunder and lightning in a case like this.

The Black Mask laid his hand lightly on Pinkus' shoulder, and asked in a melodious voice:

"Your name is Pinkus, my good man?"

"Good God, now he acts as if he had never in his life seen me," thought Pinkus, "and he has disguised his voice. Well, I am curious to know what new deviltry he is contemplating now."

That Pinkus was of an inquisitive turn of mind, even on occasions like the present, it is hardly necessary for us to recall to the reader's mind.

On the stranger's perceiving that he received no answer, he looked around in the room, took a chair, drew it close to that of Pinkus, and seated himself on it.

"You do not know me Mr. Pinkus?" began the Black

Mask. "I divine it from your surprise. Well, it is rather a difficult matter to know a man who wears a mask."

"What a serpent!" thought Pinkus; "now he wants to persuade me that I do not know him."

When, after a pause, the Black Mask again received no answer, he said:

"I think that I am not wrong in presuming that about nine years ago a little boy, born of Christian parents, was intrusted to your care."

"Just listen to that hypocrite!" thought Pinkus; "he plays with me like a cat with a mouse!"

But still Pinkus was mute. Again the Black Mask waited for an answer, and at last grew impatient.

"Pinkus," said he, shortly, "can you not answer a polite question by 'yes' or 'no'?"

"Now," thought Pinkus, "he is at least coming out in his true colors," and he answered:

"Yes, gracious sir."

The Black Mask drew a breath of satisfaction, and continued:

"Can you tell me the particulars of the manner in which the child was delivered to you?"

"That you probably know as well as I do," returned Pinkus; "you have your sport with me!"

"That I do not, Mr. Pinkus; but if it pleases you to think I know it, do so; it is probably known to every inhabitant of the Ghetto. I imagine that I know it, but still wish to hear it once more from your lips. I assure you that this will not result to your disadvantage."

"Aha!" thought Pinkus, "he is alluding to the money; he wants to revel in my pain, in letting me relate this accursed story. However, it is better for me to accede to his request; he might else increase his demand. Shall I commence at the beginning?" asked Pinkus, aloud.

"Yes," returned the Black Mask. "Proceed just as if I knew not a syllable of the whole matter."

Pinkus related his adventure, which we sufficiently know, and growing warm as his recital progressed, forgot that he was only repeating what he thought his auditor already knew, and that the latter acted the principal part throughout the whole story.

When Pinkus had finished, he asked, with the satisfaction of a child after reciting some fairy tale:

"Did I do well, gracious sir?"

"You are an excellent story-teller, Mr. Pinkus, and I am deeply indebted to you," returned the Black Mask; "but permit me to put another question: is the child still with you?"

"Now it is coming; God have mercy on me," thought Pinkus, wringing his hands, while he cried in a whining voice: "Oh, believe me, gracious sir, for God's sake believe me——"

The stranger seemed surprised at this outburst on the part of Pinkus, for he arose from his chair and said:

"Why should I not believe you, Mr. Pinkus? did I express any doubt as to the truth of your story?"

"Now he is speaking in another tone again," thought Pinkus, and in the same whining voice said: "He is gone, as sure as I live he is gone!"

"Who is gone?" asked the Black Mask, hastily seizing Pinkus' hand, which the latter, who feared a repetition of the scene of yesterday, as hastily withdrew. "Tell me, tell me," asked the Black Mask, anxiously.

"There is not much to tell," moaned Pinkus, "and I am not to blame. It is solely the fault of the president, and the whole matter lies on his conscience; for he wanted the child, who lived on the charity of the congregation, to earn something, therefore he was sent to the city to peddle rolls."

"Rolls? A fair-haired boy? beautiful as an angel?" hastily asked the Black Mask, seizing Pinkus so violently by the shoulder that the latter grew quite breathless with fear. Then the stranger seemed struck by some sudden thought; for, hurling Pinkus, who was clinging to his cloak, away with such force that he flew into a corner, he rushed off with the speed of a roe.

Greatly astounded, Pinkus came forth from his corner and thanked God for his respite. But the poor man's joy was but of a brief duration, for in about two minutes the door of the little dwelling was again pushed open, and the Black Mask re-entered.

"Well, Jew," he cried, in a voice which brought Pinkus to his knees, "have you the money which is to save you and your accomplices from the gallows?"

"There," thought Pinkus, "now he speaks in his usual manner and tone of voice. I must have recourse to pleading. Gracious sir," he began, "but now you were so amiable—not at all impolite, and did not mention the money—I thought you had given up all idea of it."

"Did I not tell you yesterday that I must have the money to-day, else I would bring down destruction on all of you?"

"Yes, gracious sir, that's what you said yesterday; but to-day you did not say a word about it."

"Are you mocking me, rascal?" cried the Black Mask; "do you want to make a fool of me?" and he approached Pinkus so menacingly that the latter drew back affrighted.

"But, gracious sir, just recollect. Nothing is further from my thoughts than a jest. Hardly two minutes have elapsed since you left me."

The Black Mask was startled for a moment; then he said to himself: "Terror and anxiety about the money appear to have turned the Jew's head. I will speak more guardedly, else the whole project may turn out a failure."

"Attention, Pinkus," said he aloud; "collect your thoughts, reflect, and answer the questions I shall put to you."

"Speak, gracious sir, and if I can I will answer."

"When did you last see me, Pinkus; when last speak to me?"

"Not quite ten minutes ago, gracious sir."

"Reflect, Pinkus, reflect; you are mistaken."

Pinkus thought, "I can do him the favor of pretending to think." He cast his eyes to the ground, and assumed the appearance of one deeply sunk in thought. Was not every moment he could delay the catastrophe a gain? But suddenly he uttered a cry, and pounced on something that lay on the floor with such fury that the Black Mask recoiled, fairly terrified.

Pinkus picked up—a black glove!

"Here, here," he cried, triumphantly, "this you dropped, gracious sir, when you were here awhile ago."

The Black Mask started, contemplated the glove, and furiously cast it away from him.

"Have you the money, Jew?" he roared; "then give it to me, and quickly."

The Black Mask was trembling violently.

"Pardon, gracious sir, but you must have patience for a few days; the money——"

"Never mind," broke in the Black Mask, "you need not procure it; I do not require it any more."

And quicker than he had come, the Black Mask left the room and house of Pinkus.

Barely ten minutes afterward, and while Pinkus was still racking his brain as to the cause that events had taken such a fortunate turn, the president of the congregation entered his dwelling.

"Well," said he, "was the Black Mask here?"

"Yes," returned Pinkus.

"And did he ask for the money?"

"He did; but, as I was excusing myself for not having it, he assured me that he was in no need of it any more."

"Remarkable, very remarkable, indeed," muttered the president. "First the man raises such a row about the money, and then quietly resigns it."

"Yes, indeed, it is a miracle."

"That comes of awaiting things calmly, and never acting hastily," said the president; "no one ever repented of waiting."

"No, no," cried Pinkus, whom the president's waiting had provoked more than once; "this black glove is the cause of it," and he showed it to the president. "Hardly had I shown it to him, when he began to tremble, and hastily asked for the money, as if he were in a great hurry. When I declared to him that he must have patience for a few days, he cried out, in visible terror, that he had no more need for the money, and that I was not to mind it. Then he hastened off."

The president regarded the black glove on all sides, but could discover nothing remarkable about it. It was simply a black glove—nothing more.

"Do you know, Pinkus," said he, at last, "it cannot be denied that the ways of God are miraculous, and that it is remarkable that such a piece of black stuff should have averted a *gezerah* to our people. I will take the glove with me, and the congregation shall keep it as a memento of their deliverance. Let us summon the congregation this evening for a special service, and render thanksgiving to the Lord for our miraculous redemption, and rehearse Psalm 124, which is appropriate for it, and reads thus: 'If the Lord had not been for us, Israel may now say, if the Lord had not been for us, when men rose up against us, they had swallowed us up alive, when their wrath was kindled against us. Then the waters had overwhelmed us, the stream had gone over our soul. Blessed be the Lord, who had not given us a prey to their teeth. Our soul hath escaped as a bird out of the fowler's snare; the snare is broken and we are escaped. Our help is in the name of the Lord, who made heaven and earth.'"

CHAPTER XXXIII.

THE BLACK MASK AT HOME.

The Black Mask's carriage stopped before a splendid house in the most aristocratic quarter of the city. The servant sprang down and assisted his master to alight. Then he ascended the steps and opened the door of the house.

The Black Mask entered a lofty hall which was supported by marble columns, and from the center of which a staircase, constructed of the most costly wood, led to the upper stories. The inlaid floor was covered here and there by Persian rugs.

The Black Mask ascended the stairs, and was met at the top by a servant who said:

"Sir, a large number of patients are assembled in the anteroom, and are anxiously awaiting your arrival."

The Black Mask, making a motion of impatience with his hand, followed the servant, who led the way to a large room, the folding doors of which he slid back and announced:

"The doctor."

The murmur of voices which the doctor had heard before the doors were opened ceased instantaneously as he entered the large room which was almost filled by persons who had come to beg succor and health for themselves or dear ones belonging to them.

The mask which the physician wore contributed no inconsiderable share to his popularity; as people did not think him a man like other men, but believed him to be of supernatural origin.

The Black Mask looked around the room, and his attention seemed attracted by a young girl, the most shabbily dressed person in the room, for he signed her to follow him.

He preceded her into his study, which adjoined the waiting room, and before he seated himself at his magnificent writing-desk, drew up a velvet arm-chair for the poor girl, who was quite subdued by the splendor of all she saw.

"What ails you my child?" he asked in a friendly tone.

"Ah, sir," began the girl, "I do not come for myself, but in the name of my mother, the poor Widow Hammer, whom you visited some four weeks ago. She is ill again.

All the washing she has lately done has been too much for her strength."

The physician questioned the girl as to the particulars of her mother's illness, and after reflecting for awhile said:

"I know very well what medicine will be best for your mother. I recollect that she is the mother of four children, of whom only you, my good girl, are able to assist her in her endeavors for their support."

"Till now I tried to do so, sir; but since my mother is sick I am compelled to remain at home," returned the girl, the tears entering her eyes.

The Black Mask drew some coins out of his purse.

"Here, my child," said he, "this I think is the medicine that will help your mother. Tell her that she must not go out to wash any more this winter, and when she has taken all this medicine come again, I have more of it."

He pressed her hand, and she felt three or four coins glide in it. Ere he could prevent it, the girl had seized the good physician's hand and covered it with kisses and tears. He signed to her to go, and, her face radiant with happiness, the girl obediently left the room.

The door was immediately reopened, and a servant in livery looked inquiringly into the room.

"Are there more poor people, Jacob?" asked the Black Mask.

"No, sir, only an old Jew who is dressed rather poorly."

"Bring him hither."

"I beg your pardon, sir, but the noble gentlemen, who have already murmured at the act of showing them into the same room with the common people, will be horrified that an old Jew has the precedence before them."

The Black Mask stamped his foot and said sternly:

"Do as I bade you. Any one who is not satisfied with my rules is at liberty to withdraw."

The servant vanished; and that he had spoken only in the

interest of his master was soon very evident. Loud murmurs became audible, chairs were pushed back, the door of the hall violently slammed several times, and the Black Mask could distinctly hear the curses and maledictions aimed at the beggar of a Jew, who dared penetrate into the house of such a celebrated physician, the excuses the poor Jew made, and his offer to immediately and gladly leave the room, if it so pleased the noble gentlemen.

The Black Mask rose angrily and appeared at the door as the tumult was at its height.

"Gentlemen," he cried in a voice of thunder, and immediately there was such silence that the fall of a pin might have been heard. "I desire that you either conform to my rules or dispense with my advice."

He approached the Jew, whose face was covered, for he was weeping, grasped his hand, and drew him into his study.

This was too much for the noble gentlemen, who one after the other left the waiting-room. The servant announced this with a grieved face.

"Never mind, my man," answered the Black Mask; "they'll all come back soon enough. If I, as physician, cannot teach them that all men are equals, then no one can do it."

He now turned his attention to the Jew, and fairly started as he caught sight of his face.

"What is your name, my good friend?" asked he, with trembling voice.

"Isaac Kline," answered the Jew.

"Are you from this city?" the doctor continued to question, holding his hand tightly pressed on his heart.

"No, no; I come from a great distance. Your honor has probably never heard the name of our village, although your fame has penetrated to us. Its name is Immenfeld, a small, insignificant place, which was formerly famous for its castle. The man who is in charge of it now never gave us a coin to earn yet. In former times," continued the Jew, loquaciously, "we thought we would be happy if we only could get rid of the baroness, but since she is gone, the whole castle seems to have gone to sleep."

We cannot say if the physician was interested in the Jew's talk, or if he was thinking of something else. He allowed the old man to ramble on, and the latter had ceased a long while before the physician raised his head and inquired:

"Well, my good man, what leads you to me? Are you sick?"

"No, not I," returned Isaac Kline. "I am the sexton of the Immenfeld congregation; the most important person of our community, the president, is afflicted with a dreadful disease. No one could help him, and he was quite hopeless, until he heard of you; then he said to me one day:

"'Isaac,' said he—my name is Isaac, your honor—'go to the city, to the Black Mask'—that is what the people call your honor;—'tell him of my sickness, perhaps he can help me.' I waited over the Sabbath, for on that day I have to be on my post in the synagogue, and the journey, I knew, would take me a whole week; and then I went to an old woman—a little woman she is, and she used to nurse the sick people before the duke granted her a pension, no one knows why; since that she lives very comfortably, very comfortably, indeed, and—what was I going to say? Oh, yes—I went to her, and said: 'Mrs. Bonafit,'—goodness! what is the matter with you, sir? Flies? Yes; they are very annoying; I guess we will have rain soon. Well, I said to Mrs. Bonafit that she should go and take care of the president during the absence of Isaac (meaning myself); for the president's wife—peace to her ashes!—is dead.

"Mrs. Bonafit, although she is not very strong now, went with me immediately, and she is taking care of the president until my return. Of course she does not need to do it, for she has quite a large pension from the duke; but she is very fond of the president, because he never allows any one to slander her boy, who was a real good-for-nothing, and who ran away the day before his *Bar-Mitzvah*. (But I beg your pardon! you do not know what a *Bar-Mitzvah* is). Then Mrs. Bonafit, who always wanted to persuade us that her boy was no good-for-nothing, probably made it up with the president that a *Ba'al-Shem* should come to the village.

"Your honor knows what a *Ba'al-Shem* is? A *Ba'al-Shem* is—well—a *Ba'al-Shem*. Now, the *Ba'al-Shem* really did come, and she says that he told her that her son Joseph (his name) was in a good place, and that great things were in store for him.

"Now the old woman is waiting for her son, just as we are waiting for the coming of the Messiah, and she firmly believes that the good-for-nothing, who once associated intimately with an apostate, will yet do her and his congregation great honor. However, it is more than nine years since then, and no one has heard anything of the boy.

"All mockery and all dissuasions are in vain. Old Mrs. Bonafit has implicit faith in her son, and always says:

"'My boy will come back, for the *Ba'al Shem* has said it.'

"And thus she has grown old and gray, and in due course of time will sink to everlasting rest, but her good-for-nothing will not come back."

The Black Mask had jumped up from his chair and walked excitedly up and down the room all the time that Isaac Kline, the sexton of Immenfeld, gossiped away, with his eyes, as is the custom of old people when talking, directed toward the floor. He had so lost himself in his reminiscences, that he could not remember for what he had come hither until the Black Mask reminded him of his errand.

"Ah, yes," said he, "your honor must excuse me, but I get excited when I think of that good-for-nothing of a boy; for he has a mother who may be compared to Sarah, Rebecca, Rachel and Leah. Well, the president is paralyzed in all his limbs, and has not been able to stir for the last year. I am to ask you if anything can be done for him? He is the richest man in the congregation, and if you cure him will pay you anything you demand."

"I must see the man."

The doctor said this slowly, and as if the resolve had cost him much thought.

"How is that possible, your honor? We cannot fetch him here."

"I—I will go there!"

"To Immenfeld? It takes a whole week to go there and come back."

"Yes, and if it were to take a year, I must go there," said the Black Mask, in a voice which seemed to Isaac to have an angry sound.

"When will your honor come?" asked Isaac, subdued.

"I know not; to-day, to-morrow, next week, some time or other, but come I will most surely."

The Black Mask sank into a chair, and to all appearances paid not a particle of attention to all of what the old man continued to talk. At last he arose, and, without taking the slightest notice of his visitor, left the room. Passing through the waiting-room he ascended the stairs to the second story. Here also the floor was covered by costly carpets and the walls lined with precious paintings.

The Black Mask walked to the extreme end of the corridor and there softly opened a door and entered a room, the windows of which were darkened by thick curtains. Still the outlines of a little white bed and the bowed form of a woman sitting beside it could be plainly distinguished.

"Margareth," said the Black Mask, approaching the bed on tiptoe, "how is the little fellow?"

"Still very feverish. Will you not see for yourself?"

The Black Mask drew back the curtains, and the bright rays of the sun broke in and flooded the bed in a sea of light. A little boy lay on it, his cheeks flushed by fever, his eyes almost closed. Long golden curls framed in the lovely face. Wondrously beautiful must the child have been when the ruddy hue of health instead of the flush of fever glowed on his cheeks and his eyes, now covered by their long lashes, looked merrily and joyously into the world. At a sign from the Black Mask the woman arose, and he sat down at her place and took the boy's hand in his. He examined the pulse, then, dubiously shaking his head, sighed heavily.

"This fever has not left him for nine days," said he. "That accursed rascal's blow must have affected the child's brain. To be so near to port and suffer shipwreck! Oh, it is terrible. My art has its limits; I can do no more; my prophecy will prove a disgraceful failure. After ten years of vain search I will place the dead child in its mother's arms. God only, and one man can help here."

The door was opened softly, and a servant cautiously put in his head.

"Sir," said he, "a Franciscan friar is desirous of speech with you. I tried to turn him off; but——"

"Where is he? Where is he?" asked the Black Mask, hurriedly.

"Here, here, my son!" cried a joyous voice at the door.

"God be thanked, Father Anselmo!" cried the Black Mask, rushing forward, and the next moment the friends were locked in each other's arms. "Father Anselmo, the Lord in his great mercy sent you hither. You came not a minute too soon."

CHAPTER XXXIV.

THE THIRD VISITOR IN IMMENFELD.

HELPLESSLY stretched out on a couch, and powerless to move a limb, lay the president of the Immenfeld congregation; that first personage of the community who has been brought so often before the reader, but whose name has not as yet been mentioned. Let us atone for this neglect, as otherwise it might become difficult for the patient reader to distinguish the many persons we have introduced to him. The president's name was Raphael Ben Dan.

At his bedside sat a frail little woman, one whom we have seen several times before, and who is patiently waiting for her truant son, as is Israel for the Messiah, with a firm and implicit belief. Ah, we know the good soul as she sits there, her back bowed with age and cares, her eyes reddened by much weeping, her good-natured face crossed by deep furrows, her forehead covered by some stray white locks which had escaped from the confinement of her close-fitting black cap. It is the mother of Joseph Bonafit, that good mother of an unworthy son, as Isaac Kline, the sexton, had said to the Black Mask.

Mrs. Bonafit nods sleepily now and then, only to start up in affright and stare into the night-light, which consists of a small wax taper stuck into a piece of card, the whole swimming in a glass of oil. Wide awake, she stares at the little light for half a minute, then slowly, slowly her head droops again, and she is off in dreamland. 'Tis no wonder the good woman feels tired, and drops off to sleep, though she had resolved to keep awake never so firmly, for the watchman, also an old acquaintance of ours, is just calling out the twelfth hour. The sick man groans, the little woman starts up and looks confusedly around for a moment, then she remembers where she is, and says, in her still melodious voice:

"Rabbi Ben Dan, did you say something?"

"Good Mrs. Bonafit, how long is it since Isaac Kline came back from the city?"

Mrs. Bonafit reflected for a while, then said:

"It was a week last Friday."

"And what day is it to-day?"

"Just now the watchman called out the twelfth hour; that is the beginning of Thursday."

"So it is nearly a fortnight, and still the physician does not come. Oh, a body can die, and be buried twice over, before ever such a doctor even thinks of keeping his word."

"He will come," said Mrs. Bonafit, consolingly. "You must remember that such a distinguished man's time is fully occupied, and that he promised more than we dared hope for—his coming to see you."

"Many thanks for that," cried Ben Dan, peevishly; "Isaac told him that I was rich, and could pay him well, so the sacrifice on his part is not so great."

"How can you talk so?" returned Mrs. Bonafit, reprovingly; "as if the great doctor could not gain as much, or perhaps more, did he remain in the city instead of coming here."

Ben Dan must have perceived the force of this argument, for he did not answer. Mrs. Bonafit began to nod again, and all was soon as quiet as before her conversation with the president; suddenly she started up with a cry of terror. The blast of a post-horn—a fanfare—resounded shrilly through the silence of night.

"Mrs. Bonafit, Mrs. Bonafit," cried the sick man, anxiously, "as I hope that God will restore me to health, I believe that this is the doctor, the Black Mask."

"Where? where? Who?" asked Mrs. Bonafit, her senses not quite collected yet.

Again the post-horn sounded, and the rattling of a coach could be plainly heard coming up the street to the president's house, where it suddenly ceased.

"Praise be to God," said Mrs. Bonafit, "he has really come."

Quickly she set her cap straight, fastened the kerchief at her neck, and hunted for one of her slippers which she had dropped while napping. When she at last recovered this, she had much ado to get it on the right way; then she wasted several minutes in looking for the torch, which at that time was the only substitute for a candle. When she at last found it, and was holding it over the wax taper in the glass to light it, several loud knocks resounded at the door, and so startled the good woman that she dropped the torch into the glass, which extinguished the light, and total darkness reigned in the room.

"Good God, how very awkward!" cried the sick man, much provoked by the nervous little woman.

"I can't help it," she returned, apologetically; "the *Srore* (distinguished person) has quite upset me."

"Please open the door, Mrs. Bonafit; the man is capable of going off without seeing me."

"In the dark? How can I bring the man into such Egyptian darkness?"

"Just so; you can lead him in; and then the carriage lantern can be brought," cried the president, angrily.

(The reader has probably not forgotten how difficult it was at that time to strike a light.)

Mrs. Bonafit immediately tripped down the stairs, and drew back the bolt from the door.

In the faint light which the carriage-lamp diffused, Mrs. Bonafit saw standing before her the imposing figure of a man, the upper part of whose face was concealed by a black mask.

Many words were not wasted. Mrs. Bonafit felt herself pushed back into the dark house and—terror almost deprived her of her senses—a number of glowing kisses were imprinted on her wrinkled face. Then her hands were seized and fervently pressed, and the figure, which she now of course could not at all distinguish, drew her through the hall and up the stairs to the sick-room without once stumbling. Mrs. Bonafit was quite beside herself. The doctor had kissed her—her, a pious old Jewess; the crime appeared enormous! Then she comforted herself that it had all been a mistake, that the kisses had not been intended for her. Still, she was provoked at such behavior from a distinguished physician who had come to pay a visit to a sick man. All these thoughts flashed across the little woman's mind as she stepped into the sick-room with the stranger.

"Why is there no light here?" now asked the latter, in an extremely melodious voice.

However, he did not wait for an answer; but stepping to a faint square of light at the opposite end of the room, which he rightly divined to be the window, he opened it, and called out:

"Jacob, bring up the carriage lantern."

Shortly after, the servant entered with a lantern, and the stranger bade him light all the branches of the Sabbath lamp.

Soon the little room was ablaze with light, and the stranger attentively regarded the little woman, who ascribed his curiosity to quite another cause, and was elated by the thought how much the strange doctor must feel ashamed of his mistake, at having kissed an old Jewess.

"Sit down, my good woman," said the stranger, in a friendly tone; "standing is not good for old bones."

"Why does the man's voice tremble so?" asked Mrs. Bonafit of herself, as she drew up a chair and sat down.

"How are you, my good woman?" asked the Black Mask, and his voice vibrated strangely.

"You mistake, sir," Mrs. Bonafit ventured to say, rising from her chair, courtesying, and quickly seating herself again, "I am not the patient; he lies there on the bed."

The Black Mask quietly took this correction, approached the bed, and proceeded to examine the sick man.

"Can you give me hope?" asked Ben Dan, when the doctor had finished.

"Yes, with God's help; and if you closely follow my instructions, I believe that you may be completely restored to health. But the means will cost you a considerable sum; for you will have to construct certain buildings, for which I will give you the plans."

(It may here be remarked that the Black Mask prescribed Russian vapor-baths for his patient; these were not in vogue, even then little known, and in such a remote part in Germany as Immenfeld, not even dreamed of.)

"Further," continued the doctor, "I am decidedly against your being attended to by a woman. Women are not strong enough to properly care for a sick person like you. If you wish to get well, you must not by any means suffer a woman to be your nurse. Besides," proceeded the doctor, "it is cruel to permit such a frail old woman to sit up all night. She must have her share of sleep."

Why did the stranger's voice, which had been so firm while giving the sick man his orders, now tremble again?

"Excuse me, doctor," said the sick man, "I did not summon the woman; we are old acquaintances, and, so to say, friends, if the president of the congregation and a poor woman may be called friends;"—this very complacently;—"so good Mrs. Bonafit insisted on being my nurse."

"Is the good woman obliged to do this for her support?"

"Not at all; our gracious duke has granted her a pension, on which she can live very comfortably."

"I now hear this for the second time," muttered the Black Mask, and drew forth a memorandum book. "I must make a note of it, and try to find out how this came about."

The doctor arose, and said:

"I will remain in the village till to-morrow morning, as I do not like to leave now. Have you a good inn here?"

"Not in the Jews' lane; but there is one in the village," answered the president.

"But I should prefer to stay in the Jews' lane; I do not wish to wake any one in the village."

The president reflected while he said:

"I really cannot recommend a lodging here, as they all leave much to be desired in respect to comfort. I once kept a spare room for guests, but since my illness this has been put to other use. However, Mrs. Bonafit has a neat little room in the upper story of her house; she has prepared it for the reception of her absent son in the case of his return."

"Mrs. Bonafit, I think that is your name," said the doctor, "will you not put your son's room at my disposal to-night?"

Mrs. Bonafit would have been glad to say no; but how could she, a poor humble woman, dare to reject the request of such a distinguished man? The denial would have remained sticking in her throat. She therefore courtesied acquiescently, and the doctor took her hand and pressed it so fervently that the poor woman almost shrieked.

"Come, my good woman," said the Black Mask, "show me your house, and my little room, and take a few hours' rest. My servant will watch with the sick man for the remainder of the night, and to-morrow he can procure another nurse."

The doctor ordered his coachman to take the carriage to the village stable, posted his servant beside the sick man's bed, and left the house with Mrs. Bonafit. The good woman could not marvel enough at the care with which the stranger led her, and avoided every stone and gutter in their way. Arrived at the house, Mrs. Bonafit took from her pocket the door-knob, which replaced the key, inserted it in the door, and pushed the latter open.

As it was dark in the house, she begged her guest to wait outside until she had struck a light, and entered her little dwelling. When, after persistent blowing into the coals, she at last succeeded in getting a light, to her no little astonishment she saw the stranger sitting at the table, his face buried in his hands, and his body trembling convulsively.

"Are you ill?" asked Mrs. Bonafit, anxiously.

"No, no, my good woman, I feel chilled from the cold night air; please show me my room."

Lighting the way, Mrs. Bonafit crept up the stairs and led the stranger into a small room. All that a mother's love could do had been done to beautify the little room. A dazzling white bed took up one side, the walls were covered with pictures, and a glittering copper ewer stood on a little washstand, beside which hung a finely embroidered towel, the only one of such splendor that Mrs. Bonafit possessed; it was the one that her husband had always used at the *Seder* on the eve of passover. A wooden stool was covered with gayly colored chintz, which gave it quite the appearance of a cushioned arm-chair. In short, all that her poverty permitted had the good mother done to decorate her child's room. Mrs. Bonafit set down the lamp and said:

"Here, worthy sir, shall my son lodge when he returns to me. I hope it pleases you. I am certain that he would like the room very much."

"It pleases me as much as if I were your son, my good woman, and just to make it seem true, I say to you goodnight, mother dear."

"Just so, just so he used to say," muttered Mrs Bonafit, thoughtfully contemplating the strange doctor. "Goodnight, sir," said the old woman, starting from her dreamings, and soon the stranger heard her carefully descending the dilapidated stairs.

Mrs. Bonafit had a remarkable dream that night. She dreamed that the door of her room was softly opened, and there entered a young man of great beauty, who much resembled her Joseph, and yet in figure and walk looked like the strange doctor. Very cautiously and on tiptoes he approached her bed, bent over her and kissed her on the mouth twice. Mrs. Bonafit dreamed this so vividly that she murmured the name "Joseph" in her sleep, and thought to hear her son's voice reply, "Mother, dear mother." Then he seemed to weep. Again he turned into the doctor, who, with a black mask over his face, walked backward to the door. Suddenly the rattling of a carriage awoke the widow from her dreams. She hastened to the window, and was just in time to see a coach and four vanishing around the corner. On the table Mrs.

Bonafit found a well-filled purse and a letter. She opened the latter and her eyes fairly blazed as she recognized the Hebrew characters of her son. She read:

"Mother dear! My friend the Black Mask promised to deliver this. I neither disgrace you nor the name of an Israelite. I have commissioned the doctor to kiss you, mother dear, a thousand times for me. Your Joseph."

"So he did not make a mistake after all," said Mrs. Bonafit, her conscience considerably eased. "But now, quick to the president, he must know this."

CHAPTER XXXV.
THE TRIUMPH OF EVIL.

THERE was grief and sorrow in the beautiful villa of the Count of Weiden. Since the Black Mask had left the count the latter had grown worse and worse, and the beautiful countess was quite beside herself with grief at the thought of her husband's approaching death. She had done all in her power to preserve the life of the old count, who had already passed the age usually allotted to man, three-score and ten, for she loved him dearly, and patiently bore all his humors and petulancy. She had warmly welcomed the woman who, according to the sibyl's prophecy, was to come from the East, and had so come, although at sight of her a secret shudder of dread had overcome the countess. She consented to the woman's demand, that the count should be left wholly to her care, and despite the sibyl's phophecy that death would soon carry the old man away, believed that this woman would keep the fell destroyer at bay.

And when time passed on, and the old count still lived, she was certain that the woman from the East had effected this wonder. She had but one grievance against her; this was that the woman violently opposed her wish to send for the Black Mask, of whose wonderful cures every one was speaking. The woman called the Black Mask a quack, an adventurer, and succeeded in inspiring the count with an intense antipathy against the mysterious physician. This had no little to do with the cold, sarcastic reception the Black Mask had met with on his visit to the count.

When the Black Mask had taken his leave, the countess spoke sadly of the hopes he had given her in regard to her lost child. The woman, who was present at the time, grew livid with rage. She maligned the impostor in such terms that the fastidious countess fairly shuddered with dread and disgust.

"I know this man well," said the woman, "and could have unmasked him long ago. However, it is none of my business, until he stretched forth his hand to a family which I prize and love beyond all things, that of your honorable selves. My lady, do you know for what reason this man constantly wears a mask? He is branded on the forehead."

The count and countess looked at each other in surprise.

"How do you know this, my good woman?" said the countess, not yet wholly convinced.

"In a city in the East, he was convicted of a dreadful crime, and condemned to bear forever a Cain's mark on his face. The hangman branded him on the forehead. I recognized him the moment I saw him, and that was the cause of my panic. Whoever trusts in him is lost."

Thus spake and warned the woman who sat at the bedside of the count. The count and his wife had not yet recovered from the consternation into which the woman's disclosure had thrown them, when the knocker on the front door resounded three times in rapid succession, and a servant brought in a handsomely engraved card on a silver salver. The countess took up the card, and said coldly:

"Tell the Black Mask that he cannot be admitted, as the count does not wish to see him."

The servant departed, but soon returned, bringing a letter on the selfsame salver.

The countess opened the letter with trembling hands.

She could not account to herself why it put her into such a state of agitation. As she read, her face flushed and paled alternately; she arose hastily, and said to the nurse:

"My good Martha, would you be so kind as to leave us alone a moment?"

"Why so?" asked the count, "does the letter contain a secret?"

"No," said the countess, in confusion, "it is from the Black Mask."

"And you attach so much importance to it as to desire this good woman to leave my side?"

"But," timidly answered the countess, "I only wished it in order to spare the good woman some vexation. He speaks of her in no very flattering terms."

"Oh, then I would urgently pray you," said the woman, with an expression on her face that an impartial observer would have construed as that of ill-concealed terror, "to read to me that part of the letter concerning me, as probably he has it in mind to drive me from here, in order to gain a fair field for his game."

"Be easy, my good woman, he will not succeed in this," said the count, in a low voice, for he felt indescribably weak.

"Oh, God," cried the countess, "this letter contains tidings which would have filled me with happiness had I not heard the disclosure of this worthy woman. Listen, my husband, he writes that he has kept his promise; that our child is found."

At these words the woman was overcome with terror, and could not regain her composure for a length of time; finally she said, in a constrained voice:

"Please read the miserable rogue's letter aloud."

The countess glanced at her husband, and as he expressed no dissent, she read:

"Most Honored Countess:—

"Suspecting that I would not be admitted to your presence, as a demon holds guard at the bedside of your husband, and banishes all good spirits thence—a demon whom I think I know, although I caught but a momentary glance of it, I have prepared this letter, in case of such emergency. How gladly would I have called to you the words which I must now write: Happy mother, your child is found. God has rewarded my exertions with success. He guided me in my search for the child. He is a beautiful fair-haired boy, your perfect image, madam. I came near losing him after I had found him, for he was sick, so sick that I despaired of his recovery. But God has preserved him, and I will place him in his mother's arms, if you, gracious countess, will come to my dwelling, either in my carriage or your own.

"With all respect for yourself, and best wishes for your husband, I subscribe myself,

"THE BLACK MASK."

The nurse sat on her chair in a rigid attitude. Her eyes were wide open and staring into space. Her hands, convulsively clasping each other, lay on her lap. She had the appearance of one totally overcome by terror. The countess observed the woman's remarkable looks, and said:

"Martha, for God's sake what ails you?"

The woman opened and shut her mouth several times in a vain effort to speak. At last she stammered:

"Gracious countess, do you believe a word, a single word, that the impostor writes?"

"Would I be so composed did I believe it, Martha?" said the countess. "No, no; the man is, in truth, an impostor. The only thing I cannot comprehend about the matter is, for what reason he plays that game with me."

"But I comprehend it, my lady, I fully comprehend it," shrieked the nurse, now fully recovered from her terror. "God in his mercy has protected you. He wanted to commit the same crime for which he received the brand of Cain on his brow—he wished to capture you, in order to send you to Turkey to be sold as a slave."

Incredulously as this statement would have been received by another person, the countess, whose nerves were unstrung by the many strange things she had heard, gave it full credence. Nor was that which the nurse had said an impossibility, for at the commencement of the last century women were kidnapped in Hungary and Austria, and sent to Turkey to be sold as slaves.

The countess sank, half-fainting, into a chair, and the nurse had enough to do to so far restore her that she was enabled to pull the bell and command the servant to tell the Black Mask never to molest them by letters or visits again, unless he wished to have the police set on his track.

"Yes, yes," said the countess to herself, when the servant had departed to fulfill her command, "if this woman had not come I would now be in that bad man's power, and the House of Weiden would have ended in disgrace and bondage."

It seemed as if the count's vital powers had but survived till the moment when he sent from his door the child he had so long and anxiously sought, for they now rapidly decreased. He fell from one fainting-fit to another; it was plain that the hand of death lay on him. The doctor, who had been hastily summoned, shook his head at sight of the patient, then bade the countess and the nurse to leave the room.

"My friend," said he then, "you are a man, and doubtless you are prepared for what I have to tell you."

"I know what you are about to say," said the count, very composedly; "you wish me to settle my affairs with the world, and make my peace with God."

"Yes; man has to die some time, and when that time comes it beseems him to close his account with earth and heaven."

Some more consolatory words the doctor said, then left his patient, while a priest took up his position by the bedside. The count was perfectly calm, but the countess was lost in grief. The last sacraments were administered, and the dying count called his nurse, who immediately stepped up to the bed.

"I have something to request of you, my good Martha; do not forsake my wife, for you have been appointed her guardian by a higher power."

"Never, never will I leave your wife," sobbed Martha, "never, until I have seen her coffin-lid close over her sweet face."

"That will probably not be the case whilst you live, my good Martha, for my wife is still very young."

"Who can say at what time we shall be summoned?" sobbed Martha; "the younger may precede the older."

The count lay quiet awhile, as if lost in thought; then he said:

"Call my wife hither, Martha, and then leave us alone."

The countess came, and threw herself on her knees by the bed. The count comforted her, and said:

"See if we are alone, my love."

The countess arose, looked around the room, opened the door, and glanced into the hall. She forgot, however, to look behind the fire-screen. She returned to her husband, who placed his cold hand on her beautiful golden curls.

"May God protect you, my love, when I am dead," said the count. "You were always a faithful, loving wife, though I was an old man and you a blooming girl when we clasped hands in marriage."

"I loved you, my husband," sobbed the countess; "you were so noble and so good. When my poor parents—whom, alas! I never knew—when they died, you, in your kindness, took pity on the forsaken orphan."

"I often spoke to you about your parents," continued the count. "I told you that you were the daughter of a poor nobleman, who was a friend of mine, and as such I introduced you at court."

"Yes, my husband, but you never mentioned the name of my parents."

The count was silent a moment; he was very weak indeed. After a pause, he said:

"I do not want to part from the world and enter the presence of God with a lie on my lips; therefore I must tell you, my dear wife, my angel—oh, my thoughts are going from me—yes, yes, my wife, I must make a disclosure to you. It may grieve you—grieve—but I cannot die—with a lie on my heart. God has already—punished me for it—our child—he took my heir from me. Quick, my love—come nearer—listen—before it is too late. You are not—not the daughter of a nobleman—not the daughter of a baron—you are the daughter—of a—Jew!"

A double shriek rang through the room, and there was a heavy fall. The countess lay on the floor in a swoon; the count's arms hung helplessly from the bed. His eyes were glassy and wide open—he was dead. The last sound he had heard on earth was the cry which his wife and another person had simultaneously uttered. This other person now came forth from behind the fire-screen. It was Martha, the nurse. She raised her clinched hands at the dead man and fainting woman. She ground her teeth, gasped for air, and then fairly howled the words:

"A Jewess! a Jewess! Ho, ho! the child of a Jewess shall never inherit the estates of Weidens.

"Oh! I knew it; the Black Mask is right; the child lives—the little Jew is not dead. I know now that Kuno lied, that he deceived me; but I will take care that the child shall never be acknowledged. Now the old man is dead, my task begins. Rejoice, Jewess! No one shall dispute your place in the family vault of the Weidens; and it shall be my greatest pride once to be buried beside the baptized Jewess, when I shall have wrested the inheritance from your son, and given it to mine, who is not the descendant of Jews."

CHAPTER XXXVI.
TWO IMPORTANT DISCOVERIES.

THE duke was in a very bad humor this morning. For the last few years he had been suffering with the gout, which, however, did not prevent his rising at his customary early hour and settling himself in a comfortable chair. Thence he issued all commands and gave ear to all visitors. This morning, for the first time since he could remember, he was unable to leave his bed, the old soldier's limbs would not obey his will any more.

After the duke had uttered a considerable number of maledictions, had half pulled out his mustache with rage and had hurled a cup of chocolate at his valet's head, it suddenly occurred to his mind that perhaps Benrimo could cheer him up a little. Accordingly the duke commanded:

"Tell Benrimo to come here!" in a voice as if he were leading a troop to storm a battery, and the twelve gentlemen in waiting rushed off for this oil which was to soothe the agitated humor of h.s royal highness.

Benrimo was standing with his head and hand encircled by his phylactery, his face turned toward the east, repeating the *Shemorah Esrah*, when the duke's deputation burst into the room.

All began to speak at once, but as suddenly ceased when they saw Benrimo's occupation, for so sincere was the devotion with which the Jews in former times performed their prayers that it excited the respect of all Gentiles.

The *Shemorah Esrah* is a prayer consisting of eighteen benedictions, and while reciting this no Jew allowed himself to be interrupted, were the danger ever so great. Thus it was with Benrimo. Although he knew that something extraordinary must have occurred to bring all the duke's attendants into his room, he quietly continued his prayer, hobbled three paces back and as many forward at its close, and then began to say the closing prayers, during which he unwound his phylacteries, folded them artistically and placed them in a little bag. When he had accomplished all this, he turned around to the waiting gentlemen; and now that his face had become visible, we see that it is the same Benrimo we knew in Immenfeld, his hair a little grayer, but otherwise not at all altered.

"Good-morning, gentleman," said he, in a cordial tone.

He was interrupted by a perfect storm of entreaties to come to the duke, who felt very unwell, and was besides in such a bad humor that there would certainly be broken panes and broken heads in the palace before long did not the worthy interpreter (the reader will remember that this was Benrimo's office) hasten to him immediately.

Benrimo seized his crutches and proceeded to hobble away as speedily as could be, but this seemed slow work to the impatient gentlemen, who had already been kept waiting so long; at a sign from one they seized the old man, lifted him on their shoulders and carried him in triumph to the door of the duke's room. This was done so rapidly that the worthy interpreter had not even time to be astonished before the door flew open and he found himself in the presence of the duke.

"Why did you not come sooner?" asked the duke, frowning ominously.

"I was in the presence of the King of all kings, and could not sooner take my leave," answered Benrimo.

This happy answer smoothed out the wrinkles on the duke's brow.

He had his old comrade take breakfast and then sit down beside his bed, all which Benrimo most faithfully did.

Then, in compliance with the duke's earnest entreaty, he lit his pipe and soon the room was filled with fragrant clouds of smoke.

"My friend," began the duke, "I feel that I have not much of life left in me; soon, very soon, you will sit on my bier, attired in all your military equipments. I have adjudged you this post of honor."

"Pshaw, your highness, while there's life there's hope," returned Benrimo, vigorously pulling at his pipe; "such a little twinge of gout cannot place stout, vigorous men like you and me on the bier all in a minute. Your highness knows that I have been troubled with this sickness, though, of course, I have the advantage of your highness, inasmuch as I can have the gout only in one foot."

His highness could not resist a smile, and the gentlemen in waiting rejoiced to see a gleam of light break athwart the dark cloud of his ill-humor. But their joy was of short duration, for suddenly turning to them the duke said:

"Drones, what do you stand there and stare at me for? Away! Benrimo is enough company for me!"

Much crestfallen, they vanished, and the duke and Benrimo were left alone.

"Benrimo," said the duke, "if I were not ashamed, I would send for the Black Mask and hear what he says about my sickness."

"Your highness may do that without scruple," returned Benrimo; "he is said to be an excellent physician; the city continually sings his praises."

"Yes, but—Benrimo, I am almost ashamed to say it—there is something supernatural about the Black Mask!"

"H-m, h-m!" muttered Benrimo; "what have you heard about the Black Mask that is supernatural?"

"Well, my valet told me that he was seen at the same time in three different places in the Ghetto."

"Nonsense, your highness; some one, who knows how ready the Jews are to believe in miracles, has played off this practical joke by imitating the Black Mask's dress."

"You may be right, Benrimo; I never thought of that, although it is so probable. In your case, my friend, the talmudical proverb proves its truth: 'Where there is Torah, there is wisdom,'" said the duke, fairly relieved.

After a pause, Benrimo began:

"Concerning this physician, there is a question which I wished to ask you long ago: Why do you not command this mysterious doctor to lay aside his mask and show himself as other people do?"

"I have given him express permission to wear such a mask."

Greatly astonished, Benrimo returned:

"Then your highness knows him personally?"

"I? No; not at all."

"Did he petition your highness?"

"It is altogether a very odd affair, and I am surprised to think I did not confide it to you long ago. But I have grown very forgetful of late," said the duke. "When I think over the matter, it only heightens my distrust of the Black Mask."

"All this excites my interest, your highness."

The duke was much diverted by his friend's curiosity, and purposely hesitated in order to increase Benrimo's impatience. At last he said:

"Go to my desk, and look for a yellow paper which looks and smells very mildewy. When you have found it, read it; it will partly explain the matter to you."

Benrimo searched among the duke's papers, and soon found the one he had described to him.

"This actually smells as if it came from the grave," said he, slowly. "Doesn't it?"

"Well, just read it."

Benrimo read:

"From the grave of the physician, Rabbi Isaac Mundolfo, in Rome:

"If his highness, Francis XII., still thinks of the service the undersigned once rendered him, he will permit the latter's deputy to go about in his highness' city with a mask on his face.

"Isaac Mundolfo,

"Died in the dungeons of the Inquisition at Rome."

Benrimo was about to express his contempt of such a plain piece of forgery, when he suddenly recollected that a person of his faith was mentioned in it, and he did not know in what relation the latter stood to the duke. He therefore dissembled great astonishment, and uttered several ejaculations indicative of surprise.

"Yes, yes," said the duke; "it is astonishing; all the more as there is truth in the letter. This Isaac Mundolfo was the most eminent physician in his time. You know that I like learned Jews, and I visited this one in his dwelling, in the Ghetto, every time I went to Rome. I owe my recovery from a very dangerous sickness to him. On some idle pretext he was thrown into the dungeons of the Inquisition, and there he is said to have died."

"Who brought this letter to your highness?"

"A most remarkable messenger—a Franciscan friar, who declared to me that Mundolfo had given it to him, for he had long ago foreseen that some misfortune threatened me and my country, and that this Black Mask could avert it, if I placed no obstacles in his way."

"The old gentleman is beginning to be a little childish," thought Benrimo; "but I will be silent for the present, and try to discover the purpose of this matter, which is nothing but a lie from beginning to end."

Aloud he said:

"And does not your highness wish to send for the Black Mask after such a warm recommendation?"

"What do you think, old friend? Come, tell me."

"I would certainly have him come, for it is not to be denied that there is something curious about this matter."

"That is just what I think; and you, Benrimo, shall yourself go and summon him. Listen, old friend," continued the duke. "Formerly I did not give the least credence to such wonderful tales, and now I am perfectly set on them. How comes that?"

"Old age is the cause of that;—and weakening of the mental faculties," he added, under his breath.

A short silence ensued.

The duke broke this, by saying:

"Now that old age is coming on me, I have thoughts which never troubled me before, and I wish nothing more ardently than that I had an heir to succeed me. It vexes me to think that my flourishing little country, which I have kept in such good order, will fall to the emperor."

"Yes, your highness, I believe you; but it cannot be altered."

"If I had not been so obstinate things might have been otherwise. But I could not acknowledge my brother's marriage, although his wife was of a noble English family. He wrote the most touching letters to me from America; I, however, was hard-hearted enough to withhold my sanction. He fell in battle, and I never heard anything of his wife again. Probably she is dead."

"Did your brother leave any children?" asked Benrimo.

"I never knew that he had any; and even if this was the case, it would be too late now to institute a search for them. It is better so, for my subjects are reconciled to the thought of reverting to the emperor after my death, and no one ever knew of my brother's marriage, excepting myself. Let us drop this disagreeable subject, Benrimo. Go, see if there are any letters or petitions for me. If so, send them here."

Benrimo rang the bell, and a servant came in loaded with letters. The duke, according to his usual custom, took them up one by one, and after reading each, handed it to Benrimo, with some observation or other, which the latter marked down on the margin. Suddenly the duke uttered a cry of surprise.

"Look here," said he, agitatedly; "tidings of my brother; he left a child, a son, who is now in this country. He came from America with his mentor, for whom he begs leave to be admitted to speech with me. As credentials he has inclosed the letters I wrote to my brother at the time."

Benrimo looked at the letters. They were genuine, there was not a doubt about that, he knew the duke's hand too well. He silently handed them back.

"Well, why do you not rejoice with me? Do you doubt the genuineness of these letters?"

"For the present—no. It all depends what the future will bring forth, your highness. As soon as your highness is well enough to leave your bed, you had better see this man."

"Oh, you unfeeling, hard-hearted man," said the duke. "In the evening of my life God grants my most ardent wish, and you speak of waiting and the future. No, no, my Benrimo, you have not spoken wisely this time. Ring the bell, quick, I am in a hurry."

Benrimo silently did as he was bid. When the servant entered, the duke called him:

"Is the person who brought this letter still in the anteroom?"

"Yes, your highness, a very remarkable man, with a face as red as copper."

"That is he, that is he; bring him in," cried the duke, excitedly.

Shortly after, the humpbacked, strangely dressed man whom we once saw in Duke street entered the room.

He immediately sank on his knees by the bedside and said with a foreign accent:

"The Red Arrow is a great chief, but bows the knee before the hoary chieftain of the pale-faces."

The duke's eyes shone with joy. Benrimo remained quite passive.

"Welcome, stranger yet friend; arise! What good tidings do you bring?"

"The Red Arrow brings the white chieftain greeting from the great white warrior long ago went to the pleasant hunting-grounds of his white brethern, and greeting from the squaw of the great warrior, and from the White Eagle Alfred, the noble son of the white chieftain, whom his white brothers called 'Wimmerstein' and his red brothers the 'White Panther.'"

"And where is your ward, the White Eagle?" asked the duke, who had great difficulty in understanding the figurative speech of the Indian.

"The Red Arrow knew not if the White Eagle would be welcome to his relative; therefore he sped on in advance to see and question if his eyes would look with favor on the White Eagle."

"Hasten, my friend, hasten," cried the duke, almost beside himself, "I have perchance but a few more days to live, and much still remains to be done."

The Indian seemed very well acquainted with court etiquette, for, without answering a word, he bowed, and stepping backward to the door, left the duke's apartment.

The duke opened his mouth and was about to address Benrimo, who was sitting very thoughtfully by the bed, and smoking very industriously, when the servant once more came in with a handful of papers.

"What are those, Klas?" asked his highness, provoked at his interruption.

"Death-warrants, your highness," returned Klas, in a sepulchral voice.

"I shall sign no death-warrants to-day, Klas. But stay. Whose are these? You seem to have a perfect pile of them."

"They are the warrants of the captain's band."

"Give them here, Klas—there, hold the inkstand; these rogues have troubled me enough. For years and years they rendered my country unsafe, and just to-day, I will send them to the gallows, so that my successor will find the land purged of them. But where is the warrant of the ringleader, Trumpcard?"

"Does not your highness recollect that he was not captured, and that the police scour the country for him in vain?"

"Oh, yes," said the duke, continuing to write assiduously; "I recollect; my head is so weak nowadays. Who put us on the track of these rascals?"

"A complete list of the criminals with the place of their concealment was sent to the head of the police."

"Yes, yes, Klas, I recollect; it must have been one of the band who betrayed them."

"One of the band—they call him Devil's Fred, and he

is the most expert counterfeiter of them all—maintains that it was Trumpcard himself who betrayed them."

"Perhaps, perhaps," returned the duke absently, his thoughts again wholly with the Indian.

"Does your highness know," said Klas, gathering the signed death-warrants, "that Devil's Fred says he knows who Trumpcard actually is?"

"Who, Klas?"

"I do not believe it myself," said Klas, hesitatingly, "all the more as the rest of the band concur in the statement, but still it may be so."

The duke had become attentive again; he knew Klas' peculiarity of hesitating, when he had anything disagreeable to communicate; therefore he said:

"Do not be afraid, Klas, speak out."

"Well, then, do not let it startle your highness," said Klas; "Trumpcard is—so Devil's Fred says—no other than Egmont of Weiden, the expelled cadet."

"Just heavens!" cried the duke, and Benrimo almost fell to the floor, for in his fright he had forgotten his wanting leg, and had sprung up from his chair.

CHAPTER XXXVII.
TWO OLD FRIENDS FORM AN ALLIANCE.

FOUR weeks had elapsed since the events described in the last chapter. Through the whole duchy the surprising news was spread, that a nephew of the duke had come from America, that he would probably be the successor to the throne, and that the duke even had it in mind to resign in favor of his nephew, as soon as his acknowledgment by the emperor had taken place, for which he had already instituted all necessary steps.

The young prince, as a matter of course, was domiciled in the duke's palace, and all who had seen and conversed with him were charmed by his amiability and condescension.

In truth, this young prince was a most beautiful young man. The color of his face was somewhat dark, as were also the curls which fell to his shoulders; his figure was rather delicate, a small mustache adorned his upper lip, and gave a saucy appearance to his face. His eyes indeed might have been better; they were too light a blue, and protruded a little too much from their sockets.

As in all extraordinary cases, many stories circulated concerning the prince and his uncle, the duke. Thus it was whispered about that the prince, on the occasion of his being presented to his uncle by the humpbacked Indian, had trembled very much, and been hardly able to keep his feet; and it was even maintained that terror had forced drops of perspiration to his brow, which had been plainly seen by people who were present at the time. The presentation had taken place in the duke's bedroom, as his impatience would not permit him to put it off until such time when he could be able to leave his bed.

Of course the youth's agitation was ascribed to the impressions made on him by the uncle he had never seen, his ignorance of court life, and the astonishment with which the splendor of all he saw filled the "half-savage," as he was universally called. Gradually, however, this uneasiness disappeared, especially when the duke, after attentively regarding him for awhile, cried out:

"Truly, I would have acknowledged this young man as my nephew, without any other proof than the striking resemblance he bears to my deceased brother."

A few veteran officers who had known the duke's brother did not concur in this opinion; but who would dare dispute a duke's word? Besides, the duke, who was brought up with his brother, ought to remember him better than people who had but casually seen and spoken with him.

Another of the prince's peculiarities was that he rejected all the attendants the duke assigned to him, and refused to inhabit the splendid suit of apartments in front of the palace which had been selected for him. He took possession of a few rooms in a side wing, and was attended only by his mentor, the old humpbacked Indian, who guarded him jealously, and lay before his door at night, with his tomahawk within reach.

Again the prince, though of a jovial temperament, was possessed of such delicate nerves that he could not bear to see a doctor beside a sick-bed, and invariably hastily retired when the duke's physician was announced.

The latter had now for some time been the Black Mask, whom the duke had summoned on the day after his nephew's arrival. Since he had submitted to his treatment the duke's health had improved noticeably, and he hoped soon to be fully recovered.

* * * * * *

The Black Mask sat in his office, waiting for those who come to him for help. A fair-haired boy was playing about the room; from time to time he ran up to the doctor, who seemed in a very thoughtful mood, caressed him and chatted with him. Each time the latter was the case, the doctor would reprove the child for the jargon he spoke in, and repeat to him the proper way it ought to be said, which the boy, however, never remembered.

"Why can't a pody speak like they to in the Ghetto?" asked the boy, impatiently.

"It is not proper for you to do so, my son," returned the Black Mask, gently. "I have already told you that your parents are of noble lineage, and you will soon be restored to them. By that time you must be able to speak in a manner which will not make you an object of ridicule to all Gentiles."

"I am no count," cried the boy, peevishly; "I am Pinkus' poy from the Ghetto, and I suppose you'll pring me pack there when I am well again."

The doctor was about to return an answer, when the door was opened, and a servant ushered in Benrimo.

"Welcome, thrice welcome, my dear sir," cried the Black Mask, joyously, stretching forth both his hands to the old gentleman, and leading him to a chair, while he sat down beside him.

"I suppose you are curious to know the cause of my

coming here to-day, doctor? I have not only learned to prize your skill, but, taking such a liking to you, I feel that I can confide in you. Your voice sounds as familiar and pleasing to my ears as the voice of an old, tried friend; and yet I am certain that I never met you before. I have come to-day to take you into my confidence, albeit a man as old and as experienced in the ways of the world as I ought not to trust his secret to a man whose face he has never seen, not to mention the fact of his not even knowing his name."

Without returning a word, the Black Mask applied a silver whistle to his mouth, and its shrill sound soon brought a servant to the room.

"Take away the child," said the Black Mask.

Benrimo's attention was attracted to the child, and expressing his admiration of the boy's beauty, he asked:

"Is this your child, doctor?"

"No; it belongs to an acquaintance of yours, Rabbi Benrimo!"

"Of mine? To whom? I cannot remember having ever seen the boy."

The physician raised his hand, and took off his mask for a moment.

"Great Heavens!" cried Benrimo, "is it possible; you are——"

"Sh—sh," said the physician, replacing his mask; "now you not only know my face, but my name. Well, why do you not embrace me, sir?"

Tears gushed from the old man's eyes as he affectionately embraced the young physician.

"But, tell me, how has all this come about?" asked Benrimo, after he had somewhat recovered from his astonishment and joy.

"At the time when this mask falls from my face forever, all will be made clear to you, Rabbi Benrimo. But now that you know, you can trust in me; tell me the purpose of your visit."

"Listen, then. I am afraid that all is not as it should be, about the young prince."

"Indeed!" asked the Black Mask, astonished, "what gives you reason to think so?"

"Well, on the whole there is actually nothing to make me think so, but still I suspect him."

"Why, are not the proofs of his identity sufficiently satisfactory?"

"Yes, and no," said Benrimo. "A person will not wait twenty years, if he thinks he has pretensions, to a throne. The duke is ill, and not so sound in judgment as I, else he would have been struck by this, as well as by many other matters that surprise me."

"But have you not drawn the attention of the duke, whose right hand you are, to this?"

Benrimo sighed, then said:

"Since the prince and his Indian are at court, my influence with the duke has decreased daily, and it will not be long ere he will grow altogether tired of the interpreter, and send him to the Ghetto."

The Black Mask reflected silently for awhile, then said:

"I really have no opinion in this matter, for I have not even seen the young prince."

"That, also, is another of my observations. However engrossed in conversation the prince may be, when you are announced, he leaves the room in strange haste. His pretense that he cannot bear to see a physician beside a sick-bed is perfectly ridiculous; I cannot help thinking that he has some cause to fear you, and for this very reason I wish that you could see him."

"I can remember the Indian very well," returned the Black Mask, thoughtfully. "I saw him when he arrived in the city, but at that time, the pretender was not there, or else I took no notice of him in the crowd. The Indian did not seem at all out of the way to me."

"Well, the prince is so all the more, and I entreat you to see him."

"But how can I bring this about, if, as you say, he always hastily beats a retreat when I am announced?"

"Come with me now. The prince is generally with his highness at this hour. I will tell the servant to announce me only; you shall step in behind me."

"But what cause shall I state for a visit to the duke at this unusual time? It is now late in the afternoon, and I always go to him in the morning."

"Tell his highness that you wish to change the prescription you gave him this morning. He will take the excuse graciously."

"That will do," said the Black Mask; "come, let us go immediately."

The servant helped the Black Mask on with his cloak, and he and Benrimo entered the carriage which rapidly conveyed them to the palace. As Benrimo had planned, they did.

The physician entered the duke's apartment behind Benrimo, and was so well covered by the latter's colossal frame that both were in the center of the room before he was observed.

The young prince was chatting in a lively tone to his uncle; but when his eyes fell on the Black Mask, who appeared to have risen from the ground before him, he broke off in the middle of a word, and fell into a violent fit of trembling. His hands shook as with an ague, and his eyes protruded even more than usually from their sockets.

The duke, very much astonished, though not displeased, asked what brought his doctor at such an unusual hour; the latter answered as Benrimo had bidden him, without, however, for a moment turning his eyes from the young prince, who grew more and more embarrassed.

As Benrimo had said, the duke was well pleased with the doctor's excuse, the latter's care gratified him. He began a conversation with the Black Mask, during the progress of which the young prince endeavored to slip off, but the doctor maneuvered so skillfully as to gain a perfect view of his face before he succeeded in escaping.

Had the Black Mask heard what the prince muttered as the door closed behind him, he could not so composedly have continued his conversation with the duke.

Benrimo impatiently awaited the time when the duke would dismiss his physician; when it at length arrived, he begged for permission to accompany the Black Mask.

"Well," asked he, when both were once more in the carriage, "do you know the prince?"

"I know him."

"Is he a prince or an impostor?"

"He is an impostor," briefly answered the doctor.

"Will you unmask him?"

"When the time will have come, yes. But, Rabbi Benrimo, as you value your life, and the lives of thousands of Jews in this city, betray not a syllable of what I have told you."

"I can be silent," Benrimo solemnly said.

The Black Mask invited Benrimo to come to his office, when the latter again saw the beautiful fair-haired boy, and immediately recurred to the former conversation about him.

"My dear doctor," began Benrimo, "you said before that this child belongs to one of my acquaintances. Will you not explain this more clearly?"

"Certainly; he is the heir of the Count of Weiden."

For a moment Benrimo looked at the Black Mask in silent amazement. Then he said:

"How comes it that you have him here?"

The Black Mask proceeded to relate how he had found the child in a tavern laying lifeless on the floor, had taken it home, and, with the aid of another doctor, restored it to health.

"More I cannot tell you, for an oath I once took begins to lay its fetters on my tongue," continued the doctor.

"You need tell me no more; I guessed the rest long ago, and counseled the Countess of Weiden to fly from the machinations of the Baroness Weiden and Baron Witzleb, although at the time I did not mention these by name. I was certain that none but these had stolen the young heir, in order to gain possession of his inheritance."

It was now the Black Mask's turn to be astonished.

"That reminds me," said he, smiling, "of the explanation you once gave to a little boy about prophet and prophecies."

"But why do you not restore the child to its mother, who would certainly welcome him most gladly?" asked Benrimo.

"She does not want him," said the Black Mask. "I offered the child to her at the time her husband was still living; she rejected it, and threatened to complain of me to the police did I not leave her in peace."

"I cannot comprehend this," ejaculated Benrimo.

"Oh, it's easy to comprehend it; she thinks I am an impostor; a woman whose evil aspect aroused my disgust the first time I saw her, has probably maligned me to the countess."

"And can you imagine who this woman is?" asked Benrimo, in suspense.

"Yes, at least I suspect it."

"Well, I am quite certain," cried Benrimo, "this woman is the Baroness Weiden."

"I thought so, too; but this woman occupies the position of a servant, and I believe that she is some creature commissioned by the baroness."

"No, no; it is she herself in some disguise," cried Benrimo. "The sooner she is unmasked the better; the countess is in bad hands."

"Where are you going?" cried the Black Mask, as Benrimo rose hastily from the chair.

"To the Countess of Weiden, my friend."

"At such an unseemly hour?"

"And were it midnight I would go! God be with you, my friend." And Benrimo hobbled off as fast as he could.

Hardly an hour subsequently, Benrimo's carriage again stopped before the physician's house. The servant could not assist him up the stairs fast enough for his impatience. The doctor was in his private room, to which the servant did not dare to admit Benrimo; but the vigorous old man pushed him to one side, and opened the door.

He hesitated a moment when he saw a Franciscan friar in the company of the Black Mask. But the latter hastily arose and asked:

"For God's sake, what has happened?"

"Hasten, hasten—the Countess of Weiden is dying!"

The physician seized his hat, and turning to the monk, cried:

"Come, Father Anselmo. We require your assistance!"

The three hastened down-stairs as fast as Benrimo's crutches would permit, and a minute later the carriage was rolling at a furious rate of speed over the stone pavements of the city streets, out into the country.

CHAPTER XXXVIII.
ALMOST TOO LATE.

BENRIMO's carriage drew up before the portals of Count Weiden's park. The porter opened the gate, and the vehicle rolled rapidly up to the villa. Before the Black Mask, who was the first to alight, had time to raise the knocker, the door was opened, and a woman, apparently anxious and inquisitive as to the cause of such noise at an hour so unseemly, made her appearance. Hardly had she recognized, by the light which streamed out from the wall, who it was that stood before her, than she uttered a loud cry, and attempted to close the door; but the Black Mask, who had anticipated this maneuver, opposed her, and, assisted by the exertions of his two friends, who had by this time joined him, the door was soon pushed open, and the three entered the house.

When the woman perceived that she could not keep

back the intruders, she broke into loud cries of "Murder—thieves—fire!" which soon brought a number of domestics, both male and female, to the scene of disturbance. But here were three powerful agents which prevented their interfering, and, like the knights of the fairy-tale, turned them into stone. First, a monk, a person who at that time was regarded by the lower classes with the most profound veneration; then the well-known "interpreter" of the duke, a man to whom one had but to turn if desirous of a favor from the duke—and such a man might not be insulted with impunity; and, lastly, the mysterious Black Mask, the terror and delight of all ghost-loving gossips.

The united population of the city would have been powerless against this extraordinary trio—what, then, could these few servants do?

When the woman saw the impression this dreaded trio produced on the servants, she endeavored to slip off, but felt herself held by a strong hand, and, looking up, caught sight of the face, distorted by rage and contempt, of Father Anselmo.

"Lead us to the sick-bed of the countess," he commanded, in a stern tone, "or I, who have recognized you, will hang you to the posts of this door with my own hands!"

With a tottering step, and firmly held by the enraged friar's hand, the nurse ascended the stairs. The physician and Benrimo followed, while the trembling domestics, who had not yet recovered from their terror, brought up the rear. The woman led the way into a room which was dimly lighted by a lamp hanging from the ceiling.

On a couch could be indistinctly seen a female figure, writhing in pain.

"Lights!" shouted Benrimo, in a voice as loud as if he were commanding a battalion.

The servants rushed off, and soon the room was brightly lit up. Father Anselmo and the Black Mask stepped up to the couch, regarded the lady, and simultaneously cried out:

"Poisoned!"

The terrible word was taken up and repeated by the pale lips of all assembled in the room.

"We come too late," muttered the Black Mask; "she is already unconscious."

"I almost fear so," said Father Anselmo; "if my new remedy fails, she is lost."

The friar drew from his habit a small case, and, opening it, disclosed about one hundred tiny vials. His practiced glance immediately found the one he wanted; with a sure hand, he poured a single drop on a spoon, and, mixing it with a little water, infused the portion into the mouth of the countess, while the Black Mask held apart her rigidly closed teeth. But suddenly Father Anselmo seemed to recollect something, for he looked searchingly about the room; she whom he sought had vanished.

"Away!" cried he to the servants, who were still in the room; "away! search for the woman who conducted us hither! You ought not to have let her go, for it is she who poisoned the countess. Look for her, and if you find her, clutch her firmly, for she must be delivered up for justice."

The servants immediately dispersed, and soon their searching steps and low cries to each other could be heard echoing in the spacious house.

Father Anselmo took up his post at the lady's head, and the Black Mask stood at her feet, attentively marking every breath that passed her pallid lips, while Benrimo was leaning on his crutch in the center of the room. It was a touching and at the same time an unearthly scene—two mysterious men, the one with his face enveloped in the folds of a monkish cowl; the face of the other covered by a black mask, sternly and sadly watching by the couch on which a blooming, high-born woman struggled with death; and in the center of the room the colossal figure of Benrimo—in whose gold-embroidered uniform, and many decorations, the lights danced and sparkled—standing solemn and motionless, like a statue of war, whose business is death, bewailing the sacrifice of this fair young life.

The moaning of the suffering lady, and the ticking of the clock against the wall, seemingly hastening on to keep pace with the flying pulse of the sufferer, were for a long, long time the only sounds that broke the dread silence in the room, in which Death waved his freezing pinions.

Suddenly there was a thrilling, awful cry, apparently from the most remote part of the house, and this was repeated by many voices. Immediately after, rapid steps were heard approaching the room, and several servants came in with deadly pale faces, and related, with trembling lips, that the nurse, after long searching, had at last been found in one of the attics, where she had concealed herself behind a pile of rubbish. Hardly did she find herself discovered than she darted with the agility of a cat to the gable-window, and, before any of them even thought of the possibility of such an undertaking, climbed out, and, with a dreadful cry, precipitated herself from the roof.

There was a trampling of feet ascending the stairs, and Father Anselmo, hastening to the door, beheld a ghastly burden, which was being slowly borne in his direction. He signed to the bearers to deposit it on the floor of the hall, and, bending down, proceeded to examine it. He drew off the cap on the head, and, stroking back the brown hair, he was not greatly astonished to find it remaining in his hands, while scanty whitish locks came to view beneath it.

At the same time two voices cried:

"The Baroness Weiden of Immenfeld."

Yes, it was indeed the woman whose crimes were about countless, the woman who had once ruined a whole family because its head would not abet her in crime, the woman who had wished to let the Jewish widow and her son starve in her dungeons, the woman who had murdered her relatives to gain for the son, who had attacked her, an inheritance which was not rightfully his; and this woman now lay a mutilated mass on the floor of the corridor which led to the room where her latest victim, the Countess of Weiden, lay struggling with death.

"God is just!" said Father Anselmo, as he arose from the dead body and signed to the servants to bear it away. They returned in silence to the sick-room; not a word was exchanged concerning the dreadful discovery that had just been made; the suffering lady absorbed all their attention. There was no sensible improvement in her condition, and Father Anselmo tried another drop of his elixir.

Once more the physicians sat in stern silence by the bedside, while Benrimo, who had taken a seat at the table in the center of the room, carelessly played with a silver casket that stood on it. It was not locked, the lid fell back, and disclosed a number of papers.

Benrimo absently glanced at them, when his eyes were suddenly riveted by something he saw on one.

Seizing it, he unfolded it, and was soon absorbed by its contents.

"Remarkable, most remarkable!" he muttered again and again, "where have I heard the name mentioned in this baptismal certificate? Strange, strange! a Jewish name and a Christian certificate. Where did I hear—ah! I recollect, the duke spoke of it in connection with—with—I have it—with the Black Mask."

"Doctor," said Benrimo, almost loud, "can you tell me something concerning the name Isaac Mundolfo?"

The Franciscan Friar and the Black Mask started violently, and both arose, when a low cry from the couch diverted their attention.

The sick lady lay very quietly, the convulsions had ceased, and her large blue eyes were fixed with a conscious but inexpressibly terrified expression on the Black Mask,

Soon they wandered to the friar, and with a pleading look at him turned again to the object of her dread. The latter immediately understood her, and stepped back, though very unwillingly. The friar signed to him and Benrimo to leave the room, for the sick lady had whispered to him that she wished to prepare for death. She could not think otherwise than that the monk had been sent for to hear her last confession. Father Anselmo, in order not to excite her, humored her wish and prepared to listen.

In the meanwhile Benrimo and the Black Mask who had retired to an adjacent room, conversed, as may be easily imagined, about the events of the evening, and the sudden end which had been put to the Baroness Welden's machinations.

Benrimo now thought it high time that he should be told something of the Black Mask's adventures, and his astonishment knew no bounds when he heard things which he would never have even dreamed of as being possible. His life in comparison seemed a mere cipher.

But the Black Mask did not tell Benrimo that Father Anselmo, for whom the old soldier conceived a most intense veneration, was a baptized Jew, and Benrimo was greatly surprised that a Franciscan friar could act so unselfishly, and commit such a sin as to tear a proselyte from the arms of the Church.

The night advanced, and still all was silent in the sickroom. The two friends grew uneasy as hour after hour passed and no news came from the patient. One of the servants slipped in every now and then to inquire about their mistress.

At last the sun already threw its first rays on the beautiful landscape and on the villa, which looked so calm and peaceful, and yet held much crime and suffering within its walls; the Black Mask's anxiety would permit him to wait no longer, and he arose and crept to the door of the sick-room where he listened intently for some sound. Suddenly he started and drew back hastily.

Benrimo anxiously asked:

"Did you hear anything?"

"Yes, I heard the heavy sobs of a man, and a woman's convulsive weeping. Oh! it must have been a dreadful confession to make a man like Father Anselmo shed tears."

"Who can know," returned Benrimo, "what dark deeds lie buried in the heart of man, not to be revealed until the last day shall bring them to light? But let us speak of something else; it always oppresses me to think that a person, in order to get rid of the load of his consience, confides it to the bosom of another, thus making him an accomplice and part bearer, as it were, of his burden. For this reason I always consider confession as a desecration of the human heart; it demoralizes the one who confesses, and makes a priest, who is conscientious, unhappy for life by overwhelming him with the dark secrets of his fellow-being; while it gains for the unprincipled priest a terrible dominion over those whose secrets he knows."

"Father Anselmo is not of your opinion," returned the Black Mask; "he maintains that all the grandeur of the Catholic Church consists in this, and that by this means she gains the allegiance of her subjects."

"Then Father Anselmo thinks as I do," eagerly returns Benrimo; "in the confessional lies the might of the Catholic Church, and that is just the misfortune. In Rome every word becomes known that a prince or minister has intrusted to his father confessor, and the Pope holds the destinies of nations in his hand, being enabled by betrayed secrets of the confessional to govern kings and princes as if they were puppets, while leaving them to think they act only according to their own royal pleasure. But let us drop this subject; tell me, rather, what you know concerning the name Isaac Mundolfo?"

"Whence know you that name?" returned the Black Mask, "and what leads you to think I know anything of it?"

"I heard it for the first time when the duke spoke to me about you. His highness permitted me to read a letter signed by the name of Isaac Mundolfo. This evening I found a paper that lay in a casket in the sick-room, and on it was written the name Isaac Mundolfo. My curiosity being excited by this, I unfolded the paper and found that it was a baptismal certificate, drawn up at Rome in favor of——"

The shrill tinkle of a bell resounded from the sick-room, and the Black Mask hastily followed the summons, while Benrimo, whose curiosity in regard to the name of Isaac Mundolfo was again disappointed, hobbled after him and found him politely waiting at the door of the room, which they now both entered together.

CHAPTER XXXIX.

FATHER AND DAUGHTER.

When Benrimo and the Black Mask entered the sick-room, they found Father Anselmo sitting beside the couch of the countess. His right hand held both the lady's, while the other lay affectionately on her beautiful golden curls. Although Anselmo's eyes were swollen with weeping, his face bore an expression of indescribable bliss, while the blue eyes of the countess rested with infinite love and veneration on the monk's countenance.

"Do not be afraid, my love," said Father Anselmo, softly, as he observed the terrified look that crept into her eyes as she caught sight of the Black Mask, "this man is my friend, and all my secrets are known to him; I have more confidence in him, than in any other person in all the world, and his name will yet become famous in the land. He was maligned to you because he knew the designs of your enemies and wished to frustrate them; look at him as your brother."

"You regard me with astonishment, my friends," continued he, turning to Benrimo and the Black Mask; "yea, God has performed a miracle; join me in praising Him, but not that God to whom I and this patient sufferer seemed devoted, not that God who incites men to persecute and harm their fellow-beings, but praise the only and mighty God of Israel, who has vouchsafed me, the apostate, the happiness of finding my child. Yes, yes, Joseph, down with your mask, that my Ella, my beloved child, may look into your dear honest eyes; I have found her; the Countess Matilda of Weiden is Ella, the daughter of Isaac Mundolfo!"

The Black Mask tore the covering from his face, and, falling on his knees before the countess, kissed her delicate hands amidst streaming tears, while the sick lady looked with astonishment at the manly beauty of the young man's face, and could not suppress a faint smile as she thought how dreadful her imagination had pictured it.

Then Joseph repeatedly embraced his dear teacher, and old Benrimo was made acquainted with the remarkable destinies of father and daughter.

"God is great," said he when he heard all; "and as it is written, he gathers his people from the ends of the world. 'Who turneth the heart of the fathers to the children, and the heart of the children to the fathers.' How wonderfully has He ordained it that three Jews meet at the sick bed of a fourth who was robbed from them, and thus every foreign element is excluded."

Joseph felt the pulse of the countess and became convinced that she was out of all danger, although so weak that she could hardly utter a sound. Then he whispered to Father Anselmo that he required his advice in an important matter; the reader will easily imagine in what.

When Father Anselmo arose to accompany Joseph from the room, the countess pleadingly whispered the word—

"Father!"

The monk pressed his hand on his swelling heart, as he heard this word from the mouth of his recovered treasure. For years and years he had been used to being addressed a hundred of times daily by the title "Father," yet this single whispered appeal held more of happiness to him than the numberless times he had been called by that name.

"Be composed, my dear Ella; I shall soon be back; in the meanwhile Benrimo, who proved himself your friend years ago, shall take my place by your side."

Anselmo and Joseph—the latter resuming his mask—repaired to the room in which the latter, with Benrimo, had passed most of the night, and here teacher and pupil again embraced each other in overflowing joy.

"I know why you wish to speak to me," then said Father Anselmo; "you wish to bring her son to the countess, to my Ella."

"You have divined it, my dear teacher, and I wish to know if this can be done without danger to her?"

"Till now," returned Father Anselmo, "I have carefully refrained from mentioning the child to my daughter. The scenes of this night; her confession, which made me the happiest man in the world, by revealing to me the secret her husband had told her with his dying breath, and our subsequent recognition of each other, have so exhausted her little strength that more excitement would certainly prove dangerous. I have not even disclosed to Ella who her nurse really was, nor the dreadful death she met with. I will now take leave of Ella for a few hours and repair to your house in order to prepare all necessary medicines for her. There we can discuss this matter more at length."

"Very well, I shall wait for you."

The morning was now far advanced, and a servant came to summon the gentlemen to a breakfast which had been prepared for them. The sick lady also partook of a few morsels, and then a messenger was dispatched to the city to notify the authorities of the events that had transpired in the villa (regarding the suicide of the nurse, etc).

The Black Mask—for now that he has resumed his mask we must call him so again—sent another servant to his house for his carriage and Margareth, the nurse who had waited upon the little boy. When she arrived, he bound her to silence concerning her little charge, and having given her all due instructions, and seen her installed beside the lady's bed, he urged his friend to depart. Benrimo, also, who did not wish to miss his morning prayer, pressed Father Anselmo to go.

When the latter bent over his daughter's couch to take leave of her, she twined her arms around his neck, and kissing him tenderly, whispered:

"Father."

For Benrimo and the Black Mask she had a warm pressure of the hand and a sweet smile.

When the three companions and allies in all that is good and noble were in the carriage, the Black Mask said:

"Father Anselmo, you still owe me a continuation of the story you once told me concerning Isaac Mundolfo."

"Yes, yes," said Benrimo, "I should like to know in what manner the name Isaac Mundolfo is connected with——"

But it seemed that the old gentleman was never to have his curiosity appeased, for Father Anselmo, apparently quite disregarding these words, said:

"I understand you, my son; you think, and rightly think, that my daughter has solved me the riddle how she became a countess; but as I cannot tell you this in the presence of this gentleman, whom it will not interest, as he does not know all that has gone before, I commission you to make him acquainted with my story whenever he will have the time to listen to it, and I will then tell the continuation to both of you."

The carriage had by this time reached the ducal palace, and Benrimo was set down at the main entrance. Father Anselmo accompanied the Black Mask to the latter's house. Arrived there, he patiently awaited the opening of the door, and with youthful agility flew up the stairs to the boy's room.

The little fellow was still asleep, but Father Anselmo's kisses awoke him. Hardly had he opened his eyes and seen the figure that bent over him, than an expression of dislike came over his pretty face, and he muttered:

"Go away; you're a Galah (priest)!"

"Ah!" said the friar, softly, "the blood betrays itself Jewish blood will run in the veins in the third and fourth generations." Then he said, aloud:

"Don't you like a Galah?"

"No, no; they are bad to the Jews in the Ghetto; they dislike all of them, and treat them badly."

"But I have been told that you are no Jew."

"Yes, so they said to me, and called me a Christian; but I always felt like a Jew, and always kept the commandments of God. And," the boy continued to chat, "I have been told that I am a count. Oh, what nonsense! I know that a Jew can't be a count."

"Wouldn't you like to be a count?"

"If I must be a Christian first, I don't want to be a count. I've got a Hebrew name, and I dislike the Galahim."

Father Anselmo smiled, well pleased, then he said:

"What is your name, my child?"

"Benoni—that means child of pain, Pinkus says, for I caused Pinkus much grief."

"Would you like to have me for your grandfather?" softly asked Father Anselmo, kissing the struggling boy.

"If you will not be a Galah, I shall like to have you for a grandfather; but if you want to be my grandfather, you must give me a mother; for, while all the boys of this street have mothers, I had none. First, Pinkus was my mother, and now comes a Galah and wants to be my grandfather. Oh, how silly!"

Father Anselmo held out his hand to the boy, which the latter very reluctantly took, and then descended with him to the laboratory, where he prepared the medicines for the Countess of Weiden.

The Black Mask had driven out to visit the duke and his other patients. When he returned home, he found

Father Anselmo waiting for him, with a rather serious face.

"What makes you look so gloomy, father?" asked Joseph, wonderingly. "I should think you had no cause for it."

"I am just thinking how it will dampen my Ella's joy—she who is so extremely accomplished, and used only to the most refined society—when we will bring her her child in such a neglected condition. Why, the boy speaks in a manner used only in the Ghetto, although he possesses a good deal of natural wit."

"That is certainly unfortunate, father; but the mother's love will speedily overlook such a fault, especially as it is one which may be corrected in a few months."

"But it will lessen the mother's joy considerably at first."

"You are mistaken, father. Was the Countess of Weiden ashamed to acknowledge her father because he is a baptized Jew?"

"No, no; she made me happy by the joy which she displayed, although she confessed that when she first heard the story of her birth the shock caused her a fainting-fit."

"Well," returned Joseph, "just put yourself in the place of a highly accomplished lady, the wife of a count, and, as she believes, the daughter of a baron, and the poor lady's horror will not seem so improbable to you."

"You are right, my son, as you always are—but what does the servant want?"

The latter announced Benrimo, who immediately after made his appearance, and briefly saluting the Black Mask, hastened to the monk, seized both his hands, and heartily pressing them, cried in a warm tone:

"Permit me thus to express my pleasure at making your acquaintance, Rabbi Isaac Mundolfo. I have shed tears over your unhappy past, and sent a thanksgiving to the Almighty, who had at last blessed you with happiness, as misfortune was tired of persecuting you further."

"You know all?" asked Father Anselmo, surprised.

"Yes," interpolated the Black Mask, "the good old gentleman would not allow me to leave the palace ere I had—of course, under the seal of the greatest secrecy—told him all your story, Father Anselmo, as you had yourself commissioned me."

"And you have come to hear the continuation, all that relates to my daughter, Rabbi Benrimo? Well, so be it."

Father Anselmo drew from his habit a book bound in Morocco leather, and said:

"This book contains notes by Count Weiden's own hand, and was, together with her baptismal certificate, found in a casket by the countess, after her husband's death. She marked those places which had reference to her, and thus I was enabled to read all connectedly in a few minutes.

"The count during his sojourn in Rome, while walking one day past the palace of the Inquisition, remarked a number of people assembled before the chapel close by. On asking what was going on within, he received the answer that a Jewish child was just being baptized.

"Rendered inquisitive by this, he entered and pressed forward to the front, where he caught sight of a beautiful little girl. Although it could walk and speak, it seemed to have no comprehension of the solemn ceremony in process. The count, though a bachelor and no longer young, took such a fancy to the child that he resolved to adopt it and take it to Germany with him. He had no great difficulty in procuring the child, for the Inquisition was anxious to force people to baptism, but did not much care what became of them afterward.

"When the count had convinced the holy fathers that he was a good Catholic, and presented a letter of recommendation from his country's embassador, the child was delivered to him, together with its baptismal certificate, which stated that Ella, the daughter of the Jew Isaac Mundolfo, had received the name of Matilda in holy baptism.

"He traveled about with the child, had her most splendidly educated, and everywhere presented her as the daughter of a deceased noble friend. When Ella attained to years of womanhood, she was of startling beauty, and as the count feared that some young man might deprive him of her, he married her himself, and after having very easily gained her consent, her loving heart asking no more than always to stay with the man who had been so kind to her. Although their married life was unusually happy, the count, after the mysterious disappearance of his son, began to reproach himself in secret for having married a Jewess, even a baptized one, and looked upon the loss of his heir as a punishment for his sin.

"However, he never let the countess suspect anything of this; he loved her far too much for that, and it can be ascribed only to the pangs of his conscience and to ease his heart that he disclosed to her with his dying breath the secret of her birth. That is all I have to read in the count's diary," concluded Father Anselmo.

"But, father, you once told me that when you inquired for your child you received the answer that the name of the gentleman or family who adopted it was not known," said the Black Mask.

"And that with truth, my son," returned Anselmo; "the priests had no intention of putting me on the track of the count, and exposing themselves to the danger of being deprived of a convert. But now, my son, lend me your carriage, for I want to visit *my daughter.*" Father Anselmo uttered the last two words with such loving pride, that both his auditors were overcome with emotion.

CHAPTER XL.
THE COURT-PHYSICIAN TO HIS HIGHNESS.

THE apartments which the young prince and his mentor inhabited were situated, as already told, in a side wing of the ducal palace, and had been newly furnished in honor of the prince.

It was dusk, and the prince, who suffered no attendants near him, had just with his royal hands lit the wax-lights on the silver chandelier.

He threw himself peevishly into an arm-chair and impatiently turned the leaves of a book. His meeting with the Black Mask had left a very unpleasant impression, which he could not efface, upon his mind. He was awaiting his mentor.

The prince never felt easy or safe when the latter was not near, and only reluctantly allowed him to leave his side; but the Indian was obliged to go out now and then in order to procure the funds requisite for their style of living. It is true that the duke had put his treasury at the prince's disposal, but the Indian would not permit him to accept anything, as this might easily bring the duke's enthusiasm down to zero, as poor relations are never agreeable to their wealthy kin.

"So soon, my prince, as you are publicly acknowledged and proclaimed successor to the throne," said the mentor, "you may, for all I shall say to the contrary, dip as deeply as you will into your uncle's purse, but not before. Leave all to me; I have good friends who advance me all I need without charging any interest."

So now the Indian was absent on one of his expeditions, which he had said would take him longer than usual, for he had to journey to a remote convent near the boundary to procure money.

It was yesterday that the prince had met the Black Mask in the duke's apartment, and since then he had kept in his room, giving out that he felt ill, but wished for no visitors, least of all for a doctor.

The prince was desirous of conferring with his mentor before he again ventured into the presence of the duke. For this reason he was so vexed at the Indian's absence.

At last the evening was far advanced, and the prince had given up all hope for the night, when he thought he heard a peculiar knocking at the door which led to his apartments. The room in which he sat was the last of the suite, and all the doors were locked from within.

The young man sprang with alacrity from his arm-chair, and unlocking all the doors, at last beheld the humpbacked Indian whom he had anxiously expected. The latter silently followed him back through all the rooms, carefully locking each, and having reached the last, he locked this also, and with a sigh of relief stretched himself, suddenly appearing of more than medium stature.

"God be thanked that you have come, Red Arrow," said the prince, not at all astonished by this transformation; "never, never have I so longed for your return."

"For Heaven's sake, what has happened?" asked the Indian, in very plain words, not at all the figurative speech he displayed at court; "nothing disagreeable, I hope? Or has the prince committed some piece of folly, and jeopardized his faithful Indian's head as well as his own?"

"Nothing of the kind, Red Arrow—Red Devil I should prefer to say; I was surprised yesterday by the Black Mask."

"Well?" asked Red Arrow, anxiously; and his eyes almost started from their sockets with dread.

"Well, apparently he did not recognize me."

"What do you frighten a body so for, my prince?" very angrily said the mentor.

"I did not know you could get frightened so easily," mockingly said the prince; "I am sure he does not know you, and your fear of him is truly childish. I have every cause to avoid him, for he not only saw me once, but hit me." And the prince gnashed his teeth.

"That has nothing to do with it!" cried the Indian, angrily; "the man intimidates me; and the first time I ever saw him I was overcome by a presentiment that he would conduce to my misfortune—a presentiment which has become partly true, as he is the cause of my having had to relinquish the money from the Jews."

"Yes, so you said once before; but you did not tell me in what way he prevented you."

"I will tell you that at some more opportune time. I do not feel in the mood for it to-day."

"Why? Did you not get any money in the convent you spoke of?"

"Oh, yes; but I did not bring it with me. A confederate is going to fetch it to a certain tavern you know of, to-morrow. The prior did not have as much as I needed on hand."

"In your place I would have chosen another spot, my faithful mentor," said the prince, thoughtfully; "the prince's attendant is known all over the city, and ought not to be seen in a thieves' tavern."

"O most worshipful prince," returned the mentor, mockingly, "do not think I am so foolish as to go there in my character as an Indian. I did not go to the convent as such. I have a very pretty disguise, in which no one suspects the prince's faithful redskin. To what end have we the house in Duke street?"

"That is what I wish to say. But we have strayed from our subject, the Black Mask. What shall we do in regard to him?" asked the prince.

"Yes, yes," returned the Indian, in a low tone; "a few inches of cold steel between his ribs would put him nicely out of the way; but you cannot summon resolution enough for a steady thrust!"

"I have sworn to kill him," said the prince, gloomily; "I perceive very well that there is not room for both of us in the world."

"Well," said the Indian, artfully, "do you want to wait until he makes the same discovery, and puts you out of the way?"

"No, by heavens!" cried the prince, threateningly; "I shall watch all his going in and his coming out, and stab him as I would a dog, and were it only for the evil he did me by restoring the old duke to health and delaying my succession to the throne."

"So be it," cried the Indian, stretching out his hand; "your hand on it."

The prince gave his hand, and excusing himself on a plea of fatigue, retired, not to bed, but to form a plan of attack on the Black Mask.

The Indian threw a contemptuous glance after him, and muttered:

"Coward, you have not even the courage to stab a man in the back."

Then the red man drew a pistol from his embroidered belt, took a tomahawk from a drawer, and lying down before his prince's door, placed both weapons within reach.

The next day passed like all others; the prince had summoned up all his courage and remained with the duke even after the physician was announced. It would have been better for his peace as well as his temper had he retired as usual. On the preceding day, the doctor had told the duke that he would take his leave of him on the morrow, as he now considered his highness fully restored to health.

When the Black Mask entered the duke's apartment, he found Benrimo there as usual, and to his intense astonishment, the young prince.

The duke advanced to meet the physician—a proceeding contrary to all court etiquette—and in an exceedingly gracious manner held out his hand.

"I bid you welcome, my dear sir," said his highness, "and herewith hand you your patent of office as court-physician to the duke of Wimmerstein."

The duke took a roll of parchment which Benrimo, who had likewise arisen, held in his hands, and presented it to the Black Mask.

"This office which I have now conferred on you, entitles you to come to court at all times, and to attend all public banquets; of course you will ever be a most welcome guest at the private table of your sovereign. The

name in this patent has been left for you to fill in, as
Benrimo tells me that you do not wish it to be known."

The Black Mask—also quite in opposition to court
etiquette—kissed the duke's hand and stammered his
thanks; but his highness said:

"Do not thank me, my dear sir, thank old Benrimo,
for he is the manager and contriver of it all. I did not
know of any way in which I could express my gratitude
for the restoration of my health; he it was who advised
me to surprise you in this manner."

The Black Mask hastened to Benrimo, and was about to
kiss his hand, but the old soldier warmly embraced him
and whispered in his ear:

"I betrayed your name to the duke. I spoke to him
of you years ago. Although he said to fill it in, it is
written there by his own hand."

The new court-physician took leave of his highness,
and departed to visit his other patients.

That afternoon several criers, each provided with a
large bell, walked through the streets of the city and proclaimed to the people that his Highness Duke Francis
XII. had pleased to allow his old court physician to retire on a pension, and conferred this position on him so
well known in the city as the "Black Mask."

This news likewise soon spread to the Ghetto. A
proclamation had been sent to the president of the congregation, who could read it very well, and transcribed it
into Hebrew characters for the sexton, Wolf. The latter
passed through all the streets crying it aloud, his lips
quivering and growing quite pale every time he came to
the words "Black Mask."

It cannot be said that the inhabitants of the Ghetto
were particularly pleased to hear what honor was done to
this ominous and mysterious personage; they therefore
received the tidings with great indifference and callousness, conceiving that, if it foreboded no harm for them,
it certainly promised no good.

The news of this distinction burst upon the young

prince like a bombshell. The days on which it had been schemed were those the prince had passed in his apartments, so it came upon him quite unprepared, and put him into an ungovernable rage. Shortly taking leave of his uncle, he hastened to his room, where he found the Indian comfortably smoking his pipe. Breathlessly he related all to his uncle, and swore in a most unprincely manner. But the hunchback only shrugged his high shoulders and said, mockingly:

"And will my white Young Eagle never show his claws to the creeping Black Snake?"

"By Heaven!" cried the prince, clinching his fists, "this black bat shall never eat at the duke's table; I will take his desire for it away. And that old accursed Jew, that one-legged toad; I shall wait with him until my idiotic uncle is dead and buried; then I'll accuse him of high treason and have him cut and quartered!"

"Trisected, my son, you mean to say," mocked the Indian; "you can only have him cut into three pieces, as he is short of a fourth."

"And you can make bad jests at such a time?" yelled the prince, his face quite distorted with rage."

"Why not?" returned the Indian, very coolly; "I rejoice to see how excellently you can play the part of a sovereign, at least in so far as it concerns the quartering of obnoxious courtiers. However," continued he, "I have no more time for you now; I must go to the rendezvous you know of to get my money."

The hunchback put on his cloak and departed. Evening was fast coming on when the left the palace.

The prince enveloped himself in a large cloak, concealed a glittering two-edged dagger in his bosom, and went out directly after his faithful Indian. He had summoned up all his courage, and sworn death to the Black Mask. The prince had purposely assumed no disguise, for he knew that, were he not caught in the very act of committing the deed, no one would think of accusing him of murder, nor even lay hands on him, however near to the scene of it he might be found.

Of course he directed his steps to the street where the Black Mask resided. At this time of day, the physician was usually at home. The prince knew the house, and his design was to ask for the Black Mask and announce his rank. The former would then, as etiquette demanded, come to receive his distinguished visitor in person, upon which the prince would stab him, and then cry for help, as if some one had attempted to murder him, and by mistake hit the doctor.

But at the door the would-be murderer was told that the doctor was not at home, and would not return before midnight, as he had gone to the country. The prince was exceedingly disappointed. All the courage he had summoned up, and the cunning plan he had contrived, were rendered useless, at least for this evening.

He strolled down the street and turned into Duke street, the only one in the city that was illuminated. This was done by means of lamps hanging from chains stretched obliquely across the street. At that time people did not know such a luxury as our illuminated streets. Whoever had occasion to go out at night carried a lantern, or, were he rich enough, had one carried before him. Only the main streets were scantily lighted in the manner we have above described.

The prince halted before the house he had inhabited on his arrival in the city, and deliberated whether he should go in and wait for the Indian's return with the money.

At this moment, a person carrying a lantern came slowly up the street. The blood stagnated in the prince's veins. He took up his position in the shadow of the stairs. The person coming up the street had a mask on his face, and was of slender figure. All this the lantern plainly showed. Now he was but two paces distant from the house where the prince stood—he advanced a step — yes, it was the Black Mask. Now—heavens and earth!—

he placed his foot on the stairs of the house in which the prince once lived, and—a dagger glistens in the uncertain glow of the lantern, and the next moment is plunged deep into the back of the Black Mask.

A thrilling cry broke the silence of the night; the lantern fell to the stone pavement, shivering into a thousand pieces; the tall, slender figure swayed back and forth and fell, face upward, close to the lantern light that still flickered feebly on the ground.

"Wretch!" muttered the trembling murderer, "I must know your face!" and, bending down, he tore off the black mask.

As if himself pierced by a hundred daggers, the murderer recoiled, and howling pitifully, fled away into the night.

CHAPTER XLI.
THE HAND OF GOD.

ON the afternoon preceding the evening on which the events related in the last chapter occurred, Father Anselmo thought the time had arrived for presenting her long-lost child to his daughter. She had by this time fully recovered from the attack on her life, only a lingering weakness remaining, and this Father Anselmo had not considered a sufficient obstacle to prevent his informing her of her prospective happiness. The countess most willingly and gladly believed her father, and with glowing cheeks and beating heart was awaiting her boy's arrival. Every time she heard the rolling of carriage-wheels she rushed to the window, every unusual noise made her tremble. But Anselmo and the Black Mask had prepared a surprise for her.

The countess was again at the window, intently and longingly looking down the road which the Black Mask's carriage must pass, when she felt a light touch on her shoulder. She turned quickly. Before her stood Anselmo and the Black Mask, holding between them a beautiful, golden-haired boy, who was looking up with an embarrassed and even frightened mien at the tall, handsome lady.

For a moment the countess remained motionless; then, uttering a joyful cry, she sank on her knees, and drawing the child to her heart, stammered, amidst convulsive weeping:

"Yes, yes; you are my only one, my darling, my Hugo!"

The boy, who had never been even looked at, much less embraced, by so elegant a lady, was quite at a loss how to act; but finally, having nothing else to do with his arms, he twined them around the lady's neck, who almost smothered him with her caresses. At last the lady arose, and sitting down on a sofa, drew the child to her side.

"You are lovely, my Hugo," said the lady, smiling through her tears, and attempting to draw him on her lap, against which the child struggled violently, deeming it a shame for such a big boy to sit on any one's lap. The countess repeatedly kissed the boy, who did not dare to utter a remonstrance. She quite forgot that he must be intimidated by her imposing appearance and the splendor of all her surroundings, though he had seen pretty rooms in the doctor's house.

"Why do you not speak to me, my Hugo?" asked the countess, with a tender accent.

The Black Mask and Father Anselmo both trembled as the boy began:

"My name is not Hugo; my name is Benoni, which means child of pain, because it was bad for Pinkus when I came to the Ghetto, and bad for all the Hebrews."

The blood retreated from the face of the countess as she heard this dreadful jargon proceed from the coral lips of the boy. She could hardly believe he had spoken.

But soon her motherly love gained the victory over her pride, and closely embracing the boy, she said:

"Then you shall be called Benoni by me, my darling

child; for you are my child of pain also. Will you not acknowledge your mother, my son?"

"I should have liked to have had a mother long ago; in the Ghetto they said I was a Christian, and that Pinkus was my mother and my father too."

Although the lady still made a wry face when the boy spoke, the first stroke had been the worst.

"Do not be uneasy, my Ella," said Father Anselmo; "this gentleman," continued he, pointing to the Black Mask, "spoke even worse than our little Benoni; half a year cured his fault, and the tender care of a mother will correct it still sooner."

"I must confess that it surprised me," said the countess, smilingly; "but I ought to have been prepared for it, as you, my father, told me where my boy had been reared."

"And this discovery frightened you, my Ella," said Father Anselmo, tenderly.

"If you want to be my mother, you must 'bensch' me every Sabbath and every 'Jomtob,' as the boys are 'bensched' in the Ghetto; no one would ever 'bensch' me."

The countess looked inquiringly at the two gentlemen. She had not understood a single word.

"Benoni asks you if you will bless him as the Jewish mothers bless their sons—a religious act which is of more importance to them than any other."

"Yes, yes, my son," said the countess, the tears rising to her eyes; "yes, yes; may God in his mercy bless you for ever and ever!"

"That's not 'bensching;' that's what the Galahs say," cried Benoni, disappointed; "you can't 'bensch' aright, because you're not a Hebrew mother."

The countess grew pale and pressed her hands on her heart. The boy had hurt her by the reproach which he had in all innocence uttered.

"O, my father," cried the countess, painfully agitated. "teach me to pronounce the blessing this child asks for."

"Lay your hands on your boy's head," said Father Anselmo, in a low, moved voice, "and try to say after me: 'Y'simcha Elohim K'Ephraim v'chi M'nasseh!'" (God make you great, like Ephraim and Manasseh!)

Repeating word for word, the countess blessed her child, and never did Jewish lips pronounce a blessing with more fervor. The boy looked wonderingly from his mother to Father Anselmo and back again; then breaking forth into a loud, merry laugh, he exclaimed:

"God's wonder! since when can a Galah bensch, and a mother, that wants to, not be a real mother?"

"Be comforted, my son; your mother will exert herself to become a good Jewish mother, and you will never again have cause to complain of her ignorance in the old faith."

Anselmo and the Black Mask exchanged a look of surprise; the countess intercepted it, and said quickly:

"Yes, my father, and you, sir, to whom I owe this happy hour, listen to my vow. If God grants me life I shall return to the religion of my fathers, from which I was torn by violence. May God, the Lord, strengthen me in my resolve, and my husband forgive me for not wishing, when my time comes, to rest by his side in the family vault, but to be buried on the mounds where my ancestors found peace after a tortured life."

* * * * * *

It was late in the evening when the doctor's carriage turned into the city. He had deposited Anselmo at the station, for the latter's furlough had expired, and besides he did not wish to remain away any longer from his patients who were in great need of his care.

The coachman drove through Duke street, for this, as we have already mentioned, was pretty fairly illuminated. Suddenly he stopped the horses. At first the Black Mask took no notice of this, but when the stoppage lasted too long, he put his head out of the carriage window and perceived that a great concourse of people in the street was the cause of the delay.

At the same moment a policeman in uniform stepped up to the carriage, and saluting its occupant, said:

"Will you please alight for a moment? A heavily wounded man lies in yonder house, and the police surgeon is nowhere to be found."

The Black Mask immediately left the carriage and followed the policeman into the designated house.

On the sofa in a room on the first floor lay the figure of a man with pale face and closed eyes. All the lights of the chandelier were lit and the room was so bright that the doctor, coming from the darkness of the street, was at first dazzled.

Approaching the sofa he cast a look at the wounded man, then recoiled in amazement, and was obliged to lean against the wall for support.

"The ways of God are marvelous!" muttered he, when he had somewhat recovered.

He sent a policeman to the carriage for his case of instruments, and when it was brought, proceeded to examine the wounded man and probe the wound. This did not take long.

The doctor answered the questioning looks of the bystanders by a sorrowful shake of the head. He then bound up the wound, and put his patient in an easier position. When this had been done the policeman bade all the bystanders to leave the room, and remained alone with the Black Mask.

"How long has the wounded man still to live?" he asked in a whisper.

"A half an hour, perhaps."

"That is not long," returned the policeman; "I am afraid we will not even find out his name."

"Do you not know him?" asked the Black Mask, in surprise.

"No; nor have any of the many persons without recognized him."

"Well, I know him," returned the physician in a whisper; "it is Baron Kuno of Witzleb."

The policeman stared at the Black Mask, then said:

"Excuse me, but the man you say has been lost track of for years. We were once in search of him as the murderer of a monk."

"Nevertheless it is he," said the physician, almost aloud.

Their attention was now drawn to the sofa whence deep moans proceeded. The wounded man had regained consciousness, and when he caught sight of the Black Mask his face, which was already the hue of death, assumed a pitiably terrified expression.

"Be easy, baron," said the Black Mask, soothingly, "I am not here as your enemy, but in the character of a doctor. I am not more to be feared than any other man; my mask was never the shield of evil deeds."

"But mine was. Oh, sir; your mask is the cause of my death; for I feel I must die," said the baron, feebly.

"But how can the mask of this gentleman, our most honored court-physician, be the cause of your death?" asked the policeman.

The wounded man turned his eyes on the policeman, who stood at the head of the sofa, and a mocking expression glided over his features.

"Ah!" said he, "police!" But you come too late. Baron Kuno of Witzleb will never follow you into a prison; he has always outwitted you, and does so still!"

"It is not proper for you, in your critical state, to speak in such a strain," said the policeman, gravely.

"Just this may prove to you that I am no common man," said the baron, groaning; "in one respect I have remained true to my ancestors—I have always been courageous—not like that coward——"

Here the baron's thoughts suddenly reverted to the cause of his sad plight, and fixing his eyes on the Black Mask, he said:

"For the reason that your mask is so convenient, and you are permitted to wear it in the city, I often made use of it, not only to evade the police who are still searching for the murderer of Christian, but to conduct some little affairs of my own. The wound I received was intended for you; a friendly mistake inflicted it on me."

"Do you know your murderer, baron?" asked the policeman.

Again a mocking expression rested on the baron's face, and, without turning to the policeman, he said:

"Of course I do."

"Will you name him, that he may receive the punishment of the law?"

Again the baron glanced at the Black Mask, then said in long-drawn tones, partly because his wound pained him, and partly to make a proper impression on his hearers:

"Yes, gentleman—I know him—it is Egmont of Weiden—the Trumpeard—the captain—of the band——"

At this point the physician raised his mask, and the baron's face assumed a ghastly look; then raising himself on his couch, he stretched out both his hands; and with all the strength still remaining in his lungs, cried out:

'God be merciful to my poor soul! The dead forsake their graves—help!—he—lp——!"

A stream of blood gushed from his mouth, and he fell back on his pillows. The policeman had followed the baron's frightened glance, but saw nothing but the figure of the Black Mask standing quietly at the foot of the sofa.

Two minutes later, Baron Kuno of Witzleb was dead, and the murder of Christian revenged.

The Black Mask, to all appearances quite composed, entered his carriage, and gave the order: "Home."

The next morning the city was full of the news that Baron Kuno of Witzleb had been foully murdered by his wicked nephew, the former captain of the band whose members had all been executed.

At the same time the police were busy looking for the Indian, the hunchbacked mentor of the young prince, who had mysteriously disappeared the day before, and who, in the city so strange to him, might have met with some fatal accident.

CHAPTER XLII.
EMPEROR AND PHYSICIAN.

Duke Francis was speaking eagerly to his favorite, Moses Benrimo. His subject was the mysterious disappearance of the hunchbacked indian, who, despite all the exertions of the police, could not be found. Benrimo could have told his royal master what had become of the prince's mentor, but he had promised the Black Mask perfect secrecy, and intended to keep his word.

"The loss of his faithful companion has affected my dear nephew, the prince, very much," said the duke. "He seems quite unsettled, totters about like a drunken man, and hardly dares come near me. Then what must he think of my government and my courts, when on the same night one man is murdered and another disappears? Do you know, Moses, I believe I have grown too old to govern—the sooner I retire and abdicate in favor of my nephew, the better it will be for all parties."

Benrimo was about to answer, when the servant announced the duke's nephew. The latter entered, hastened up to his uncle, kissed his hand, and inquired about his health.

"You come at the right moment, my Alfred," said the duke, much pleased; "I was just speaking of you."

"It gratifies me to hear that your highness holds me worthy of a thought."

"Why should I not? You are the only remaining branch of our family, and I thank God daily that he has let me live to do you justice. But you must promise to grant me the favor I shall now ask of you."

"Speak, your highness, I promise to grant anything in my power."

"Collect your faculties, my Alfred: do not be so lost in grief at the disappearance of this half-savage. It does not become a man who is destined to govern a people to mourn like a woman at a loss which cannot even with justice be termed a loss, for your mentor may return at any moment."

"No, your highness, he will never return," the prince quietly answered; then sorrowfully continued: "You cannot comprehend what this man, whom you, my uncle, call a half-savage, was to me. He replaced father and mother in a manner which never caused me to feel their loss, and I never can cease to grieve for him."

"God forbid that I ever should require this of you," returned the duke. "I honor gratitude in any shape, and you would show a bad heart indeed did you desire to forget this man. But I wish you to arouse yourself from this inaction, for I am about to roll a heavy load on your shoulders. My special messenger to the emperor may return soon—nay, this very day—and then, my Alfred, I will invest you with the rights of reigning duke, and retire for the rest of my days to private life."

Benrimo observed a sudden flash of triumph gleam across the prince's face. It quickly vanished, however, and the young man, assuming a grieved expression, said:

"Why do you wish to resign the crown, my uncle, and burden me, who am still so young, so inexperienced, with a load that may easily become too heavy for me? I would rather see your highness hold the reigns of government for another quarter of a century, for no one else can so well govern this beautiful little country."

The duke smiled in a superior manner—he evidently felt much flattered.

"My dear nephew," said he, "you must not think that I will leave you to wander alone through the mazes and labyrinths of difficulties which attend so arduous a position; I will ever be at your side and advise you, as long as God grants me life."

"May this be still many, many years, is my heartfelt wish," cried the prince warmly.

"I believe you, my Alfred, I believe you."

At this moment the door was thrown open, and a servant announced:

"Count Albinger, special messenger to his highness."

"You are welcome, count," joyously cried the duke, rising in great excitement from his chair, and walking forward to greet the nobleman, who was still dusty from his long ride.

"What news from the capital?" continued the duke; "is his majesty well and still favorably inclined toward me?"

"Yes, your highness," returned the count, "his majesty sends you gracious greetings by word of mouth. Other particulars are communicated in this document."

With a low bow the messenger handed the duke a letter, sealed with the imperial seal, and then, bowing again, took his departure, walking backward to the door.

"Will your highness permit me to retire?" asked Prince Alfred, as the duke was about to open the letter.

"Remain here, and you also, Moses."

The duke's eyes flew over the document; but the joyous haste with which he had begun to read, gradually turned into a displeasure bordering on rage.

"Bad news?" asked the prince, watchfully, and he moved uneasily on his chair.

"It cannot exactly be called bad news," said the duke, peevishly; "on the contrary, at any other time the announcement which this letter contains would have made me happy. Just think, the emperor is coming here. His majesty is about to travel through his domains, and so will take occasion to visit me, and learn to know my heir personally."

The prince again begged for permission to retire, and this time it was granted.

When he had left the apartment the duke said:

"Moses, I am excessively vexed; can you imagine why?"

"Clearly, your highness, most clearly: the emperor hates the idea of losing so glorious an inheritance, one of the prettiest provinces in the German realm, and on which he had surely counted, so he makes some excuse and comes in person to see if he cannot discover a flaw anywhere."

"My old Moses, I see that we still understand one another," returned the duke, smiling lightly. "Yes, it is so, and what do you think is best for me to do?"

"The best policy, your highness, would be to put a good face on the matter, receive his majesty very cordially, and persuade him to acknowledge your heir."

"He can't avoid doing this last, Moses, but he may previously put many difficulties in the way."

"For this reason your highness ought to receive his majesty with the utmost cordiality."

"Yes, we will do so, old Moses," said the duke, and arose from his chair, thus signifying his wish to be left alone.

*　*　*　*　*　*

All the city was in a state of great excitement. The emperor was to come, an event which had not happened within the memory of the oldest inhabitant. And particularly this emperor, of whom all the world spoke and wrote, the most condescending and affable man that ever graced a throne, was an object of curiosity to every one. Even in the Ghetto the emperor was anxiously expected, for his majesty had done much to improve the social condition of the Jews in his own realm. Thus here the streets and houses were decorated with flags and garlands, and even triumphal arches were erected, although the Jews were pretty well convinced that the emperor would not set foot in their quarter.

The morning of the day on which his majesty was expected dawned most promisingly. The troops at the duke's command were drawn up in long columns, awaiting the arrival of the distinguished visitor. The duke, with his nephew, and most of the court, had driven to meet the emperor without the city. The officers of the duke's household, to which, of course, Benrimo and the court-physician beloged, were assembled in the ducal palace. The duke would have liked to take his physician with him; but firstly, the latter was not of noble extraction, and secondly, no one durst appear before the emperor with face covered. It is true, he might have commanded the doctor to lay aside his mask, but we know that he did not dare to act in direct contradiction to what the mysterious epistle of Isaac Mundolfo had requested him.

Benrimo and the Black Mask sat in the duke's apartment, engaged in conversation. It must have been of a very entertaining nature, for Benrimo nodded and smiled incessantly, while the court-physician was merry and in good mood.

Suddenly the report of a cannon was heard in the distance, and another and another followed in rapid succession; his majesty, the emperor, had arrived.

Benrimo and the physician took up their position at a window, in order to see the emperor, who might now at any moment reach the palace.

Their surprise was no less great than that of the crowds who had assembled to see all the splendor the emperor would display.

His majesty sat beside the duke in an open carriage. Of the immense retinue that had been expected, nothing was to be seen; the emperor must have left it behind him somewhere, most probably in the capital. His majesty himself was dressed very simply in a plain blue coat, on the left side of which a diamond star, the only indication of his rank, glittered brightly. His three-cornered hat, raised in salutation to the crowds in the streets, was decorated only by a cockade, representing the various colors of his provinces.

The emperor appeared to be not much over thirty, and his face expressed great nobleness and kindness of heart.

When the carriage stopped at the gate of the palace, the duke and prince hastened to alight in order to conduct his majesty to the apartments prepared for him.

The Black Mask uttered a cry as the emperor's foot touched the ground. Benrimo turned in surprise, and asked the reason of it.

"My God! Do you not see that his majesty has sprained his ankle?" exclaimed the Black Mask.

This must have been the case, for the emperor limped very noticeably. The cheering crowds remarked it also, but imagined this was his majesty's usual gait.

Before long hasty steps became audible in the corridor leading to the duke's apartment, and anxious voices cried:

"The court-physician, the court-physician!"

"I knew it," said the Black Mask, hurriedly buckling on the sword which had come to him with his new dignity, and with which the duke himself had invested him, "I knew it;" and snatching up his hat, he hastened into the corridor. Arrived at the door leading to his majesty's apartments, he paused, took off his mask, then entered.

The emperor sat on one chair, and had his foot elevated on another. An expression of pain rested on his fine features as the physician entered. The emperor made a sign, and all present excepting the duke left the apartment. In the confusion attending to this, no one, not even the duke, had noticed that the physician was without his mask, and the latter, hurriedly approaching the emperor, bent so low over the injured foot that his face was quite hidden from view.

The emperor, however, threw a sharp, searching glance on the physician's countenance, and was not only agreeably surprised by its expression, but so pleased with the sculptured beauty of his features, the large, shining black eyes, and high, intellectual brow, that he uttered a gratified:

"Ah!"

"Do you require assistance, doctor?" anxiously asked the duke.

"No, your highness, thanks," returned the physician, as he skillfully examined the emperor's foot.

While uttering these words, he had glanced up a moment, thus turning his full face to the duke, who, now also beholding it for the first time, could not repress a cry of pleased surprise. The emperor, however, took it to be a cry of sympathy, and not wishful of causing the the old gentleman any needless pain, he said in a kind voice:

"My dear duke, I by no means desire you to remain a witness of this somewhat painful proceeding, and grant you permission to leave me."

The emperor's slightest wish sufficed for a command, according to the etiquette of that time, and the duke, sighing heavily, retired without uttering a contradictory word; a thing which was also held in bad repute.

Hardly had the door closed behind the duke, when the physician, raising his fine eyes to the emperor's face, said:

"Will your majesty permit your most submissive servant to wear this mask in your majesty's presence?"

"Is it some vow you have made?" asked the emperor, graciously.

"But for a few days more, your majesty, then I will show my face to the whole world," returned the doctor, in an apologizing tone of voice; "I do not wear it because I have anything to be ashamed of, but only because, without this disguise, I cannot unmask certain criminals who have found access to the duke's court, and infested it."

"I believe you, my friend," kindly said his majesty, "your face speaks for the truth of your assertion, and I hope that you will tell me the whole story when you have succeeded in your exertions, for I love court intrigues, as long as they are not played in my court. Resume your mask. I permit it."

The physician thanked the emperor, who again admonished him not to forget to tell him the story of the intrigue, resumed his mask, and admitted the noblemen who had been appointed for the emperor's service during his sojourn at the palace, and who had till now been waiting in the antechamber.

When the emperor had been carefully helped to bed, the physician assured him that his foot would be quite healed in, at the most, three days, and prepared to depart, but the emperor, heedless of all etiquette, called him to the bed and bade him lower his head.

"Keep the prince from my bedside, my dear doctor," whispered his majesty, "else my foot will heal but slowly; the fellow has a perfect rogue's face."

"At your majesty's service," answered the doctor, and his mask moved as if he laughed beneath it.

It was with the greatest envy that the noblemen surrounding the emperor's bed heard his majesty call after the departing physician:

"Doctor, do not forget to look after me again to-day!"

CHAPTER XLIII.
TWO UNMASKED INDIVIDUALS.

As the physician had predicted, the emperor's indisposition lasted but a few days, and during this time he, at his majesty's express desire, visited him several times daily.

The duke also visited the emperor, and had many conversations with his majesty about the succession to his crown, and when the duke already believed everything to be in the best order, the emperor suddenly said:

"Tell me, my dear duke, would it not perhaps be better to wait awhile before acknowledging your nephew, and see if he is good for something? You might else repent having acted so hastily."

The duke was astounded.

But yesterday the emperor had agreed to everything, and the time for acknowledging the heir had been appointed for the following week, when the emperor would be well enough to participate in the festivites which were to celebrate the happy event.

Of course the duke did not know that the emperor had had a long secret conference with the court-physician, and even had he known this he would never have imagined that the succession to the throne had been the subject of their conversation.

"Your majesty," said the duke, hardly able to conceal his vexation, "I think we had better not speak of this any more. You have appointed the day and the matter is settled. I have deliberated long and carefully, and think it best, of course with all due submission to your majesty."

"Well, well, my dear duke," returned the emperor, "do not excite yourself; I only wished you to think the matter over again. However, if you desire it, all shall remain as we settled yesterday."

Hardly had the duke retired when the court-physician was announced.

The emperor called out to him:

"Well, my dear doctor, have you seen to everything?"

"Yes, your majesty, the superintendent of the police will be here immediately, and as your majesty commanded, in a suitable disguise."

"Very well, my dear doctor; be sure I will not forget that it is by your means that I have not only detected an impostor, but regained this flourishing province, this pearl in my imperial crown."

The Black Mask bowed in silence.

A gentleman was announced, and on his producing a card which he could have obtained only from the emperor, was immediately admitted to his majesty.

The Black Mask respectfully took his departure.

Some of the noblemen whispered to each other that the strange gentleman was no other than the superintendent of the police in disguise.

They puzzled their brains as to the cause of his visit to the emperor, but finally, as they were not positive that it was really he, concluded to drop the subject.

It was remarkable that this gentleman came again in

the evening, this time accompanied by several others, all of whom were immediately admitted to the emperor.

Then a messenger was sent to the duke, and soon the latter also repaired to the emperor's apartment. Finally, the Black Mask arrived in his carriage, alighted, and entered the emperor's apartment without even being announced.

The duke was somewhat surprised to be summoned to the emperor's presence at so late an hour, and still more surprised to find the superintendent of police and several strange gentlemen in his majesty's company.

The emperor cordially welcomed the duke, and bade him to be seated. The Black Mask's arrival, later on, did not strike the duke as being at all out of the way, as he had observed with joy that his court-physician had become a great favorite with the emperor.

"My dear duke," began the emperor, "I am sorry to say that I have a disagreeable communication to make to you, which, however, you must not ascribe to my selfishness or any desire to be your heir. On my word as a nobleman, it would have made me happy to grant the wish of your heart, but the one whom you deem your nephew is an impostor."

The duke grew pale. He arose hastily and put his hand on his sword. His majesty likewise arose, and said:

"Duke, if what I have just uttered prove to be untrue, I will give you satisfaction in a duel, forget that I am emperor of the holy Roman realm, and consider myself simply nobleman."

"But," returned the duke, with quivering lips, "why must I, who have seen the most incontrovertible proofs, be mistaken, and not your majesty?"

"That will quickly become clear to you, my dear duke," cried the emperor, greatly moved by the old gentleman's anxiety and embarrassment, and wishful of ending the unpleasant scene as soon as possible. "Please send for the prince, and I will then leave it to you, duke, to accuse me of lying."

"But is all this to proceed in the presence of these gentlemen?" asked the duke, peevishly, pointing to the strangers, and the superintendent whom he had recognized.

"This gentleman," said the emperor, pointing to the court-physician, "is not unworthy of your confidence, and the others I have summoned for protection of my person. They are acquainted with the whole case."

The duke put a silver whistle to his mouth, and its shrill call soon brought an officer, who held guard at the emperor's door, to the room.

"Will your majesty please to give him your commands?" said the duke, in a vexed tone.

"My good captain," said the emperor to the officer, "first of all, see that all the guards, within and without the palace, leave their posts. Then issue the order, in my name, that for the next two hours no servant or officer, whoever he may be, shall pass through or loiter on the corridors and stairs of the palace, nor within some distance of them. When you have seen that these orders are rigidly executed, do you yourself retire to the barracks and stay there two hours, after which you may resume guard at my door. There, now go."

"But, your majesty," cried the duke, now actually frightened, "what do all these orders portend?"

"My dear duke, I wish to spare you, who have a life full of honor and nobleness behind you, the scorn and ridicule with which the common masses would overwhelm you; hence these preparations."

The duke heaved a heavy sigh, a presentiment began to dawn on him that perhaps the emperor was right, and he had not been sufficiently careful in regard to his nephew.

The emperor turned to one of the strange gentlemen:

"Go to the alleged prince's apartment and bid him to come to his highness who is in my company. Be sure that he obeys this order."

The gentleman bowed, and passed through the now

empty corridors of the palace to the prince's room. The officer had strictly obeyed the emperor's command; the sentinels and guards were all relieved of their posts, and only here and there a person might be seen hurriedly speeding to his apartment.

The gentleman, on reaching the first floor of the prince's suite, knocked somewhat loudly. The prince immediately answered, asking what was the matter, and several bolts were pushed back. Steps approached the door from within, and the prince again inquired what was wanted at so late an hour.

"His highness, the duke, has fallen seriously ill, and wishes to see the prince," was the answer.

There was a hurried running to and fro, then one more bolt was pushed back in its socket, and the prince appeared, the most lively joy depicted on his countenance, not as if he had just been informed of his uncle's illness, but as if some happy news had been imparted to him.

"Does the duke's illness excite any anxiety?" said the prince.

"Yes, considerable," returned the stranger, "in all probability a throne will become vacant this night."

"Then hasten, my dear sir," cried the prince, accelerating his steps, for of course he had misunderstood the stranger's words, and interpreted them to his own desire. Despite his agitation, the prince was struck by the fact that all the corridors were empty, and not a guard within sight. He asked the reason, and the stranger again gave a very plausible excuse.

"It annoys the sick duke to hear steps in the palace," said he.

"But whither are you conducting me?" asked the prince, as they passed the duke's apartments.

"His highness is with the emperor; he was taken suddenly ill there."

The prince's steps grew more lagging, he did not like the emperor, who had never vouchsafed him a gracious word.

At last they reached the emperor's antechamber, which likewise, to the great astonishment of the prince, was quite empty and deserted. He stepped back in order to let the stranger announce him.

The latter, however, contrary to all etiquette, pushed him into the room. The bells from the tower of the palace had just clanged forth the hour of midnight.

As the prince entered the room, he saw before him the emperor, the Black Mask, and several gentlemen who were unknown to him.

"Where is my uncle?" asked the prince, also very contrary to etiquette, for in the presence of the emperor only his majesty might ask a question.

"Here, my nephew, here," cried the duke, stepping forward.

"I thought your highness was ill," said the prince, moving a step backward.

"That was only a jest," answered the duke. "I wished to see if you would follow my call."

In the meanwhile his majesty whispered to the Black Mask:

"If you should be mistaken!"

"Your majesty, I will answer for it with my head," was the firm answer.

The prince, who began to grow rather uneasy, now said:

"Then your highness will permit me to retire again?"

He turned, and to his consternation beheld the stranger who had conducted him thither, and three others dressed exactly like him, forming a living wall before the door.

All present could now observe the violent trembling of the prince, even the duke, who cast a wondering look at the emperor.

At a sign from his majesty, the Black Mask stepped up to the prince and said slowly:

"Murderer of Baron Witzleb, I know you!"

The prince swayed back and forth like a reed in a

storm, and cast helpless glances around the circle of bystanders. A gentleman who had till now stood beside the emperor came up to the prince and, unbuttoning his coat, displayed the uniform of the superintendent of the police.

"Prince," said he, "we are looking for Egmont of Weiden, *alias* Trumpcard."

"Mercy, gentlemen, mercy," cried the prince, falling on his knees.

"Why are you so terrified, prince?" said the police superintendent, stepping closer to the kneeling prince, "your hair is perfectly erect with dread."

With a bold, rapid movement he seized the prince's hair, and the next moment the curly wig and false mustache lay on the floor, while pale yellowish locks, in truth standing on end, came to view.

The duke uttered a cry and fell on a chair.

"My God!" stammered he; "why, this is Egmont of Weiden, the expelled cadet!"

"Yes, your highness," said the Black Mask, "and the Baron Witzleb whom he murdered, was the Indian mentor."

"Then the letter from Dr. Isaac Mundolfo really spoke the truth, and the Black Mask has averted utter shame and disgrace from my head," moaned the duke.

Suddenly the unmasked robber and murderer sprang from his knees, and raising aloft a dagger, jumped furiously on the Black Mask, who barely avoided a thrust; but at the same moment the four men at the door fell on the prince, disarmed him, and bound his hands.

"The police has now its lawful prey," said the emperor, "but I do not wish this young rogue's name ever to be mentioned, nor that he ever shall gain opportunity to speak for himself. You, police superintendent," continued his majesty, turning to that gentleman, "do with that prisoner as I have secretly instructed you to-day!"

The officer bowed silently.

"If I could but take revenge on you, masked serpent,"

shrieked Egmont, "I would not care if the hangman tore me to pieces."

"The time for revenge is past, Egmont of Weiden," said the Black Mask, "the war which the two boys at the swamp declared against each other is at an end."

He took off his mask, and looked steadily at the pinioned man.

The latter thought for a moment, then broke into an awful howl. He had recognized his enemy.

"Joseph Bonafit," shrieked he; "why did I not think of you before?"

"Let there be an end of this," cried his majesty, sternly; "one of you go in advance and put all the lights out, so that none who may perhaps have been eavesdropping see this procession and draw conclusions therefrom. Cover the face of the prisoner—here, take the court-physician's mask, he has need of it no longer; the struggle is at an end.

The police agents, for such were the four unknown, led the prisoner away, and the emperor comforted the duke, who was crying like a child.

"Gentlemen," at last said the emperor, "let us swear that the events of this night shall never be divulged by any of us."

All, even the duke, raised their hands, and solemnly took this oath.

* * * * * *

In the city, as well as in the whole duchy, the news soon spread that the duke had had a quarrel with his nephew; that the latter had solemnly relinquished all pretensions to the throne, and gone back to America, whence his Indian mentor had preceded him weeks before, as Europe and its manners did not suit him. There was ridicule at the expense of the police, who had been so foolish as to search so long for the Indian.

On the day after the eventful night above described, an imprudent servant gossiped about the strange orders that had been issued in the palace. But when this chatty person was sent to prison for several years, every one suddenly forgot all about what transpired in the castle that memorable evening. For a long time the police still sought for Egmont of Weiden, the Trumpcard; of course, without success. The emperor's commands had been strictly executed, and no one ever heard anything of Egmont again.

But it was worthy of remark that, since the departure of the prince, the celebrated physician known as the "Black Mask" went about with his face uncovered, and charmed all beholders by its beauty and gracefulness. All who had till now refrained from coming to him, being withheld by dread of his mysterious mask, streamed to him in crowds, and, much sensation as the "masked" physician had created, that of the "unmasked' exceeded it by far.

CHAPTER XLIV.
THE REALIZATION OF A DREAM.

THE poor old duke never recovered from the effects of the blow which the events we have just related proved to him. The emperor, two days before his departure, was obliged to come to the duke's sick-bed to take leave of him. The court-physician was in the room, and Benrimo, leaning on his crutches, stood sorrowfully at the window.

When his imperial majesty had spoken a few words of cordial sympathy to the duke, he asked the permission of his highness to let the noblemen and officers, who were waiting in the adjoining rooms, enter.

The duke, too weak to speak, nodded acquiescence. The doors were immediately thrown open, and the apartment was soon filled with officers and noblemen in glittering, gold-embroidered uniforms.

"Gentlemen," began his majesty, "it is the happy prerogative of an emperor to reward magnanimity, noble-heartedness, and, what we prize above all, erudition, wherever we find them. We, the emperor, now making use of this privilege, intend to add a pearl of price to the nobility of this province, and all Germany; one which can only tend to heighten its luster; and we hope that all of you will esteem and love this new member.

"Kneel, Dr. Bonafit!" commanded his majesty, drawing his sword.

Full of happy confusion, and pressing both hands on his heart, the physician dropped on one knee.

The emperor lightly laid his sword on the kneeling man's shoulder, and said:

"Rise, Joseph Bonafit! By right of this blow, we create thee Count of Immenfeld!"

Intoxicated with joy, Joseph rose slowly from his knees, and the emperor, according to the custom in vogue and an old usage, clasped him for a moment in his arms, while he whispered:

"The title of count for the pretty duchy you have preserved for us, and we shall further remember you in kindness."

With bitter-sweet faces the noblemen and officers in the room followed his majesty's example, and embraced the new nobleman. Had they known what we know—that Joseph was of lineal descent of the Patriarch Abraham—their sentiment would have turned honey into vinegar.

The emperor departed, but had proceeded no further than the next town when a courier overtook him, with the sorrowful tidings that his highness Duke Francis XII. was dead.

Two days after his majesty had left the city, he returned to it and was quietly welcomed by the people, as well as the nobility, soldateska and burgher militia, who were now his subjects.

The duke's body was already laid out in state, and, as his highness had wished, Benrimo, attired in all his military equipments, held watch beside the bier. It was a prerogative he could not surrender. At the foot of the bier, attired in all the splendor peculiar to a nobleman of his time, stood Count Joseph Bonafit of Immenfeld, the court-physician of the late duke.

The emperor advanced with uncovered head, devoutly folded his hands, and pronounced a short prayer for the dead duke.

The scene was very solemn and impressive. The high, spacious room was completely draped in black, the pictures of the old dukes seeming to look sorrowfully down on the last descendant of their lineage, and the many lights which, despite their brilliancy, were inadequate to light up the gloomy surroundings.

The bier, richly decorated with black cloth and silver; the double row of burning wax-lights around it; old Benrimo sorrowfully leaning on his crutches, and the erect, handsome figure of the court-physician on one side; on the other, the great sovereign of the German realm in full uniform, and with head lowered before the dead body of his vassal—truly, such scenes engrave themselves upon memory!

* * * * * *

The funeral of the duke had taken place, and his remains were resting in the family vault of the Wimmersteins.

Benrimo still lingered in the deserted palace, and was treated by the servants with all the respect they had shown him heretofore in the lifetime of the late duke.

The emperor had also domiciled himself in the palace, and expressed his intention of staying there until he had selected a suitable governor for the duchy, which now constituted one of his provinces.

The emperor knew all about Benrimo, who had been introduced to him by the late duke. His majesty was a stranger in the city, and not admiring the pedantic councilors of the duke, he one day sent for old Benrimo, and remained closeted with him a considerable time.

These conferences were continued several days in succession, and the result was that Joseph, Count of Bonafit, of Immenfeld, was summoned to his majesty. When, after a long interview with the emperor, Joseph left him, he tottered like one intoxicated, but his face was radiant with pride and happiness.

Entering his carriage, he called to the coachman:

"As quickly as possible, to the villa of the Countess of Weiden."

"Perhaps Father Anselmo is there," he whispered to himself.

When the carriage stopped before the villa, Joseph leaned eagerly forth, and beheld the meager form of Father Anselmo at one of the windows. The servant barely had time to announce the Count of Bonafit before the latter rushed into the room and threw himself into Father Anselmo's arms.

"My teacher, O, my dear teacher, my dear Rabbi Mundolfo!" cried Joseph, enraptured, "I have reached the goal of my ambition!"

"Be composed, my dear count," said Anselmo, respectfully, and modestly releasing himself from Joseph's arms; "joy must be taken, like medicine, in small doses."

"Father Anselmo," cried Joseph, "if you will not call me by my name—that name by which you learned to know me—I would rather that I had remained plain Joseph Bonafit."

"Well, well, my son, honor to whom honor is due; I did not want to hurt you; on the contrary, I love to call my pupil by his title of honor. But you wish to tell me some news."

"Well, listen, and convince me that I am not dreaming, my honored, my beloved teacher; his majesty has just appointed me governor of the Duchy of Wimmerstein, which is now one of his provinces," cried Joseph, breathlessly, and again embraced his teacher.

"Praised be God forever and ever!" said Father Anselmo, solemnly.

He dispatched a messenger for his daughter and her child, in order to inform them of the truly surprising and glad tidings.

When Joseph, late in the evening, left the villa, where

he had passed some delicious hours, and returned to the city, he found all the streets and squares splendidly illuminated. On his questioning in whose honor this was, he received the answer that it was for the new governor whom the emperor had that day appointed, and who was no other than "*the Count of Immenfeld, the former court-physician of his highness, the friend of all the poor.*"

"Did I still wear my mask every one would know me," muttered Joseph; "now but few recognize me. This is the case with all men; if they were to lay aside the mask they wear all their lives, their best friends would not recognize them; for every one wears a mask, and only feels comfortable behind it."

It was a beautiful autumn day. The Jews in the Ghetto had that morning gone for the first time to *Seli'hoth* in the synagogue.

It was the day on which the new governor was to take the oath of allegiance, and just eleven years since the poor Widow Bonafit awakened her Joseph before dawn of day to send him to *Seli'hoth*, with his father's big *Ma'hsor* under his arm; as we have related in the first chapter.

The troops had been called in from all parts of the province, in order to make as extensive and splendid a parade as possible in the city.

The four weeks' mourning for the duke was over, and the streets were gayly decorated with flowers, bunting, and flags, as at the time when the emperor entered the city for the first time. The people crowded the streets since early morning, and shouted and cheered regiment after regiment as it passed, amid the blair of trumpets and the beat of drums, to the place of festivity.

A squadron of cavalry kept guard before the palace gate and repelled the importunate crowd.

When the appointed time arrived his majesty the emperor stepped forth from the palace; about a pace behind him the newly appointed governor of the province, in richly embroidered uniform, his sword studded with jewels at his side, a glittering diamond star on his breast, and his plumed hat in his hand.

The people enthusiastically shouted "hurrah!" quite carried away with admiration at the manly beauty of the governor.

He looked like a Greek god; his magnificent attire enhanced his beauty a hundred-fold.

Behind these two appeared the flower of the nobility, the officers and councilors of the court, all arrayed in the utmost splendor. Among these was Benrimo, who was carried in a chair by eight richly dressed bearers.

The whole company mounted the elegantly caparisoned horses in waiting for them, the squadron of cavalry fell into the rear, and the procession set into motion amidst the cheering of the people and booming of the cannons, and galloped swiftly to the field before the city, where the troops were to pass in review before them.

When his majesty and the governor arrived at the head of the immense column which stretched back to an invisible distance, the drums commenced to beat a salute, which was answered along the whole line; the flags were waved, the bands discoursed music, all which, however, was drowned by the cheers of the soldiers.

"Hurrah! the Emperor! hurrah! the Count of Immenfeld!"

Did Count Joseph of Immenfeld think of the morning, eleven years ago, when the alarm of the sexton's call for prayer had roused him from his sweet dream, and he had wakened with the cry: "Hurrah for the General!" and, still heavy with sleep, had fallen into his mother's arms? Did he think of it?

Probably he did; for, as he caught sight of Pinkus amid the spectators, and of the great book under his arm, on which the word "Seli'hoth" glittered brightly in the sunlight, a smile passed across his face, and a look of satisfaction rested upon it.

The Governor of Wimmerstein also observed a splendidly appointed carriage, in which sat a lady and a fair-haired boy. An old Franciscan friar sat beside the lady. The governor raised his hat, and his majesty, following Joseph's eyes, also saluted the inmates of the carriage, who, evidently gratified by this notice, bowed deeply in return.

"Who are these people, count?" asked his majesty.

"The Countess of Weiden, with her son and father," answered the governor.

"A Franciscan friar her father?" smiled his majesty.

"It is a remarkable story, and I will tell it to your majesty, if you desire it."

"Three very interesting persons," returned the emperor, again looking around, and regarding the inmates of the carriage; "tell them to come to court to-morrow, my dear count."

When the review was over the noble company returned to the palace, which was now to be the dwelling of the poor boy from the Ghetto in Immenfeld. A large banquet was prepared here, in which all, Benrimo included, participated.

His majesty remained a few days in the city, during which he took occasion to have the Countess of Weiden, her son, and Father Anselmo introduced and presented to him. When he finally departed, he left his best wishes for the welfare of the new governor and the province of Wimmerstein.

Now, at last, Joseph found time to speak alone to his old friend Benrimo. He went to his room, and, warmly embracing him, said:

"My first teacher! I owe to you not only my first step in the path of glory, whose goal I have now reached, but the summit of my happiness; for I know it was your paternal care that proposed to the emperor the new governor of the duchy."

"That is not much," answered Benrimo, with a modesty peculiar to him; "I only did it so as not to let my prophecy come to grief—for on that memorable day, before Rosh Hashanah, I said to myself:

"'If that boy is destined ever to enter upon the path of glory, he has cleared the first obstacle out of his way to-day.'"

CHAPTER XLV.

THE FOURTH VISITOR TO IMMENFELD.

THE changes that had taken place in the duchy of Wimmerstein did not greatly interest the Immenfeld Jews. After the lapse of six months, and when all the country was full of the news, the good people did not even know yet the name of the new governor.

What benefit could arise to the Jews from a new government? They had been, and were still, the Pariahs of society, the scapegoats of those in high places and dominions, and objects whose blood might with impunity be shed by whomsoever had the power and will to do so.

So the Immenfeld Jews were all the more surprised when they heard the news that the castle on the hill was to be repaired, or rather, thoroughly cleaned and brightened up, as his excellency the Governor of Wimmerstein was making the tour of his province, and thought of staying a while at this castle, whose owner was still unknown to the villagers.

It was very near the Easter holidays, and the Immenfeld Jews were so occupied by their house-cleaning and matzoth-baking, that they could not pay proper attention to the occurrences at the castle, and were quite surprised one day by the advent of a troop of cuirassiers, the body-guard of the governor.

These were quartered with the peasants in the village, while the Jews had to pay a contribution, as no soldier would harbor with a Jew, so great was their prejudice.

This arrival was a sure sign that his excellency was not far behind, and in fact the very next day a glittering cavalcade came galloping down the road beside the grave-yard. It was rather remarkable that they halted here a moment and all uncovered, while one of the troop, apparently the governor, pointed with his hand to the cemetery.

Then the cavalcade passed through the village, where the peasants had formed a lane; the Christian schoolmaster, with his pupils, sang a choral. Here the band of cuirassiers fell in with the new-comers, and soon the whole train could be plainly seen from the Ghetto, as it wound up the hill and vanished behind the gray walls of the castle.

The inhabitants of the Ghetto returned to their wonted vocation, and the nobility were soon forgotten.

But how was the president—who, by the way, had quite recovered from his illness—astonished, when toward evening a cavalry officer came galloping into the Ghetto, and asking for Ben Dan, notified that eminent member of the congregation, that the governor proposed to visit the Ghetto on the following day, and that he had better set on foot all necessary preparations.

The good president was quite thunderstruck. He immediately sent for Isaac Kline, and commissioned him to summon all the members of the congregation. In grand council it was then and there resolved, in order not to spoil the mighty man's temper, to form a lane, as the peasants had done that morning, and for this purpose to don their best Sabbath clothes.

The singing of a choral, however, was a difficulty not to be surmounted; the Jewish youths were not at all trained and practiced in singing.

Suddenly the cattle-dealer, whom we remember from the time of the Benrimo riot, started a proposition to the effect that the reader, bass, and soprano, who, on solemn days chant the prayers at the service, should supply the place of a choir, and receive the great visitors with a chant of a suitable psalm, selected for the occasion, and that they receive the officers carrying the sacred scrolls, in festive attire, with their silver-and-gold paraphernalia.

This proposition was accepted, amidst general acclamations, and the meeting adjourned.

It may be confidently maintained that very few of the

Immenfeld Jews passed a quiet night, for, as already observed, nothing extraordinary ever happened in those days that did not excite the fears of the Jews for their safety.

"What would impel a representative of the emperor to visit the Ghetto if he had not some malice in his mind?"

Thus every Jew said to himself, and every one was at a loss for a reply.

The eventful morning dawned, and quite early the members of the congregation, all dressed in their best, assembled in the lane, and were formed into two rows by the president. The children were all festively dressed, washed, and combed, and set on the door-steps, awaiting for the great things to come, while the women and maidens peeped forth from behind their little round window-panes. Even the lead-framed window of the Widow Bonafit's house was not without an occupant; for there sat the good little woman, in order to catch a sight of the glorious warriors and great nobility.

Suddenly a signal resounded from the castle-hill. The startled Jews fell into line; the three choristers prepared themselves; the sacred scrolls, as above described, carried by the officers, so as to be in immediate readiness; and the president, who bore as baton a blow-pipe (an article formerly used by housewives to kindle a fire, and consisting of a hollow wooden tube), shouldered it, military fashion.

A merry blast of trumpets sounded through the clear morning air, the trampling of horses came nearer, and the troop of cuirassiers, a band of music at their head, galloped into the Ghetto, scattering the frightened people to the right and left, considerably deranging the carefully formed double lines.

The troop passed through the whole length of the Ghetto, and stationed themselves at the foot of the hill on which the graveyard was situated. After them came an empty carriage drawn by six horses, a gayly dressed courier, running and leaping, ahead of it. This carriage stopped exactly opposite the Widow Bonafit's house.

This was followed by a splendid cavalcade, horses and riders so glittering and sparkling with gold, silver and scarlet trappings, that the Jews were forced to close their dazzled eyes, thus hardly gaining a clear sight of the most splendidly dressed rider of all, who fairly shone with gold and diamonds.

The minstrel trio sang Hebrew psalm 45, and carried the sacred scrolls with their silver paraphernalia on it, and the president, with great presence of mind, saluted, military fashion, with his blow-pipe.

His excellency smiled and touched his plumed hat, an action that charmed all the Jews, for a nobleman who laughs and salutes a Jew can have no evil intent in mind or malice in his heart.

This cavalcade also halted opposite the Widow Bonafit's house, and at a sign from the commander a rider dismounted and vanished into the interior of the house, to the no little astonishment of the assembled congregation.

But their astonishment very nearly turned into petrifaction when the rider reappeared, and speaking a few words to his excellency, the latter sprang lightly from his horse, and bowing his tall, stately form, passed through the little door into the Widow Bonafit's house.

The cavalcade now turned; the troop of cuirassiers fell in in the rear, and amidst the lively, stirring music of the band the whole procession retraced their way to the castle. However, the carriage with the six horses, a servant in attendance, and the groom, who held his excellency's horse, remained behind.

The Jews in the street formed into little groups and essayed to regain their speech, of which his excellency's visit to the widow's house had robbed them. None dared to leave the street for fear of missing something.

Let us now see what happened in the widow's house.

An anxious trembling fell upon the old and more than modest woman when she saw a splendidly dressed rider dismount and enter the house. She wished to arise, but had lost the power to do so. As the rider entered the room he said:

"Gracious lady, his excellency, the Count of Immenfeld, Governor of Wimmerstein, begs leave to wait upon you, in order to communicate some tidings of your son."

These words restored the widow's presence of mind, and in her joy to hear something of the son whose coming she still patiently and hopefully awaited, she forgot the importance of the visitor she was about to receive.

When, then, his excellency came in to Mrs. Bonafit, pressed her hand and gently forced her back to the seat from which she had painfully arisen, the widow did not feel nearly so timid as might have been expected. She was only somewhat at a loss by what title to address her distinguished visitor.

But the latter was as condescending, nay familiar, as if he were one of her young acquaintances.

The governor took a stool and sat down opposite to the widow.

"Madame," began his excellency, after waiting a while in vain for the widow to speak, "*your Joseph sends you his love; he lives, is a good, honest young man, and will soon come to you.*"

"Gracious, beautiful count," stammered the widow, "I thank you. I am rejoiced to think that such a grand gentleman knows my Joseph, but I should like, oh! how much! to see him. I believe that he is *good* and *honest*, else so distinguished a gentleman as you are would not know him; but, if it is not asking too much of your lordship, would you be kind enough to tell my Joseph that if he wants to come, he had better do so soon, for I cannot wait much longer. I have waited a long, long time, and have not got tired nor let scorn and mockery upset my faith; but God Almighty may take me to himself ere I have seen my Joseph. I am old and feeble; the grief for my boy has made me hoary before my time; I cannot consent to tarry much longer, not a great while longer, no, no!"

His excellency passed his handkerchief over his eyes.

For a while both remained silent; then the governor began:

"Madame Bonafit, you are a good woman, and will not be deceived in your hoping and waiting, your trust and good faith. Your son is among my retinue, he occupies a high position, and will come to see you, it may be this very day."

"God be praised forever and ever," cried the widow, bursting into tears.

Soon she asked:

"But if my Joseph is so near why does he let his poor old mother wait?"

"He fears that the joy of this sudden reunion may be injurious to you," said his excellency, seizing the widow's hand.

"No, no; by no means, my handsome sir; I have imagined this moment to myself for years and years, have always thought how he would fall on his mother's neck and kiss her. Yes, indeed, your lordship, and it would not even surprise me if you, noble sir, were now to say: 'Look at me, mother, I am thy Joseph.'"

Great Heaven! What was that? What had the grand gentleman done? He had thrown himself on his knees, and twining both arms around the trembling woman's neck, he cried:

"Look at me, mother, mother dear, I am thy Joseph!"

The reader will forgive me for not describing the storm of joy, the delight of recognition, the inexpressible bliss of reunion; no pen, were it ever so mighty; no painter's brush, were it dipped into Aurora's rosy glory, could produce such a scene. Every attempt would be a desecration of the mother-heart, an insult to the grand feelings God has implanted in the breast of man.

When mother and son had somewhat recovered

from their rapture and grown more composed, Joseph said:

"Now, mother, you shall leave this little house. Do you see that splendid carriage out there? In it you shall accompany me to my palace in the city. You shall recline on silk and velvet, eat from dishes of gold, servants will be at your call, your slightest wish shall be religiously fulfilled. It is all I can do for you; I would pluck the stars from heaven for you, mother dear, for you deserve it; but man's power is limited. However, your foot shall not strike against a pebble in your path; *I will make you the happiest mother, as well as the wealthiest in all Israel!*"

The mother fondled her son's hand and stroked his long dark curls, whilst she said:

"My Joseph, I am the happiest and richest mother in Israel; for since we are in *Galuth* (exile), no such bliss has ever come upon a mother, poor or rich, high or lowly; but, my Joseph, I pray you make my happiness still greater—let me enjoy it quietly and blessedly—leave me here. Do not tear me from the Ghetto, from the little house in which I was born and bred, in which I loved you and kept you in the fear of God, in which your father and I, with God's help, laid the foundation of your future grandeur. Leave me in the little house from which they carried your father to his last home; leave me where I can see, from early morning till late at night, the stone which marks his resting-place. I pray you, my son, do not tear me from my wonted surroundings, from the Sabbath-lamp which gleams brighter than any other. I am here like an old crippled tree, which all its life has contrived to feebly flourish in arid, sandy ground; were it suddenly in its old days to be transplanted to a fertile soil, it would certainly die. Oh, I pray you, my beloved Joseph, my only son, leave me here. You know I will follow you whithersoever it be, if you wish it; but do not ask it, my son, do not ask it!"

An expression of sadness lay on the son's countenance, but he perceived that it would be a dangerous enterprise, and not at all conducive to her happiness, to tear his beloved mother from the surroundings and habits that had been hers all her life.

He also plainly foresaw that the congregation in Immenfeld would now regard his mother with peculiar veneration. Then he considered that everything in the palace was not and could not be as strictly religious as his pious mother was wont to enjoy it, and this alone would 'imbitter instead of sweeten the few years she had still to live. Joseph therefore yielded to his mother's wishes, and soon perceived that he had acted wisely; for her uneasiness vanished and her joy was now complete.

Despite their intense curiosity, the Immenfeld Jews had found the time of waiting too long, and when the governor at last emerged from the widow's little house, there were but few stragglers in the street. It was quite dusk when the empty carriage left the Jews' lane, and the groom started on his way to the castle, leading his master's horse, as—to the man's boundless astonishment—his excellency had concluded to pass the night in the widow's little house.

CHAPTER XLVI.
CONCLUSION.

WHAT did the Immenfeld Jews say when they heard the wonderful story of the lost son? At first, they did not want to believe it, and who can blame their doubts?

The governor of Wimmerstein was obliged to issue a formal proclamation that Joseph Bonafit, Count of Immenfeld, and Governor of Wimmerstein, was the same Joseph Bonafit who had mysteriously disappeared the night before his *Bar-Mitzvah* (confirmation). On Sabbath Hagadol (Sabbath before Passover), the Saturday on which Joseph was to have become confirmed, his excellency came to the Synagogue, was called to the Thora, and read not only the benediction, but the whole weekly section, as it becomes a regular confirmant to do. He donated to the congregation a large sum of money for the building of a new synagogue and the paving of the Ghetto, as also for the erection of a good tavern, in which chance visitors to Immenfeld might pass the Sabbath, thus averting all possible vexation that might accrue from them to the members of the congregation.

During the Passover holidays, the great man, clad but in a simple black suit, stayed with his mother, and slept in the little room her loving hand had kept in order for eleven years.

And thus the governor passed the holidays for the ten years his mother still lived, an object of the greatest veneration to the Jews of Immenfeld. Every spring and autumn his excellency came to Immenfeld alone, leaving all his splendor behind, conducted his mother to the Synagogue at the solemn festivals, ate at her table, and slept in his little room.

All that the governor could do for the Jews was to release them from the obligation of paying certain taxes for their protection, and this was no inconsiderable relief to them. All the other tributes flowed into the emperor's treasury, and were out of the governor's power to abolish.

His excellency's first visit to Immenfeld was very nearly of evil consequences to him, and would have proved fatal to all his grandeur, had not the emperor been a liberal-minded man, and owed him a debt of gratitude.

His majesty received an anonymous expostulatory letter to the purport that he had committed something unheard of, to-wit, not only made a count of a Jew, but appointed him governor of one of the most flourishing provinces in the realm.

This was retorted to by a circular addressed to the nobility of the former duchy. The contents were as follows:

"TO THE FAITHFUL OF WIMMERSTEIN,—It is true we have been very careless, and confess it, although we are lord and sovereign of this country. We neglected to ask our loyal governor, Joseph Bonafit, Count of Immenfeld, to what religion he belonged. Etiquette forbade him stating anything that his emperor had not asked of him, and so we fell into the error with which our dear Wimmersteiner reproach us. As the harm is done, we most earnestly beg our dear subjects for forgiveness, and entreat them to make for once a trial of a scion of the house of Israel; but at the same time we exhort the nobility of Wimmerstein, under pain of our imperial displeasure, not to trouble themselves about, nor condemn the actions of their emperor in the future. Etc., etc., etc."

This circular had due effect, and no more murmuring was heard against the Jewish governor.

About two years after Joseph had been appointed governor of Wimmerstein, he received a letter in a well-known hand. It was dated France; and hastily opening it, he read:

"My Dear Son,—When two years ago we, that is, my daughter Ella, her son, and I, took leave of you, we expressed a desire to go to France, and there resume the religion of our ancestors. Greatly pleased at our resolve, you promised to insure the safety of my grandson's estates, despite our change of religion, provided we kept this secret. You have faithfully kept your word, for a courier has just brought us the deeds, drawn up by his majesty, which confirm my grandchild, Benoni of Weiden, in all his rights and property. I, together with my daughter Ella, the Countess of Weiden, and her son, have embraced the old Mosaic faith, and we are happier than ever heretofore. I shall take advantage of the first opportunity to return to you the money you realized for the diamonds deposited and concealed in the skeleton intrusted to your custody, at your departure from the convent, and sent to me. I have no need of it; for, as you well know, my daughter is very rich, and at court money may be always useful. Moreover, being a Jew, it is uncertain how long you may maintain your position as governor, although the best can be hoped for.

"My daughter has resumed her Jewish name, and my grandchild, whose name, Hugo, was known to but few, has retained the name given him in the Ghetto, *Benoni*, and it is by this I have mentioned him in my petition to the emperor.

"Now I have one thing more to ask of you, my dear son: I once bought the Castle Weiden, in Immenfeld, firmly resolved to place Jews where their persecutors had so long lorded it, and at that time, not forseeing your splendid career, I destined it for you.

"I will send you the above-mentioned money, also the purchase deeds of the castle, which are all made out in your name. I expect you to pay me the debt of gratitude you imagine you owe me by accepting this gift, and hope that, every time you go to Immenfeld, you will visit the castle, and if it be but to stay there an hour, in order to fulfill what was once a favorite thought of mine.

"Your devoted friend,

"Isaac Mundolfo."

"So dear Father Anselmo has at last found complete happiness, as misfortune was too tired to pursue him any further," said his excellency to himself, as he held the letter over the flame of the candle and carefully dispersed the ashes, for it was not advisable to risk its being read by any one; "good Father Anselmo, who, by sending me back this money, makes me one of the wealthiest men in the city. I think I will let some of it wander to the Ghetto, although the good Countess of Weiden, before her departure, restored to the Jews all the money Witzleb wrested from them, besides presenting them with a considerable sum. Of course I must also accept the Castle Weiden; this gives me almost as much pleasure as my high position, for the reason that once, at least, Israel has triumphed over its antagonists, and also because the castle was so long an object of dislike to my brothers in faith in Immenfeld.

* * * * * *

Now that we have taken leave of good Father Anselmo, nothing more important remains for us to do than to take a little journey to the Convent of St. Francis, and see how things look there. At the time Baron Witzleb was murdered, his effects were closely searched by the police, and a small paper, laid in minute folds, was found among them. This paper, on being opened, disclosed a written statement to the effect that Father Ignatius, prior of the Convent of St. Francis, voluntarily declared himself to be an accessory and accomplice of the baron.

Of course preparations were immediately made to arrest the prior. Soldiers were sent to the convent, and a police officer penetrating into the prior's cell, held before the holy man his written confession and declared him a prisoner. This was, however, unnecessary. The prior could not rise, he was struck by apoplexy. Hence it came, that none of the apathetic monks concerned themselves about the new governor; and never suspected in the person of the Count of Immenfeld the novice who, according to their opinion, had been baptized in his death-hour, and whose surname they had never known.

* * * * * *

Time, no matter how long it gives credit, at last demands its due, and no one can hope to escape the scythe.

Full five years after his young friend's wonderful elevation did Benrimo still live, revered by his one-time pupil, and honored by a repeal of the *'Herem* or anathema, into which the Jews of Immenfeld had put him, years ago. He was also most earnestly entreated by those same Jews who had once been so inimical to him to pay them a visit, but this he had never done.

Benrimo was a great support to Joseph in his cares of government, for the old man had been the adviser of the deceased duke, and Joseph often sighed with regret when he thought this old friend must once become lost to him,

Benrimo's hour came. When he felt that his end was drawing nigh, he said to Joseph, among many other things:

"My dear son, I have but one more wish, and this may, perhaps, seem curious to you: I should like to be buried in the graveyard of Immenfeld. I passed some very evil days there, and rejoice in the thought that I will be allowed to rest in peace upon yonder hill. Further, my dear Joseph," continued the dying man, "I wish, although you are now the greatest and richest man in Israel, that you will become my heir. It is not much that I have to leave, but it may not be disagreeable to you to be reminded at times of the old Spaniard. On the white margins of my folios you will find many interesting and, it may be, instructive observations, that I have noted down from time to time."

Joseph kept beside the death-bed of his old teacher, the first who had shown him the way to fame and splendor, and wept like a child. But tears will not detain the fleeting spirit, and Benrimo gently fell asleep, to awake to a better life.

Moses Benrimo's burial resembled that of the patriarch Jacob. The old hero's body was conducted to its last resting-place in a hearse drawn by six horses in sable trappings, and surrounded by guards of soldiers, while the Jews of each town accompanied the sad train to the next. The whole way the hearse was followed on foot by Joseph of Bonafit, Count of Immenfeld and Governor of Wimmerstein.

When the sorrowful procession reached Immenfeld, the Jews, who had once treated the man who now returned to them so ill, solemnly took charge of the body and buried it in their graveyard, on the *highest point* and *row of honor*.

The ten most eminent rabbis in the province said *Kadish* (mourner's prayer) during a whole year for the duke's old friend, who had no children to render him this service of love. For a whole year a lamp (*Ner Tamid*) burned in the ancestral halls of the dukes of Wimmerstein, to the memory of Benrimo, and for a whole year a guard of soldiers kept watch by the light, night and day.

Thus had Duke Francis XII. ordered in his last will and testament, and faithfully was the order executed by Joseph of Bonafit, Count of Immenfeld, Governor of the one-time Duchy of Wimmerstein.

[THE END.]

www.ingramcontent.com/pod-product-compliance
Lightning Source LLC
Chambersburg PA
CBHW022335230426
43664CB00040B/933